CLIMBING:
Training for Peak Performance

MOUNTAINEERS
OUTDOOR EXPERT
series

CLIMBING:
Training for Peak Performance

Clyde Soles

THE MOUNTAINEERS BOOKS

Published by
The Mountaineers Books
1001 SW Klickitat Way, Suite 201
Seattle, WA 98134

First printing 2002, second printing 2004

Published simultaneously in Great Britain by Cordee, 3a DeMontfort Street, Leicester, England, LE1 7HD

Manufactured in Canada

Project Editor: Laura Slavik
Editor: Don Graydon
Cover and Book Design: Ani Rucki
Layout: Marge Mueller, Gray Mouse Graphics
Illustrator: Scott Bodell
Photographer: All photographs by the author unless otherwise noted.

Cover photograph: © 2002 Jeff Schultz/AlaskaStock.com
Frontispiece: The trail to the top of Gasherbrum II, Pakistan © Clyde Soles

Library of Congress Cataloging-in-Publication Data

Soles, Clyde, 1959–
    Climbing : training for peak performance / Clyde Soles.—1st ed.
        p. cm.
Includes bibliographical references and index.
    ISBN 0-89886-898-X (paperback)
    1. Rock climbing—Training.   I. Title.
    GV200.2 .S65 2002
    796.52'23—dc21   2002008327

 Printed on recycled paper

Contents

Preface

As much as anything, I wrote *Climbing: Training for Peak Performance* because I wanted to know the answers for myself. I'm not a doctor, personal trainer, or nutritionist. Nor am I an elite climber, world-class alpinist, or Everest summiter. I'm just someone who has been playing hard in the mountains for three decades.

In my own quest for fun—silly things like climbing an easy 8,000-meter peak (Gasherbrum II, 26,362 feet), running a high-altitude trail marathon, and mountain biking a century (100 miles) in a day—I've tried to get the most reward with the least effort. So I've long held an interest in what actually works—and been frustrated with sifting through the claims.

Having lived in cosmic, hyper-fit Boulder, Colorado for twenty years, I've been exposed to nearly every form of holistic hocus-pocus and fantastic fitness fad. While editing the Performance section of *Rock & Ice* magazine, press releases flooded my mail with hype on the latest miracle supplement that would help climbers in "unbelievable" ways. Would-be authors frequently regurgitated old myths or proposed articles on the latest thousand-year-old training method for which nobody had time to collect data. I'm a firm believer that there is no such thing as Eastern, Western, alternative, or traditional medicine—just good and bad science. And that can come from any part of the world or point of view.

While recovering from a shoulder operation fifteen years ago, I began to realize the advantages of resistance training. Though looked upon with disdain by other climbers, I found that lifting weights had been well researched and proven effective for any sport that you care to mention. My aerobic playing was always sporadic and haphazard, at best. But I eventually discovered that applying a little science to my activities increased the payback in the same amount of time.

Thus I started this project with a thirst for knowledge, a healthy degree of skepticism, and a respect for the scientific process. Since I wasn't schooled in the fields covered herein, I approached them with an open mind while insisting on well-documented evidence. Some of the topics here are controversial and if you don't agree or if you question my analysis, I encourage you to look deeper (see Appendix D, Resources); a few of my own preconceptions were burst.

Though my biases may occasionally appear, there is no mention anywhere in the book of what I eat or how I train. What does or doesn't work for me, or anyone else, is irrelevant for you. As Dr. George Sheehan so aptly wrote, "Each of us is an experiment of one." It's fair to say, however, that I am not a born-again training zealot and I don't always follow all of the advice here—just enough to let me perform at the level I desire. Use this information to make educated decisions about your own life experiment. And have fun climbing better, stronger, and longer!

Acknowledgments

Climbing: Training for Peak Performance is one of the few books written at high altitude. As a subject in a physiology study, I spent eight weeks living above tree line at the Barcroft Research Station (12,500 feet; 3,810 meters) in the White Mountains of California. Many thanks to the staff and my fellow subjects for an interesting and delicious experience.

One of the scientists running the study, Sue Hopkins, has become my adviser and friend. Not only is she an M.D. and Ph.D. specializing in sports medicine and high-altitude physiology, Sue is also a former competitive cyclist and now an avid rock climber. Her mentor, Dr. Robert Schoene, also reviewed this manuscript and provided great insight. A professor of medicine at the University of Washington, "Brownie" was a climber-scientist on the 1981 American Medical Research Expedition to Everest and is a member of the U.S. Olympic Committee's Committee on Nutrition. A huge thanks to both of you!

The first chapter was also reviewed by Suzanne Girard Eberle, M.S., R.D., and Heather Nakamura, M.P.E., M.S., R.D., both of whom are athletes themselves who specialize in sports nutrition. The strength-training chapter was reviewed by Chris Wall, who has a master's degree in exercise physiology and is the head trainer at the Boulder Rock Club.

Thanks to Mountain's Edge Fitness Center, Boulder, Colorado, for the use of its facilities to shoot the photos. And muchas gracias to Mr. Ruge and the climbers who modeled the exercises: Fred Barth, Mark Eller, Michelle Moore, and Pam Roberts. Finally, thanks to the team at The Mountaineers Books for bringing this to fruition.

Introduction

This book is for climbers of all ages, abilities, and interests who wish to improve their performance. It is for weekend warriors who enjoy 5.6 (UK 4b) yet desire to lead 5.10 (5b) and for mountaineers interested in moving faster at altitude. It is for ice climbers who want to move more efficiently over frozen terrain and big-wall climbers who want to increase their stamina. Even those only interested in clipping bolts on overhanging desperates and cranking hard boulder problems can benefit.

The standard concept of training for climbing has long been, "Just climb!" While it may suffice for twentysomethings and a few gifted individuals, this philosophy has also resulted in countless climbers reaching performance plateaus and suffering recurrent injuries. Even after the benefits of specific training were recognized, many of the regimens developed by climbers were physiologically unsound; some were downright dangerous. Recent training books and articles have mostly focused on the young 5.absurd sport climber but the techniques are ill-suited to middle-aged, out-of-shape Jane Trad and Joe Alpinist.

The emphasis here is on sound nutrition and time-efficient training methods that will benefit "normal" people from late teens to octogenarians. This is based on the latest sport science—a rapidly evolving field that only began in 1927 and didn't get into full swing until the '60s. The techniques presented, when thoughtfully performed, can make you stronger and healthier but not necessarily a better climber.

As part of the Mountaineers Outdoor Expert Series, *Climbing: Training for Peak Performance* is intended to complement the other titles, which focus on technique and safety in different aspects of the sport. It is incumbent upon you to also learn how to move economically and safely in your chosen environment. Seek out these other books—they are excellent—and practice your skills.

The guiding principle of this book is that training should be fun! While some people enjoy suffering, they are the exceptions. Many of us would rather eat junk food and lay on the couch than adhere to a strict diet and self-inflict torture. Although "to train" may seem the antithesis of "to play," they can be the same thing—with the right attitude and a good understanding of what you are doing.

In general, to improve climbing performance, your goal is to enhance overall fitness and health, fine-tune aspects specific to your interests, and peak for major excursions. Another objective is to prevent injury through a balanced program of exercise.

Think of climbing, outdoor recreation, and fitness as a year-round lifestyle—not just on-again, off-again activities. Even when the realities of life intrude, keeping this perspective will prevent major setbacks in your conditioning. When you think of yourself climbing in a decade or three, and enjoying yourself even more, the efforts to improve yourself seem all that much more worthwhile.

A NOTE ABOUT SAFETY

Safety is an important concern in all outdoor activities. No book can alert you to every hazard or anticipate the limitations of every reader. The descriptions of techniques and procedures in this book are intended to provide general information. This is not a complete text on climbing or training technique. Nothing substitutes for formal instruction, routine practice, and plenty of experience. When you follow any of the procedures described here, you assume responsibility for your own safety. Use this book as a general guide to further information. Under normal conditions, excursions into the backcountry require attention to traffic, road and trail conditions, weather, terrain, the capabilities of your party, and other factors. Keeping informed on current conditions and exercising common sense are the keys to a safe, enjoyable outing.

The Mountaineers Books

CHAPTER 1

Performance and Nutrition Fundamentals

There are no easy ways to improve your climbing performance. It will always require sweat and determination. To believe otherwise is folly. But by losing the ancient dogmas and applying sport science to your efforts, the rewards will come faster and with less effort.

Whether you prefer to focus on one aspect of the climbing spectrum, or tackle them all, you can only succeed with a solid foundation of fitness. Even the luck of the genetic draw can only carry you so far anymore: a less gifted climber who trains smarter will blow you away.

PERFORMANCE FUNDAMENTALS

Nobody consciously sets out to train "dumb." Ask the average climber and they will vehemently deny their training efforts have been a waste of time—and in the next breath admit they could be doing more. Most of us are guilty of training our strengths and not our weaknesses; this is only natural.

One of the hallmarks of world-class athletes is brutal honesty with themselves, which is not the same as relentless self-criticism. You need to evaluate yourself for both positives and negatives, solicit the opinions of friends, and perhaps even hire a coach or trainer who can offer an unbiased evaluation. Find the areas where you can make the most gains, not just slight improvements, and the rest will fall into place on its own.

There is a world of difference between training harder and training smarter—the former is a path to mediocrity, the latter the route to the top. When you train and eat haphazardly, no matter how many hours you put in, you are climbing Mount Analogue and the summit will always remain untrodden.

When you establish specific goals, make a plan to achieve them, and fuel yourself accordingly, you'll get 80 percent of the reward with 20 percent of the effort. For many, if not most, climbers this higher level of performance is sufficient since they are climbing better, feeling healthier, and still have time for a life. Others will want to apply themselves to their fullest to eke out that maximum performance edge.

Don't underestimate the value of training, either. A study of twenty-four male and twenty female climbers by the University of New Mexico evaluated a wide range of variables that can affect performance on sport routes. They determined that anthropometric factors (such as height, arm span, and weight) could account for only 0.3 percent of a climber's ability. Increased flexibility was a slight help at 1.8 percent. But training accounted for 58.9 percent of a climber's performance.

PERFORMANCE BASICS

In case you haven't noticed, climbing is a sport that defies gravity. Since excess weight is a detriment, some climbers spend a small fortune on the lightest equipment (see my book *Rock & Ice Gear*, published by The Mountaineers Books, for full details). While high-tech gear can help performance, many of the climbers with the latest toys would do better to reduce their body fat.

Athletes can stay competitive and healthy down to about 5 to 6 percent body fat for men and 13 to 17 percent for women. However, that doesn't mean those are *your* optimal percentages. Many people require more fat for best performance—only your body knows what's best. With a thoughtful dietary plan, an ideal balance can be met while boosting performance.

Concurrent with losing extra fat, many climbers will benefit by building their muscles. Those who are past their mid-30s have in all likelihood lost significant muscle mass since the days of youth. With intelligent resistance training, you can maximize your strength-to-mass ratio, boost your power output, and increase your metabolism.

Another important purpose of resistance training is to strengthen the ligaments and tendons that hold bones and muscles together. Climbers are frequently plagued by injuries of these connective tissues, either from overstraining or overusing them. To increase their size and strength requires high-intensity loading and sufficient rest.

All of the above basics of climbing fitness are enhanced by cardiovascular conditioning, even if your style of climbing is not very demanding on heart and lungs. Through aerobic training you increase cardiac output, oxygen uptake, blood perfusion within muscles, breathing efficiency, and tolerance of lactic acid. All the while, you are burning calories and reducing stress.

Perhaps the most important aspect of climbing performance, and the hardest to master, is the mind. The mental games we must play with ourselves to accomplish a climb, or complete a workout, are substantial. Much of what we do goes completely against any real logic: it borders on stupidity. To persevere in the face of adversity, and make suffering fun, takes willpower; this too requires training.

PLAY HOLISTICALLY

An absolute truth of climbing performance: everything works together. Even though few people would deny this, the concept is nonetheless downplayed to the point that it is often forgotten. It's common to see folks who practically live in the rock gym, yet they never seem to improve and often nurse injuries. Most books and magazine articles only focus on one aspect of performance, typically strength, perhaps in a paragraph or two mentioning that you also need to do other things. Yet failure and frustration come from concentrating on one area to the exclusion of others.

Much has been said in sports literature in general, and climbing literature in particular, about the need for specialization. This has been summed up by the acronym SAID—specific adaptation to increased demand. The vast majority of this specialization is due to neural changes, both within the brain and the musculature. Specificity is essential for competitive athletes who have already achieved a high level of performance. It's where greatness comes from.

However, specialization can be, and often is, taken too far. For recreational athletes, it can do more harm than good—insufficient all-around conditioning and a much greater risk of injury. Though they are very good within their specialties, neither 5.14 climbers nor sub-3-hour marathoners tend to be complete (or even healthy) athletes, and overuse injuries are rampant. Recall the old truism, "Everything in moderation, including moderation."

With the exception of high-end sport climbing and bouldering, which receive most of the hoopla in magazines, there is very little that is specific about climbing. All other forms of the games we play require greater depth of strength and power, muscular and aerobic endurance. For optimum climbing performance, you need to condition yourself to handle different levels and volumes of intensity. Along with this comes greater muscular efficiency—the economy of play.

Unlike many sports, which tend to have a single peak season, climbing is a year-round activity. The focus may change with the weather or a particular trip, but there is often less of a downtime for complete recuperation. During an extended break from activity, aerobic endurance declines much faster than strength. By cross-playing—using other sports for fun and relaxation—you can maintain a reasonable level of fitness with less risk of overtraining.

THE AGING CLIMBER

Sadly, we all grow older—at least in body. With advancing age comes wisdom, and an inexorable physical deterioration. A large portion of these declines are the result of an increasingly sedentary lifestyle.

Between ages twenty-five and thirty-five, the average male gains 5 to 10 pounds of fat. Around our mid-twenties, strength and endurance begin to decline 1 to 2 percent per year; resting metabolic rate (RMR), the baseline energy requirement, decreases 1 to 2 percent per decade; aerobic capacity decreases about 10 percent per decade. Degenerating muscle fiber starts to be replaced by fibrous connective tissue (fibrosis), which reduces flexibility. Our joints stiffen as ligaments become less elastic and synovial fluid thickens. The rate of sweating also decreases with age, so we become less tolerant to heat stress.

The good news is that continued training will slow the aging process. The even better news is that you can reverse much of your losses if you've allowed yourself to slide— you *can* make yourself younger! With endurance training, aerobic capacity can increase as much for people in their sixties as kids in their twenties. Likewise, resistance training can increase muscle size and strength even when you're an octogenarian. Enjoy life—never stop playing!

NUTRITION FOUNDATION

Hang around any major vertical destination and you'll discover that many climbers have a distaste for nutrition. What we eat and drink before, during, and after a climb is seldom given much thought regarding performance. Yet serious athletes in other sports, such as running and cycling, tend to pay greater attention to proper fueling.

Partly this dichotomy exists because climbers often feel they are not mainstream athletes—and damned proud of it—and partly it's because of ignorance. Some would rather do ten thousand pull-ups than give up their breakfast of Kix cereal and Bud Light. The magazines seldom run articles on improving performance through nutrition, and few training books consider it a worthy topic.

But the truth is, you can climb better-faster-longer if you pay attention to what you eat. And it doesn't have to be bland, engineered crap either—quite the opposite.

NUTRITION BASICS

Accept that you are an athlete, no matter if you can redpoint 5.3 (3b) or 5.13 (7a). The sooner you start eating like one, the sooner you can start making real performance gains. Whether you climb for fun, demons, or profit, all aspects of the sport are athletic endeavors that will benefit from better eating habits.

As an athlete, your nutritional needs are slightly different from those of the general population for whom recommendations are normally made. Obviously, you are working more so you need to consume more calories and water. But compared to standard recommendations, climbers need approximately twice as much protein and possibly more antioxidants.

Shocking though it may sound, climbers do not need to buy specially designed "sport" foods or supplements. These products mostly offer convenient packaging but rarely provide anything that isn't obtainable from a normal, healthy diet. All too often, the marketing hype overwhelms reality. For example, minuscule quantities of supplements are often added simply as a gimmick; there isn't enough to have a real effect, or an important facilitator is left out because it's too bulky or expensive.

Diet Styles

With proper education and a modicum of restraint, an omnivorous diet is the easiest for meeting the nutritional needs of athletes. To be healthful, this features lots of vegetables, fruits, and whole grains. The preferred source of protein is seafood, some skinless poultry, and occasional lean red meat. In general, a good sports diet tastes better, and is better for you, than the average Western diet that emphasizes convenience and value over nutrition.

Although vegetarians are sometimes annoyingly righteous about their food preference, no studies show that this diet style is healthier than a thoughtful omnivorous diet. However, there is considerable evidence that a vegetarian diet is healthier than that of the general public, which dines on the overprocessed "food products" shoveled out at fast-food family restaurants and supermarkets.

From an athletic standpoint, vegetarians with the best chances of success are either semi-vegetarian (consume dairy products, eggs, and occasionally seafood and poultry, but no red meat) or lacto-ovo vegetarian (dairy and eggs but no meat or seafood). Both of these philosophies make it relatively easy to ensure adequate nutrition— if you pay attention!

Vegans, who consume no animal products of any sort, place themselves at a distinct performance disadvantage. Unfortunately, the most militant vegans are remarkably ill-informed about biology and the scientific process (hint: correlation does not equal causation). While it is certainly possible for an athlete to perform well and stay healthy on a vegan diet, this requires a great deal of knowledge and effort. Don't undertake this lifestyle choice casually; consult a sports nutritionist. A particular danger is vitamin B12 deficiency, and possibly vitamins A and D. On expeditions, the dietary constraints of strict vegans can cause problems if it interferes with meal planning for the team.

If you don't like the taste of meat or have moral qualms, that's fine. But make sure you offset the protein deficit with higher consumption of soy products (such as tofu, soy milk, and tempeh), which contain a full complement of amino acids. Incomplete protein sources (rice, beans, pasta, vegetables, fruits, nuts, and so forth), which lack adequate supplies of the essential amino acids, are also important although, contrary to the old thinking, these do not have to be combined at the same meal. Vegetarian female athletes must be even smarter about their diet because low protein, which often accompanies low calories, can result in amenorrhea (disrupted menstrual cycles).

According to Suzanne Girard Eberle, author of *Endurance Sports Nutrition,* "I meet vegetarians with unhealthy, unbalanced diets all the time—especially athletes who lack cooking or meal preparation skills or the desire to apply them. Dairy and eggs are poor sources of iron and zinc. Also, most people don't eat eggs daily (as we do with meat) or drink enough milk (3 glasses = 24 grams of protein = chicken breast the size of a deck of cards) to meet their increased protein needs. Especially for women, the easiest and most practical way to consume readily absorbable iron (and zinc) is lean red meat. Bottom line: If you want to be vegetarian and an athlete, you'll have to be extra vigilant about your diet."

DIET BASICS

The amount of misinformation about diets and dieting floating around is downright scary. Much of this is fueled by the megabillion-dollar diet and supplement industry, which would disappear if its products really worked. No wonder many of us are confused to the point of giving up.

Diet Chicanery

Somebody walks up to you and says, "I've just invented the best rock shoes in the world! They will friction on glass, edge on a dime, and jam the gnarliest cracks. No other shoe even comes close! And best of all, they're one-size-fits-all." Wouldn't you tell this hustler to get lost? Then do the same with all the diet plans that are foisted on the market. Your nutritional needs are certainly no less variable than your feet. Even if Mr. Charlatan offers his wonder shoes in different sizes, climbers know better than to think all size 43 feet are the same shape. And so it is with diets based on zones, blood types, or whatever.

The goal of nearly all diet plans is to lighten your wallet, little more. If you escape by only purchasing a book, then you're just out some time and money. The real scams are the ones that try to hook you on their products; multilevel marketing schemes are the worst offenders.

If a company's literature includes the words "secret," "miracle," "magic," "rejuvenate," "detoxification," or "adaptogen," you are virtually guaranteed there is no solid science behind the products. Testimonials and endorsements aren't worth the paper they're printed on, no matter how famous the celebrity or team. A patent only proves the company has mixed ingredients in a different ratio than anyone else. The patent offices in the United States and most other countries do not require any evidence that a product is safe or effective.

Before committing your body and cash to the latest diet fad or supplement, check the science. Skip the bull and go right to their references; examining these can save you a lot of time and money. First look at the names of the journals (are they widely read and recognized in their field?), then the years published (anything over a decade old in the nutrition world should be suspect), and finally at the title of the paper (is it relevant?). References to articles in consumer magazines or popular books are just window dressing and should be ignored.

Look up significant citations to read the abstracts on PubMed, a free Internet resource with more than 11 million medical references (*www4.ncbi.nlm.nih.gov/pubmed*); if there is anything to the claims, the research should be there. There is no legitimate reason for serious research to be hidden from peer review or the public. Assertions that the research is unpublished because it's proprietary, or that the study is in progress, are essentially the same as saying, "Give us your money and trust us, fool."

Beware the pseudoscience often found on websites and infomercials; these can be filled with technical-sounding jargon to hide the truth. The studies, if any, may be funded by the company (often poorly designed and with a small number of subjects) and published in popular magazines or obscure "science" journals that peers would never read. Often the references are outdated and don't mention follow-up studies that proved the theory wrong. Another common ploy is to take the results of a legitimate study out of context: drawing conclusions from a test-tube study (*in vitro* instead of *in vivo,* meaning the whole animal); assuming mice and rat (murine) studies will give the same results in humans; extrapolating data from geriatrics or the seriously ill to a younger, healthier population.

What many promoters fail to mention is that you can lose weight via countless schemes—but keeping it off is a different story. And most are intended for couch potatoes; few fad diets even consider the energy needs of an athlete. The Zone Diet (a.k.a., the 40-30-30 plan) is a classic example of bad science that has been thoroughly debunked yet still lingers. Another popular fad is the Atkins diet, which periodically makes a comeback but falls flat for athletic performance.

Remember too that the media and conventional wisdom are often wrong. The media loves to jump on a bandwagon long before it's ready to roll. The devil-may-care attitude for headlines has led to general confusion among the public: let's see, are eggs good or bad this week? Answer: good, in moderation (four per week). And conventional wisdom's selective memory is both amazingly long and shortsighted. (See Appendix D, Resources, before committing yourself to the latest fad.)

Defining Progress

First things first: throw away that old scale! Losing weight is not the goal. Reducing body fat while building muscle is your objective. A normal scale only provides trivial information that is often discouraging. One of the paradoxes of weight loss is that you can build muscle faster than you lose fat, especially when starting a training program. Thus you could trim a pound of fat while adding 2 pounds of muscle and a normal scale would deliver bad news when it's actually great; you're stronger and your resting metabolic rate (RMR) has increased so more calories are burned around the clock.

If you are serious about becoming leaner and meaner, purchase skinfold calipers or a body fat scale to monitor your progress in reducing body fat. The calipers (Accu-Measure and Slim Guide are two good brands) are used to calculate measurements from three to nine places on your body (more is better). However, skinfold measurements can be difficult to do on yourself and it's important to use the proper equation. Digital models are more convenient (they do the math) but not necessarily any better.

The body fat scale uses bioelectrical impedance analysis (BIA), which compares the resistance to flow of a small electric current through different body tissues. Muscle, which is 74 percent water, conducts electrical flow more effectively than fat, which is about 25 percent water. The method is effective only if you keep the variables to a minimum: same time of day (it's most accurate in the evening), same part of the menstrual cycle, same hydration level (go to the bathroom first and avoid excessive drinking). The body fat scale is much easier to use yourself—just stand on it for a few seconds after you get out of the shower—and it gives fairly consistent results. Better models offer different calculations for athletes and nonathletes; many climbers will be in the middle.

With proper technique, both skinfold measurements and use of the body fat scale provide about a 3 percent range of error. So a reading of 13 percent means you are between 10 percent and 16 percent body fat. The actual number is less important than the trend over weeks and months (not day to day).

If you really need to know your body composition, other methods (such as underwater weighing, air displacement, and DEXA scans) can be more accurate. But these cost significantly more and are not available in many places.

One rather useless measure for climbers is body mass index, derived by a formula that relates your height and weight to determine how close you are to your ideal weight; above 25 is considered overweight and over 30 is obese (BMI = lbs ÷ in² × 703). This simplistic formula does not account for so many factors that athletes shouldn't take it seriously; a 6-foot-tall muscular man who weighs 200 pounds has a BMI of 27, but you probably wouldn't call him fat to his face. This index tells you much less than standing naked in front of a full-length mirror—the true test.

Lasting Lean

Reducing excess body fat is central to better performance for many climbers. But it's well documented that radical diet plans don't work in the long run. The quicker the fix, the faster the weight will return—with a vengeance, since fat can replace lost muscle. If you lose more than 1 or 2 pounds per week, the majority of it comes from water, muscle glycogen, and lean muscle mass—not fat.

Strict low-calorie diets (such as Jenny Craig and Weight Watchers) both reduce your RMR and do not provide sufficient energy for effective workouts. Studies on healthy women in metabolic chambers show that at least 1,200 calories (1,500 for men) are required to sustain body weight without any exercise (see figure 1.1). Yet many diet plans are at or below this level and the victims are somehow supposed to lead a normal life—short-term results and long-term failure is almost guaranteed.

Pssst . . . wanna know the *real* secret to permanent weight loss? The surefire miracle formula, proven by numerous independent studies? *Burn more than you eat.* No gimmicks, no quackery, just honest to goodness sound medical advice. The critical corollary: gradually make small changes.

You won't see overnight results, and that's the point. You didn't gain the fat overnight either. By reducing your current average daily consumption by only 20 percent (perhaps 500 calories), which should be easy, you will maintain muscle mass and have energy to play hard. Since you are not making drastic diet changes, or even forsaking favorite foods, the minor alterations become acceptable and sustainable. Research has shown that eating in a brightly lit room can reduce the temptation to binge heavily during meals (dim light is disinhibiting).

The great part about basing your diet on energy balance is all the things that you *don't* have to worry about. How much you eat on a particular day doesn't matter: savor a gourmet meal if you want, just don't do it often. What counts is that the number of calories consumed in a week is less than calories burned.

It doesn't matter if you exercise in the morning or evening, before or after a meal. The minor differences in calorie burning are insignificant in the grand scheme of things. What's important is that you make regular exercise part of your lifestyle.

Don't fear the fats! This fairly recent obsession has led to bigger guts everywhere. Eating fats won't necessarily make you fat—

Figure 1.1		
Activity Level	**Exercise**	**Calories Needed Per Pound**
Low	Minimal to none	14 to 15
Moderate	45–60 min. moderate intensity	16 to 20
High	1–2 hrs. moderate intensity	21 to 25
Extreme	2+ hrs. moderate intensity	25 to 30

the body just doesn't work that way—but eating too many calories will. To make them somewhat palatable, those low-fat and fat-free "diet" foods can be packed with nearly as many calories as real food. Since many people are fooled into thinking the stuff is better for them, and it's less filling, they chow down more—and gain weight.

Finding Balance

Although permanent weight loss (for those without medical conditions) is merely a matter of consuming less energy than you expend, counting calories (the old standby of perpetual dieters) doesn't need to be a daily exercise in mathematics. Unless you are fanatical about it, there is little chance you'll include all that you consume; hidden calories are everywhere so we typically underestimate intake. On the other side of the formula, research has shown that most people tend to overestimate their energy expenditure. None of the charts that estimate calories burned by different exercises are even close to accurate (look carefully at the comparisons to see what a joke they are) and the heart rate monitor and exercise machine guesses are little better. Don't let the minutia overwhelm you.

However, it is helpful to have a general idea of the amount of calories you need based on overall activity level. Multiply your weight by the calories per pound to get a rough estimate of your daily requirement (reduce the total if you're carrying more body fat than you should). If the intensity of work is low or high, you might move a level accordingly. For example, 90 minutes of low-intensity is Moderate but high intensity is Extreme.

It's also wise to have an idea of where the calories come from, and the ubiquitous Nutrition Facts label on the packages of food you buy is a great resource: get in the habit of reading it. To calculate calories in each "serving" (as defined on the label), multiply the grams of carbohydrates and protein by 4 and the grams of fat by 9 (this last calculation is done for you). Be sure to multiply this result by the number of so-called servings you actually consume!

Disorderly Eating

It's a dirty secret in the climbing world that quite a few elite sport climbers suffer from eating disorders. Some of the men and women you might recognize from magazines and posters are seriously anorexic or bulimic. Nobody likes to talk about it—even their friends and parents are in denial. Sponsors, of course, just care about results and publicity.

This problem doesn't stop with the elites; eating disorders are widespread throughout a sport climbing community that places a high premium on low body fat (much like gymnasts, dancers, and runners). Eating disorders are a serious psychological issue, fostered by our society and the demands of sport, that affects men too. Since the victim is often unaware or unable to escape, this condition almost always requires intervention and counseling.

Young women climbers in particular face a very real danger from the female athlete triad: disordered eating, amenorrhea (loss of menstrual period), and osteoporosis (brittle bones). Individually, each of these is a serious problem; together the health risks are severe.

Climbers must be realistic in their expectations about body weight. There is only so little you can weigh without sacrificing performance and health. If you come from a long line of large ancestors, no amount of wishful thinking or starvation will make you diminutive. Your body has a natural set point that it will always try to maintain, no matter what you do. Restrict calories too much and it will retaliate by reducing RMR and muscle mass.

For an approximation of your ideal minimum weight, use the following formulas and allow a range of error of 10 percent for bone structure. Men: start at 106 and add 6 pounds for each additional inch past 5 feet (therefore, a 6-foot male should weigh around 180 and be between 160 and 195 pounds). Women: start at 100 and add 5 pounds for each additional inch over 5 feet (thus a 5-foot, 6-inch female should weigh about 130 and be between 117 and 143 pounds). If you think you can climb your best at 20 percent below that figure (144 and 104 respectively), faggetaboutit! On the other hand, you may feel just fine at 20 percent heavier (216 and 156 pounds).

Sport Eating

Since most of your meals are consumed at home, that is where you build the foundation for improving your climbing performance. No matter your diet philosophy—omnivore or vegetarian—the basics of healthful eating are the same.

In general, you should aim to get 65 percent of your calories from carbohydrates, 20 percent from fats, and 15 percent from protein. Since fats are pervasive, it's unlikely you'll actually achieve this ratio unless you carefully prepare every meal yourself, and you'll probably fall into the standard 60-25-15 guideline.

Run, don't walk, away from the advocates of a 40-30-30 diet: they won't be able to keep up with you, and they don't have any scientific basis for their nonsense. Indeed, high protein diets have been shown to result in chronic dehydration and greater kidney stress.

Considerable evidence indicates that, to maintain muscle mass (neutral nitrogen balance) or build muscles (positive nitrogen balance), most climbers need about twice as much protein as the recommended daily allowance for sedentary adults (0.36 gram per pound of body weight, or 0.8 gram per kilogram of body weight). Thus you should strive to consume 0.57 to 0.77 gram of protein per pound of body weight—a 176-pound person needs about 100 to 135 grams per day. Inadequate protein will hamper your recovery, prevent strength gains, and reduce resistance to colds and flu.

Contrary to claims of the protein-pushers, there is no evidence that consuming more than 1 gram per pound will make you huge or do anything else except drain your wallet. With a proper diet, there is no need for any outdoor athlete to purchase protein powders or most amino acid supplements.

Omnivores may even need to cut back on protein since many animal sources are also high in fat calories. Vegetarians, especially vegans, have to be more careful since they need to consume large portions of soy as well as other protein sources (beans and legumes); plants just aren't as protein-dense as animals.

Breakfast Rules

You're probably tired of hearing that "breakfast is the most important meal of the day." Moms around the world use this refrain—then fill their children up with candy (a.k.a. kids' cereal) before packing them off to school. Despite this hypocrisy, the basic advice holds true and is especially important for athletes—that would be you.

Don't even think about complaining that a climb is too strenuous if you didn't eat a real breakfast!

It isn't just a matter of starting the day off well-fueled, though that's certainly a big performance help. Eating a good-size (500+ calorie), carbohydrate-rich breakfast can reduce your daily calorie consumption without the usual diet suffering. You won't feel as much need to snack on junk food and sodas in the afternoon and are less likely to overindulge at dinner.

Cereals with milk or yogurt are still the king of breakfasts since they're convenient and contain mostly carbs with a bit of protein; adding fruits is a bonus. Although the box may be more nutritious than many of the cereals at the supermarket, you can find some healthy ones that actually taste good; it just takes a bit of looking and testing.

If you haven't made the switch yet, now is the time to use lower fat milk: start with 2 percent, then move to 1 percent, and finally see if you can tolerate skim milk or soy milk; the latter is tasty but not necessarily healthier than cow's milk unless you are lactose intolerant. In cereal, you'll hardly notice the difference and eventually won't even miss whole (3.3 percent) milk.

The main cereal ingredients should be whole grain oats, whole grain wheat, or bran flakes. When comparing the Nutrition Facts labels, first multiply the grams of sugars by 4 to get the number of sugar calories, then compare that to the total number of calories; it should be less than a quarter—though it's about half in many kids' cereals. Ideally there should be, in each serving, at least 5 grams of fiber and less than 8 grams of sugar, 3 grams of total fat, and 250 mg of sodium.

It's ironic that granola-crunchers have earned a reputation as healthy, back-to-nature types since most granolas are fairly high in saturated fats and sugars; the few granolas that are actually better for you tend to taste like cow fodder. Instead, try muesli with low-cal yogurt (but be aware that some flavored yogurts are loaded with empty sugar calories).

If cereal just isn't your thing or you need variety, there are lots of other options besides greasy egg dishes, bacon, sausages, hash browns, croissants, and all the other traditional gut-bombs that slow you down (still better than nothing, if consumed in moderation). More athletic choices include a bagel with lox and low-fat cream cheese; poached eggs and whole grain toast or muffin with fruit preserves; Canadian bacon and whole grain waffles or pancakes with maple syrup; or even a breakfast drink. Opt for fresh fruit or orange juice over that extra cup of coffee.

Midday Refueling

In terms of calorie content, lunch should be the same size as breakfast and dinner. But this doesn't have to be in one sitting. If you're going to work out in the afternoon, it's often better to eat a light lunch or simply graze on healthy snacks throughout the day, since a full stomach isn't conducive to exercise. Snacking can prevent hunger binges and maintain your energy level—no post-lunch coma.

There are lots of good midday snacks that are fast and easy: soups; fruits (fresh and dried) and fruit smoothies; raisins and prunes; low-fat yogurt or frozen yogurt; low-fat cottage cheese and carrot sticks; celery and hummus; stone-ground crackers and sugar-free peanut butter; whole-grain bread with tuna fish and low-fat mayonnaise; bagel and cream cheese; baked potato with plain yogurt or mustard; zucchini bread.

Some snacks, like low-salt pretzels, rice cakes, and air-popped popcorn, don't provide much calorie content (if you don't overdo it) or any protein, but help fill you up. Drink several glasses of water throughout the day; use a carbon filter on your faucet if taste or chemical contaminants are a problem in your area (bottled water has no salubrious effects but does cost more). Try to avoid soft drinks (diet or not), potato chips, french fries, and many of the most popular entrees served at fast-food restaurants.

If you've eaten well earlier in the day, you won't feel the need for that huge dinner that may have been your mainstay. By eating a smaller supper, you'll sleep better and wake up hungry for a good breakfast.

Dining Guides

Whether by choice or necessity, we don't always eat at home. This doesn't mean you have to give up all hope of healthy nutrition, even if you don't know what the menu means. Following a few simple guidelines can prevent fat and cholesterol overload. (Before dining out or traveling, consult Appendix A, Dining Out, for healthier meal choices.)

- Always try to cover two-thirds of your plate with carbs (vegetables, beans, pasta, rice, potato, bread, fruit), then make sure you have adequate protein represented; the fats will usually take care of themselves.

- Make fish and seafood your main priority, followed by poultry, then red meats. Select organic free-range meats to reduce consumption of antibiotics.

- When possible, opt for baked, broiled, or grilled entrees versus fried or sautéed to eliminate hidden fat calories.

- Remove the skin from chicken and trim the fat from steaks.

- For maximum nutritional value, select vegetable courses that are raw or lightly steamed versus cooked to death. If it's limp and pallid, it's been ruined.

- Don't smother baked potatoes with cheese, butter, and sour cream, but do eat the skin. Better yet, order a sweet potato; it's packed with vitamins.

- When grazing at the salad bar, go for the dark green and colorful vegetables (spinach, broccoli, carrots, peppers, tomatoes), plus cauliflower, beans, chickpeas, and sunflower seeds. Go light on the pale lettuce, celery, mushrooms, cucumbers, radishes, zucchini, and alfalfa sprouts; pallid vegetables tend to add more weight than nutrition (vitamins and fiber).

- Watch out for the heavy dressings (can add more than 800 calories) and fatty toppings (cheese, greasy croutons, marinated artichokes) that can null much of the health benefits of a salad. Request dressings on the side and then add sparingly.

Power Shopping

The bulk of your food probably comes from the grocery store, so that's where good nutrition begins. Of course, if you have a local farmer's market, by all means take advantage of it; everything is fresher, healthier, tastier, and often cheaper. It takes a little longer to be a smart shopper—you have to read the labels—but the rewards are worth it.

The main rule of thumb: the less processed, the better. When selecting breads, crackers, and cereals, always opt for whole grain instead of enriched white or just "wheat"; these have more vitamins, minerals and fiber. Brown rice is more flavorful and nutritious than white rice, which has the bran removed. Although whole-wheat pasta is slightly healthier, the traditional durum wheat (semolina) cooks better because of a higher gluten content; soy and rice pastas turn to mush.

Organic foods may or may not be healthier than that offered by the agro-chemical industry. Some of the claims by starry-eyed advocates are inaccurate or blown out of proportion, but eating fewer toxic chemicals is probably a good thing. There is no question that organic farming is better for the planet; it can even be more productive per acre of land. Unfortunately, the major food corporations care more about profits than nutrition, so they emphasize taste (add sugar), eye appeal (add coloring), and long shelf life (strip the good stuff and add the periodic table).

Every visit to the store is an opportunity to vote against spraying pesticides, depleting topsoils, contaminating water, and short-sighted greed. Now that the Pandora's box of genetically modified organisms (GMO) has been opened, there are even greater health and safety concerns, with very little assurances, about our food supply. Yet there currently are no regulations on labeling of GMOs so there is little choice about eating them. If you simply choose one additional organic item per shopping trip, the impact to your wallet will be minimal but the cumulative effect can be major. The best overall value is probably in organic meats (free-range animals grown without steroids or antibiotics) and omega-3 enhanced eggs (from chickens that eat feed high in canola oil).

Smart Reading. Pay attention to the Nutrition Facts label, not the advertising hype on the packaging. First, look at the serving size and see how much you will actually eat. Then find out how many calories are in a serving and do the math. Next find out how many calories come from fat, the total grams of fat, and the total grams of protein. The amount of sodium and saturated fats should be close to zero. With practice, it doesn't take long to scan a label to find the good, the bad, and the ugly.

Learn some of the lingo, too: "Reduced Fat" (25 percent less than the original product); "Lite" (one third the calories or half the fat, not both); and "Fat-Free" (half gram or less per serving). These products tend be less filling and guilt-free so people often eat more. Many people consume more calories and sodium than if they'd gone with the "evil" original.

When it comes to oils, they all contain about 120 calories per tablespoon but some are better than others. The ones to shun are animal fat (lard, bacon grease), coconut oil, and palm oil, all of which are very high in saturated fats. The best choices for cooking are ghee (clarified butter), olive oil, and canola oil, with peanut oil a runner-up; shun corn, sunflower, and safflower oils. Extra-virgin, cold-pressed, first-pressing oils retain more flavor and nutrients than those extracted with heat or chemical solvents but need to be refrigerated and protected from light. Fish oil isn't used for cooking but may be added to foods to boost omega-3 fatty acids; research has linked this essential fatty acid with healthy hearts.

Sugar. Among the most pervasive additives is high fructose corn syrup; it may sound healthier but it's only a cheaper form of table sugar. Other sweeteners include honey, brown or raw sugar, refined cane juice, and fruit-juice sweeteners. Products containing these are often labeled as "natural," implying they are somehow better, but they have insignificant nutritional value over table sugar (sucrose).

Probably the most common artificial sweetener, aspartame (a.k.a. Equal and Nutrasweet), is actually a molecule of two amino acids that is 180 times sweeter than table sugar but follows a different metabolic pathway. Diet sodas, usually made with aspartame, cut about 150 calories per can from your diet, and are okay in moderation (one or two cans a day). But plain old water or flavored seltzer is still the best way to slack your thirst.

All carbohydrates are ultimately broken down in the small intestine to glucose (blood sugar), which is then converted to glycogen; however, the body handles the sugars differently. While glucose is actively absorbed into the bloodstream, fructose (fruit sugar) diffuses so it doesn't provide a fast energy spike. This is good for some people, but too much fructose may cause cramps or diarrhea in others. Combined with other sugars, small amounts of fructose give a bigger energy boost than either alone. Maltodextrins are another form of sugar, called glucose polymers, that are not as sweet as many others, which allows them to be used in higher concentrations for high-energy foods and drinks.

While carbohydrates are classified as simple (1 to 5 molecules) or complex (hundreds of molecules), this does not describe how quickly they are absorbed. The glycemic index (GI, see Appendix B) is a rating system developed for diabetics to approximate how fast sugars enter your bloodstream; 0–60 is low and slow, 60–85 is moderate, 85–100 is high and fast.

Even if you are not particularly sugar-sensitive, you may benefit from using the tables to plan your meals before, during, and after a big climb or hard workout. By consuming low-GI foods prior to a long day, you can get sustained energy to carry you through. For a quick pick-me-up during the day, moderate- to high-GI foods will enter your bloodstream faster. Following a hard effort, consuming high-GI foods can restore muscle glycogen faster so you'll be ready to go again the next day.

While worth experimenting with when training, the GI charts have limited value in normal dining since comsuming fats and proteins can lower the GI of carbohydrates. Most healthy people don't have real problems with an insulin spike and the ensuing sugar crash, so there is little need to stress over the glycemic index.

Walking the Aisles

The tricks of the supermarket trade make healthy shopping more difficult. Notice how the lighting is just right (so you don't blink or squint), the music is soothing (so you'll relax and linger), and the in-store bakery and chicken rotisserie are always on (so the smell will make you hungry and buy more food). At most stores, products at eye level and the ends of aisles have paid a premium for that location. If a product is discontinued, it may have sold well but the manufacturer didn't pay the slotting fee charged by the store.

To defeat these tactics, the smart shopper prepares a list, sticks to it, and doesn't go to the store on an empty stomach. Get in, get out. Ignore the store's layout—though fresh products are often on the perimeter—and shop according to the food pyramid: start with carbohydrates, move to produce, and finish with meats and dairy. Resist the temptation of coupons and specials since you often end up buying more and getting a less healthy product. Compare the unit price on the shelves; bulk isn't always a good value.

Cereal Aisle

- Pick cereals that contain at least 5 grams of fiber and no more than 8 grams of sugar, 3 grams of total fat, and 250 mg of sodium per serving.

Bread Aisle

- Look for whole grain as the main ingredient but keep fat to less than 2 grams per slice. Pass on any white or "wheat" breads.
- Avoid the high-fat treats such as croissants, muffins, and pastries.

Produce Aisle

- Fill your basket with fruits and vegetables. Consider organic to reduce your pesticide intake. Prewashed and packaged salad mixes cost more but make your hectic life easier.
- Fresh fruit juices and vegetable juices are a tasty and convenient way to get your daily quota, though you miss out on the fiber in the real thing.

Canned-Foods Aisle

- Stock up on soups, but avoid those with a cream base.
- Select canned tuna packed in water for an excellent, low-cost source of protein.

- Canned vegetables contain nearly as many nutrients as fresh, but watch out for sugar, salt, and other additives.
- Canned fruits are often packed in syrup that is basically liquid sugar; look for ones packed in their own juices.

Ethnic Aisle

- Choose the vegetarian refried beans without the lard.
- Many pasta sauces and salsas contain a surprising amount of sodium and hidden sugars.
- Pesto sauce typically contains 50 percent more calories than tomato sauce.
- Don't make a habit of coconut milk; choose the light version if available.

Dairy Aisle

- Pick 1 percent or skim milk. Try some flavored soy milk.
- Select cheese made with skim milk. If the cheese is labeled, look for those with less than 5 grams of fat per ounce. Nonfat cottage cheese is a good source of protein.
- Yogurt is an excellent source of protein and calcium. Look for less than 200 calories, 2 grams of saturated fat, 40 grams of sugar and no artificial sweetener. The best option is plain yogurt mixed with fresh fruit.
- Butter or trans-free margarine is the best choice for daily consumption; avoid hydrogenated or partially hydrogenated oils.

Frozen-Foods Aisle

- Frozen yogurt often contains as much sugar as ice cream. Whichever you choose, try to keep total fat to less than 5 grams per serving. However, it's better to

BETTER LIVING THROUGH PLANTS

Numerous compounds in plants, generically called phytochemicals, are emerging as potential insurance against a host of diseases. It's best to get the original sources than purchasing expensive (and sometimes ineffective) supplements. Here are some of the goodies that have been identified and their possible benefits:

Plant	Compound	Action
Broccoli, cauliflower, kale, cabbage	isothyocynates, indoles	block synthesis of estrogen associated with breast and ovarian cancer; prevent carcinogens from harming cells
Carrots, cantaloupe, apricots, parsley, vegetables	carotenoids	formation of vitamin A; immuno-protection
Chile peppers	capsaicin	anticoagulant
Citrus fruit	terpenes, limonoids	prevent growth of tumors
Flaxseed, walnuts	omega-3 fatty acids	block estrogen activity; immuno-protection
Garlic, onion	allylic sulfides	reduces blood pressure and cholesterol; formation of glutathione, a powerful antioxidant
Rosemary	quinines	inhibits carcinogens
Soy milk, tofu	genistein	slows tumor growth
Spinach, collard greens	lutein	antioxidant; eye health
Strawberries, pineapple	chlorogenic acid	prevents formation of carcinogenic nitrosamines
Tea, red wine, fruits, vegetables, chocolate	flavonoids	antioxidants; inhibit carcinogenic hormones
Tomatoes	lycopenes	antioxidants
Vegetable oils, almonds, peanuts, sesame and sunflower seeds	vitamin E	antioxidant

indulge in a super-premium ice cream once a month than in a lowfat one a couple times a week.

- Select calcium-fortified orange juice and any other that is 100 percent fruit juice.
- Frozen entrees from the natural foods case or the "health" section will usually have reduced saturated fats and can be quite tasty. However, they may also be loaded with calories, so check the labels.
- Frozen vegetables are nearly as nutritious as farm fresh—and often more nutritious than store fresh—but beware the sauces.

Meat and Seafood Aisle

- Try to make the fish counter your main source of protein but check the Seafood Watch on Monterey Bay Aquarium's website (*www.mbayaq.org*) for an updated list of fishes to avoid (it's grim). Albacore tuna, catfish, halibut, mahi mahi, rainbow trout, and Pacific salmon are nutritious fish with healthy populations that are caught with minimal by-catch (other sea life) or are farmed with minimal environmental impact. (Although they may be not be bad for you, eating the following seafoods is bad for the environment: bluefin tuna, Chilean sea bass, orange roughy, Pacific red snapper, farmed Atlantic salmon, shark, farmed shrimp, and swordfish.)
- Commercially raised chickens are not kept in cages nor are they fed hormones (by law), but they do consume antibiotics. Organic and free-range chicken isn't necessarily better. Purchase skinless or remove the skin.

- Turkey is another good protein source. However, processed turkey (bologna, sausage, hot dogs) is often high in fat.
- Pork tenderloin and Canadian bacon are both fairly low in fat. Back away from the bacon and hot dogs.
- Choose lean steaks (sirloin, top round, roast beef) or extra-lean hamburger, preferably from "natural" farms. Avoid the fatty grilling steaks (New York strip, porterhouse, T-bone) and regular hamburger.

Cookie and Snack Aisle

- Journey not into the valley of temptation. But if you must stray, read the nutrition labels and try to minimize the damage.
- Most peanut butter is loaded with sugar for kids and hydrogenated oil. Select a natural brand without any additives. Pour off the oil and replace it with flax oil to get some good fat in your diet. Almond butter is also tasty, and does not contain aflatoxins, known carcinogens produced by molds that grow on some crops.
- All of the sodas and most of the fruit juices (unless labeled 100 percent) are merely liquid candy that deter people from healthier alternatives.

SUPPLEMENTS

Athletes are notorious for looking for the quick fix that will deliver better performance: the first case of Olympic organizers banning competitors for using supplements (mushrooms and animal protein) occurred in 300 B.C. Climbers are certainly no exception to the search for magic elixirs. Yet the utter disregard for health and common sense is truly amazing. On little more than rumor and bad science, North Americans and Europeans waste billions of dollars each year and get little more than expensive piss.

The truth is that most athletes have minimal need for extra vitamins or minerals simply because these are not burned by exercise and we eat more than the average person. Assuming you consume a balanced diet (no bizarre eating habits) and consume more than 1,500 calories per day, which is probable even if you're trying to lose fat, then you are probably well above the dietary reference intakes (DRI) on just about everything. Quite simply, if you gobble pills by the handful, you've been suckered.

The evidence for enhanced performance or health by supplementation of most vitamins, minerals, and micronutrients beyond dietary amounts is scanty at best—really. The body has large stores of fat-soluble vitamins (A, D, E, and K), and even the water-soluble vitamins (B-complex and C) won't show a deficit over a month of no intake. If you binge on junk food for a few days, get stressed at work, or wake up with a hangover, popping a supplement pill won't do any good. Supplementation is only beneficial for correcting long-term deficiencies from an inadequate diet.

Even the media hysteria over antioxidants has been blown out of proportion. Although free radicals (molecules with unpaired electrons) sound scary and can do nasty things in a test tube, the body is better able to cope with them than once thought. There is no solid evidence that taking additional antioxidants will increase performance or speed recovery. While antioxidants may prevent some chronic diseases, the research does not support overdoing them, or overspending on them, the way the vitamin industry would like.

The dangers of overdosing on vitamins can be greater than the consequences of not taking extra. Too much vitamin A and beta-carotene may increase the odds of heart disease and lung cancer; chronic megadoses of vitamin B-6 can result in neurotoxicity; high levels of niacin has a host of side effects including decreased fat burning and possible liver damage; megadoses of vitamin C combined with excess iron can become a pro-oxidant (increasing free radicals and oxidative damage) and cause kidney stones and heart failure; too much vitamin D can be toxic and reduce bone mass; and overdoing vitamin E can exacerbate bleeding and possibly suppress your immune system.

Likewise, megadosing on minerals can lead to unpleasant complications. As mentioned, iron can be highly toxic. Men should have a blood test for serum ferritin (more sensitive than for serum iron) before taking extra iron—and should not exceed 45 mg per day. While calcium is important, overdoing it reduces zinc absorption. High intakes of zinc can result in a copper deficiency; don't use the cold lozenges for more than a week. Magnesium can also be overdone, resulting in kidney problems. Similarly, too much chromium may interfere with iron in the

SUPPLEMENTS THAT MIGHT HELP

The Reference Daily Intake (RDI) for vitamins and minerals, from which supplement label percentages are derived, is based upon the science of 1968 (with minor changes up to 1989). However, the Food and Nutrition Board (FNB) of the Institute of Medicine (IM), made up of scientists in Canada and the United States, has developed replacement guidelines based on the most recent research, termed Dietary Reference Intakes (DRI), that started coming out in 1997.

In addition, the committees have provided a Tolerable Upper Intake Level (UL) that is considered the maximum safe level in your diet. It is termed "tolerable" because the science does not support higher dosages than the DRI.

To sum up: The FNB of the IM created the recommended daily allowances (RDAs) that the FDA used to set the RDIs that give the percent daily values now on labels. But the RDAs are being replaced by the DRIs, which are a combination of RDAs, adequate intakes (AIs), estimated average requirements (EARs), and ULs, and labels may someday change. Got that?

These DRIs are for healthy adults ages 19 to 50. They are listed in grams, micrograms, and international units. Your needs will be different if you are: younger, older, pregnant (or thinking about it), lactating, have a medical condition, or are otherwise abnormal (aside from being a climber). If in doubt, consult your doctor.

	Present RDI	New DRI	UL
VITAMINS			
Vitamin A	5,000 IU	900 mcg (3000 IU) men, 700 mcg women	3,000 mcg (10,000 IU)
Vitamin C	60 mg	90 mg men, 75 mg women	2 g
Vitamin D	400 IU (10 mcg)	5 mcg	50 mcg
Vitamin E	30 IU (13–20 mg)	15 mg	1 g
Vitamin K	80 mcg	120 mcg men, 90 mcg women	Not determined
Thiamin	1.5 mg	1.2 mg men, 1.1 mg women	Not determined
Riboflavin	1.7 mg	1.3 mg men, 1.1 mg women	Not determined

	Present RDI	New DRI	UL
Niacin	20 mg	16 mg men, 14 mg women	35 mg
Vitamin B-6	2 mg	1.3 mg	100 mg
Folate	400 mcg	400 mcg	1,000 mcg
Vitamin B-12	6 mcg	2.4 mcg	Not determined
Biotin	300 mcg	30 mcg	Not determined
Pantothenic acid	10 mg	5 mg	Not determined
Choline	Not established	550 mg	3,500 mg
MINERALS			
Calcium	1,000 mg	1,000 mg	2.5 g
Iron	18 mg	8 mg men, 18 mg women	45 mg
Phosphorus	1,000 mg	700 mg	4 g
Iodine	150 mcg	150 mcg	1,100 mcg
Magnesium	400 mg	420 mg men, 320 mg women	350 mg as a supplement
Zinc	15 mg	11 mg men, 8 mg women	40 mg
Selenium	70 mcg	55 mcg	400 mcg
Copper	2 mg	0.9 mg	10 mg
Manganese	2 mg	2.3 mg men, 1.8 mg women	11 mg
Chromium	120 mcg	35 mcg men, 25 mcg women	Not determined
Molybdenum	75 mcg	45 mcg	2,000 mcg
Fluoride	Not established	4 mg men, 3 mg women	10 mg

blood. There is some evidence that excessive phosphorous can lead to bone loss. Selenium is the easiest mineral to overdose, with toxic results.

Supplements That Might Help

Those vast aisles of bottles at health food stores and supermarkets are less intimidating once you know what to avoid. Most of the stuff is expensive snake oil. Once you have optimized your diet, you *might* be able to boost performance with additional supplements. But ya gotta plug the big leaks before fixin' the little drips! None of these can make up for an inadequate diet or overcome inefficient training—sorry, no miracles here.

Multivitamins. Even if you're doing everything "right," it's still a good idea to take a one-per-day multivitamin/mineral supplement with a meal. This will ensure that most of the essentials are covered without pushing you over the limit (remember, those DRIs are *total* daily intake). Unless you are vegan, lactose-intolerant, or have food allergies, there is no legitimate reason for the megavitamin horse pills or many-per-day supplements that the scammers swear are necessary.

When selecting a multivitamin/mineral supplement, examine the label to make sure the pill will dissolve completely—guaranteed by USP (United States Pharmacopeia) approval. A simple test is to place a pill in a half cup of vinegar and gently stir occasionally; it should disintegrate within 30 minutes. Most of the ingredients should be about 100 to 150 percent of the recommended daily value, though none will contain enough calcium or magnesium since you wouldn't be able to swallow the pill. Men should avoid iron unless you have been cleared by a blood test. Women who may become pregnant need extra folate.

Beyond these basic requirements, you can ignore the hype: there is no practical advantage of "natural" vitamins (except vitamin E); chelated supplements don't absorb better; time release isn't superior; sugar or starch are fillers that don't affect anything; liquids aren't better than pills; brand names are no better than generics as long as the quantities are right.

Antioxidants. Although the evidence for additional antioxidants is far from conclusive (much of it is based on cellular studies), it's sufficient for the U.S. Olympic Sports Medicine Committee to recommend somewhat higher dosages for athletes.

Since your multivitamin already contains the RDI of vitamin A (5,000 IU) and too much is toxic, there is no need for more. Beta-carotene is a related, even stronger antioxidant that has no DRI because supporting data is lacking. Besides, it's just one of over 600 carotenoids—eat your veggies.

Climbers might consider 250 to 1,000 mg per day of vitamin C to boost immune protection, especially during cold season or if you are doing a brutal, multiday route. But citrus fruits, strawberries, kiwi fruits, raw broccoli, and red peppers are all better sources than a pill.

Even with a healthy diet it can be difficult to meet the DRI and there may be additional benefits from 100 to 400 IU of vitamin E. The natural form (d-alpha or RR-alpha tocopherol) is about a third more potent than the synthetic version (dl-alpha or all-rac alpha tocopherol) and comes with related chemicals that may be beneficial.

BCAA. Branched chain amino acids (BCAAs; leucine, isoleucine, and valine) may help with mental fatigue and prevent muscle breakdown during 2 hours or more of endurance fun. The theory holds that high levels of BCAAs will reduce free tryptophan, which is a precursor of serotonin (the brain hormone associated with fatigue).

At present, there is no clear evidence that BCAA supplementation is more effective than ensuring adequate carbohydrates. In low doses, as is found in some sport drinks, it has no effect on serotonin and high doses can cause stomach problems. If you experiment, purchase prepackaged BCAAs, not the individual amino acids, to get the proper ratio.

Caffeine. Even if you are a habitual coffee or tea drinker, you can get a slight performance boost by supplementing with 2.5 mg caffeine per pound of body weight (about four NoDoz or two Vivarin tablets) about an hour before a long endurance climb. Because of other compounds that moderate the effect, drinking coffee is less stimulating than caffeine supplements. Recent research has shown that caffeine is not the strong diuretic it was once considered; the dehydrating effect is mild to nonexistent.

The evidence supporting caffeine as a "fat burner" is equivocal at best, though the combination with ephedrine appears more effective. These stimulants can make you wired and sweaty and should not be taken in excessive dosages or at all if you have high blood pressure. There is a risk of unwittingly overdoing it since they are hidden in many products under innocuous names (see cautions on ephedrine later in this chapter in the section "Suspicious Supplements"). The results also appear to vary widely, so many people see no positive results.

Calcium. Calcium has many functions besides bone growth, so it's important for optimal performance. Even if you are not lactose-intolerant or vegan, it can be difficult to get adequate calcium from a normal diet if you don't pay attention.

To make the quota, you need to consume three cups (24 ounces) of milk, soy milk, or fortified orange juice each day. Other good options include yogurt (one container is a third of the DRI) and tofu made with calcium sulfate (five times more calcium than regular tofu; 6 ounces meets your need). Some vegetables contain calcium but you have to eat a lot. Cheese and ice cream contain calcium but come with a price (lotsa fat calories). As a last resort, you can fill in the deficit with a calcium supplement (500 mg maximum per dose).

Creatine. Among the most talked about, and advertised, sport supplements is creatine, a naturally occurring substance found in meat and fish. While it is normally considered useful for power athletes (sprinters, power lifters, and possibly sport climbers), creatine may help to raise the lactate threshold (see chapter 3) and enhance the quality of workouts for endurance athletes too. However, you need to be more careful about hydration levels and more research is needed.

Vegetarians are most likely to see the biggest boost in performance, since their diet is lacking in creatine. About a quarter of the people who try it see no results. To prevent excess water gain, take six 1-gram doses per day for five to six days, then 2 grams per day for maintenance. There is no significant difference between the different brands of powdered or liquid creatine, except how much you pay.

Echinacea. Considerable evidence supports the claims of immune-boosting properties for this plant. It can both decrease symptoms and shorten the severity of colds and flu. Once you feel something coming on, take either the liquid or pill form of the standardized extract according to the instructions (pills don't require counting drops). Research on its preventive capabilities is inconclusive and little has been done on goldenseal, which often is mixed in.

Ginkgo Biloba. This tree has been around for 200 million years and the Chinese have used the nuts as medicine for nearly 5,000 years. Now, extract from the leaves is proving effective against problems associated with microcirculation, which includes everything from cognitive function to balance to acclimatization. Ginkgo is a powerful antioxidant and increases blood flow throughout the body (taking it with aspirin may cause problems with excessive bleeding). Research is still ongoing in many fields, but 200 mg per day (half in the morning, the rest later) seems to be effective for most people.

Glutamine. Another amino acid that might help performance is glutamine, which is normally abundant. However, levels of glutamine are severely depressed following intense endurance exercise, overtraining, and severe stress. It has been suggested, but not conclusively proven, that supplementing with 5 to 20 grams of glutamine might increase glycogen stores, improve recovery, and boost the immune system. Be warned that most "sports foods" contain nowhere near this amount, which makes its inclusion mostly for show. Glutamine absorbs best when combined with other amino acids.

Herbal Antioxidants. There are many natural sources of antioxidants, though little research has compared them against each other or simple vitamin supplements that are less expensive. When tea leaves are dried instead of fermented, which turns them black, they retain their antioxidant properties. You'd have to drink five to ten cups of green tea every day to get an effect, so extracts (125 to 500 mg per day) are more practical. Grape seed extract (50 to 100 mg per day) is an alternative to drinking red wine every day, though human studies are lacking at present.

Iron. Roughly a quarter of female athletes may be iron deficient; partly due to menstruation but also because many are vegetarians on calorie-restricted diets. Male climbers, especially vegetarians and endurance fiends, may also be iron deficient. If you are often tired and feel weak and fatigued, it may be an indication of deficiency instead of overtraining.

If you eat red meat a few times a week, there should be no problem. Many plants contain a form of iron (non-heme) that is less bioavailable, so try to purchase iron-fortified breads and cereals and consume them with a source of vitamin C. Using a cast-iron skillet will also boost iron intake.

Women can safely include 15 mg of iron in their multivitamins; however, men (and postmenopausal women) should only do so after a serum ferritin blood test. Hemochromatosis (iron overload) is the most common of all genetic disorders, affecting about one in two hundred Caucasians in North America. There is no benefit to supplementing iron if your supplies are adequate (above 50 nanograms per milliliter of blood for athletes), and it can be dangerous to do so if they are already high.

Milk Thistle (*Silybum marianum*). Reputed to protect the liver, an analysis in 2000 of all the data concluded that the clinical evidence is inconclusive but more research should be done. Milk thistle appears to be safe and has no major side effects, so it falls into the "can't hurt and may do some good" category, particularly if you drink alcohol. For preventive purposes, typical recommendations are about 280 mg of 80 percent extract per day.

Phosphorus. This mineral is used for energy production, lactate buffering, and release of oxygen to the muscles, plus strong bones and teeth. Most people get more than enough from their diet so there is little need to supplement. But a fair amount of research shows that up to 4 grams per day of phosphate salts for three to four days can slightly improve endurance. Too much on a routine basis can lead to calcium deficiency.

Protein Powder. Active climbers have a higher protein requirement than the DRI (see the earlier section in this chapter, "Sport Eating"). Most athletes on a normal diet consume adequate protein (about 1.5 grams per kilogram of body weight) and shouldn't waste money on powders. However, during periods of strength building and high-intensity climbing, supplementing with protein powders to achieve a 2-grams-per-kilogram total daily intake can help with recovery.

Whey protein, a former by-product of the cheese industry, is the most common protein supplement, but the processing can vary widely (30 to 90 percent concentrations). The most expensive form, ion-exchange whey protein isolate, may also enhance immune protection. Casein (milk curd) is another protein supplement that absorbs more slowly, which increases amino acid levels. Soy protein isolates contain isoflavones that may protect the heart. The bioavailability of all these protein sources (that is, the body's ability to use them), based on the most recent rating system, is comparable. All of these contain

BCAAs, so there is no need to do both at the same time.

The patented or proprietary protein supplements are merely different blends of various sources with scanty evidence to prove they are better than others. Virtually none of the formulations have actually been tested against each other in well-documented independent studies. Blending is a marketing trick that lets them list protein first on a label; the ingredients would be lower down (below all the sugar) if listed separately.

Glucosamine. Among the latest buzzwords in the over-40 crowd are glucosamine and chondroitin, which appear to be as effective at relieving joint pain as ibuprofen; they may even assist in rebuilding damaged cartilage. Here again, the research is preliminary but anecdotal evidence is convincing, and a recent study showed glucosamine stopped the progression of osteoarthritis. While probably not a cure for arthritis, as is commonly advertised, glucosamine/chondroitin could be worth a try if you are experiencing joint pain. However, if symptoms persist, you definitely need to see a doctor!

Non-Steroidal Anti-Inflammatory Drugs (NSAIDs). Many climbers take "vitamin I" (ibuprofen) to ease their aches and pains. While effective at reducing swelling, this exceedingly popular NSAID does not promote healing and can be more dangerous than you realize. It's debatable whether ibuprofen masks pain sufficiently for a climber to aggravate a preexisting

injury, but the possibility exists. However, combining ibuprofen and alcohol (three or more drinks per day) is known to cause stomach bleeding. Since ibuprofen is cleared through the kidneys, avoid taking it when they are stressed during ultra-endurance events. (See chapter 5 for more details on NSAIDs.)

Suspicious Supplements

In 1994 a federal law (Dietary Supplement Health and Education Act) reclassified dietary supplements so they were no longer "food additives" that were controlled by the Food and Drug Administration. This left the industry virtually unregulated regarding product claims and helped make it extremely wealthy—annual sales were over $16 billion in 2000.

The supplement companies are frantically looking for the next creatine—that product's annual sales jumped from $50 million to $400 million in just five years—and are promoting products long before they're ready for prime time. Since there is no reporting of adverse effects, the safety of many herbs and supplements is unclear.

It's a rare race package, climbing competition, or outdoor event that doesn't provide samples of "sports enhancers" and "nutraceuticals" with ingredients you probably haven't heard about. Most of these exotic ingredients are backed by little more than glowing testimonials with unbelievable before-and-after photos. Invariably when somebody claims a product gave them great results, they were manipulating several variables at once, such as diet and exercise, in addition to taking the supplement. Even if the word hasn't reached the pill-pushers at "nutrition centers," many of these popular supplements have proven to be ineffective in well-controlled studies. Don't be swayed by claims of faster or superior absorption for liquids or unique blending processes and formulations: three times zero is still zero.

Androstenediol. A prohormone one step away from testosterone. "Andro" comes in several forms (norandro, 1-AD, etc.); all have nasty steroid side effects and minimal evidence supporting the claims of muscle growth.

Carnitine. L-carnitine is used in the oxidation of fatty acids. It is marketed for improving endurance and fat loss, but substantial research shows no effect.

Chitosan. Crab and shrimp shell extract that binds with fat to prevent absorption (the "fat trapper"). Sketchy evidence, with the minus of reduced calcium and vitamin E, plus the squirts (constant diarrhea).

Chromium. This mineral has a function in insulin regulation. One company holds the patent on chromium picolinate and has promoted it heavily. Most independent studies show it doesn't aid fat loss, build muscles, or do anything else except spot-reduce your bank account.

Coenzyme Q10 *(ubiquinone).* A ubiquitous antioxidant also used in the mitochondria to create energy. Found in fish and meat, there is no evidence CoQ10 is lacking in healthy people or that it improves endur-

ance. Even the supposed health benefits remain unproven for those who are not recovering from a heart attack.

Conjugated Linoleic Acid (CLA). A slightly modified essential fatty acid found in dairy products and meat. Builds muscles, reduces fat, and protects against cancer—if you're a rat. Human research is just starting to appear; some studies show no effect while others support fat loss claims with a dosage of 3 to 4 grams per day.

DHEA. The precursor of androstenediol. Hyped as a "natural" steroid because it can be made from wild (Mexican) yams, research in humans does not support the claims of muscle building or fat loss. Furthermore, neither yams nor extract produce DHEA or progesterone in the body.

Ephedrine. A stimulant that is derived from herbs such as Ma Huang (*Ephedra sinica*) and *Sida cordifolia.* Although the risks appear minimal for healthy individuals who don't abuse it, there are many contraindications including high blood pressure. Due to the potential dangers, ephedrine is banned by most athletic organizations. Ephedrine often lurks in diet products that claim to boost your metabolism. Frequently combined with caffeine (or guarana) and aspirin (or white willow bark), this "ECA stack" can be effective for weight loss by giving you the constant jitters. Synephrine from a fruit called zhi shi (*Citrus aurantium*) has a similar effect. However, your body builds a tolerance to these stimulants and the fat will return once you stop.

HMB. A metabolite of leucine (a BCAA). Nearly all the research showing that HMB aids muscle growth or endurance performance comes from the university lab that holds the patent. Independent human studies haven't been as convincing, though more research is needed.

Glycerol. A nonintoxicating alcohol that may help you stay hydrated during endurance events in the heat. The research is far from conclusive, but there may be some benefit to 2 liters of a glycerol solution a couple of hours prior to a long climb in the sun. However, possible side effects include headaches and blurred vision due to a drying effect on your brain and eyes.

Magnesium. This essential mineral is utilized in many processes throughout the body. Some companies have suggested supplementation can enhance endurance, but little evidence supports this. Magnesium is widely available in a healthy diet; taking too much causes diarrhea.

MCT Oil. Medium-chain triglycerides are fats, with 6 to 12 carbon atoms, that act more like carbohydrates (fast absorption and quick burning). Claimed to reduce body fat and increase endurance by sparing muscle glycogen. Several well-controlled studies show that MCT does nothing and can even harm performance.

Pyruvate. The end product of glycolosis. Claimed to aid fat loss and improve endurance (the so-called "exercise in a bottle"), but this is based on a few flawed studies. No evidence exists that pyruvate supplementation is effective in the doses commonly marketed.

Ribose. A simple 5-carbon sugar that is a precursor of adenosine, used to make ATP (adenosine triphosphate). Theories abound that d-ribose supplementation will increase energy stores and speed recovery. Most of the research that showed promise was on cardiac patients, but a recent well-controlled study on healthy subjects found no effect on performance.

Vanadyl Sulfate. Vanadium (named for a Scandinavian goddess of beauty and youth) is an essential trace mineral found in a wide variety of foods that has an insulin-like effect on regulating glucose. Widely hyped for muscle building, but for nondiabetic humans, the main result is a smaller bank balance. Besides the lack of efficacy, there is a risk of toxicity.

Other Supplements. There are too many unproven supplements to detail them all. Among those that stretch the limits of scientific credulity or fiscal practicality are arginine, boron, choline, chrysin, enterostatin, growth hormone releasers, glutathione, gugglesterone, HCA, inosine, KIC, MSM, OKG, orchic substance, ornithine, taurine, and ZMA. Don't waste your money until they show a *lot* more serious proof.

Herbs of Doubt

These days, most sports food contains at least a few herbal ingredients. Usually, there is little evidence to back up the marketing; just a lot of mumbo jumbo and pseudoscience. Often there isn't even a biologically credible explanation of how the ingredient is supposed to work.

With many herbal supplements, there are risky drug interactions since they contain so many compounds—and many people don't just take one supplement but a smorgasbord. Some, such as St. John's wort, can counter the effects of prescription drugs, including oral contraceptives.

Among the most hyped category of products are "adaptogens," a term coined by Russian scientists in the 1950s, though the Chinese have used the herbs for millennia. These products are said to offer systemwide healing, stress reduction, and "balancing" without any specific site of action or detrimental effects. Unfortunately, the science behind these claims has never been verified in controlled, peer-reviewed studies published in major international journals. The promoters all hide behind vague references to Soviet or undocumented research.

Beware the testimonials for herbal products. Usually the people who offer these testimonials, even if they aren't paid, also made other fitness improvements at the same time. Many herbal products are said to take up to six weeks before effects can be seen—plenty of time for training and proper nutrition benefits to show.

Sometimes there is a grain of truth to the statements—but there often is not enough of the herbal ingredient to be effective, it's of the wrong species, or the quality is poor. Standardized extracts may be the most reliable form for ensuring you're receiving a proper dosage, but there is no guarantee you're getting what you pay for. Tests of herbal products routinely find that they contain a fraction of (or many times) what is stated on the label.

It is quite likely that some of the compounds in the following herbs will eventually prove to have merit. But at present, none of them have demonstrated their efficacy at anything except making a few people wealthy.

Alfalfa (*Medicago sativa*). A fiber-rich plant in the legume family that is commonly used as animal fodder (the name in Arabic means "father of all foods," since it appeared to make horses faster). Claims include increased energy, reduced fatigue, lower cholesterol, and liver detoxification, yet virtually no clinical evidence backs this up. One study showed lowered cholesterol from ingesting 120 grams per day, but most dosage recommendations are only 2 to 3 grams per day.

Astragalus; Huang qi (*Astragalus membranaceus*). The dried root of this Chinese herb is used, often with other adaptogens, to make energy tonics. There are no studies that demonstrate it increases performance, and evidence for immune protection is sketchy.

Bee Pollen. It's actually flower pollen collected from bees returning to the hive. Called the "perfect food" by hucksters because it's supposed to have a magical blend of nutrients. Groovy. No proof it does anything, but there is a risk of allergic reaction.

Blue-green Algae (*Spirulina; Aphanizomenon flos-aquae*). Several species of expensive pond scum that are a source of nutrients already abundant in a healthy diet that includes vegetables. Despite copious hype and fanciful claims, there are no controlled studies published in reputable journals that show blue-green algae does anything special.

Chlorophyll. Because this plant molecule is similar to human hemoglobin (it contains magnesium instead of iron), some have theorized that it speeds the production of red blood cells, cleanses the liver, and fixes nearly everything. Long on talk, pathetically short on solid science. Wheatgrass and cholorella (green algae) are favorite sources, but it takes weeks of daily consumption before it's supposed to work.

Colloidal Silver. A favorite of the charlatans, this is merely silver suspended in water that is supposed to cure everything. Silver is not an essential element, and it's only effective as an antibiotic in amounts that are toxic to humans. No benefits have yet been proven.

Cordyceps. Originally collected from dead Tibetan caterpillars, this fungus is supposed to increase energy, sexual and otherwise. So far, minimal evidence substantiates claims that it can enhance oxygen utilization and athletic performance.

Germanium. A trace element that is supposed to facilitate oxygen uptake, correct your electrical fields, and prevent cancer. There is no good evidence it is lacking in diets or that supplementation helps anything.

Asian Ginseng; Ren Shen (*Panax ginseng*). This is the classic ginseng that is claimed to improve performance and have adaptogenic properties. Though there is a lot of research on panax, much of it is poorly designed and conflicting. American ginseng (*panax quinquefolium*) is closely related but has slightly different properties.

Peruvian Ginseng; Maca (*Lepedium meyenii*). A root related to turnips that was eaten by Inca warriors before battle to boost strength and stamina. The main claim to fame is as an aphrodisiac and adaptogen though all of this is purely anecdotal; no human studies have yet to offer corroboration.

Siberian Ginseng; Ciwujia (*Eleutherococcus senticosus*). A distant relative of panax, it is also an adaptogen that is claimed to improve endurance by reducing lactate production and raising the anaerobic threshold. As the main ingredient of Endurox and PrimeQuest products, eleuthero is also supposed to burn more fat, increase muscle oxygenation, and hasten acclimatization. Sounds great but the oft-cited research is mostly from Soviet and East German sports labs from three decades ago. Recent studies in mainstream, peer-reviewed journals do not support the claims of increased performance.

Golden Root (*Rhodiola rosea*). A "second generation" adaptogen from Russia that has even less research supporting it than the "first generation" ginsengs. Increased oxygen uptake, fat burning, and mental power are some of the unconfirmed claims.

Guarana (*Paullinia cupana*). An Amazon berry that produces an overpriced form of caffeine (guaranine). Used to make a product sound exotic or natural.

Hornet Juice (*vesper mandarin japonica*). The grubs of 3-inch-long wasps digest insect meat, then regurgitate a clear liquid that serves as food for the adults. Gross, and no evidence it does anything for humans.

Maral (*Rhaponticum carthamoides*). Another adaptogen from Siberia that is supposed to build muscles, prevent muscle breakdown, and increase energy. While the claims are abundant and fanciful, the hard evidence is nonexistent.

Maté; Yerba Maté (*Ilex paraguariensis*). The leaves of this South American tree are sold as an energizer and fat burner. There are cheaper ways to get caffeine, antioxidants, and an "herbal high."

Reishi Mushroom; Ling-zhi (*Ganoderma lucidum*). Considered the king of herbal medicines by ancient Chinese, it is now marketed as a cure-all that, among other things, can prevent altitude sickness and increase endurance. Unfortunately, trustworthy studies on humans are entirely lacking.

Royal Jelly. The spit worker bees feed to queen bees is claimed to have all manner of health benefits, which is true—if you're a bee. No major journal has ever published a human study that supports the hype. There is nothing mysterious in the product, and there is a chance of allergic reaction.

Wheat Germ Oil; Octacosanol. A single study fifteen years ago showed an increase in grip strength, but little else, after eight weeks of supplementation. No other studies have demonstrated any effect that enhances athletic performance.

Yohimbe. An extract from African tree bark marketed for weight loss and as a "natural Viagra." The active ingredient is a stimulant with many unpleasant side effects. Clinical studies show the rewards are minimal to nonexistent.

Other Herbs. Look at the label on many herbal supplements marketed for athletes and you'll find a wide variety of unproven ingredients, including anterior pituitary, beet root powder, colostrum, fo ti, garcinia, forskohlin root, gotu kola, hawthorn berry, Indian berry, kava, kelp, kola nut, murira puama, nettle, oat straw extract, pumpkin seed, sarsaparilla, saw palmetto, tribulus terrestris. Caveat emptor.

FUELING THE CLIMB

For normal training and climbs, you don't need to alter your standard diet—as long as it's healthy. However, if the next day will include a very demanding route or long alpine ascent, you can give yourself an edge by eating smart in advance.

The day before the climb, have a good breakfast and a hearty lunch, with some snacks along the way so you don't feel a need for a massive dinner. Start filling your tank early by hydrating all day long and avoid alcoholic beverages that will cause dehydration; you should urinate more often than usual. Make your evening meal high in carbs but avoid gaseous foods (beans, broccoli, cabbage), especially prior to alpine climbs. It's best to stick with familiar foods that aren't too spicy so you don't have an unexpected surprise on the approach. Don't pig out since that can disrupt your sleep, which is often hard enough to come by prior to an alpine start.

Endurance athletes often "carbo load" prior to a big event to increase energy stored in the form of glycogen. After the carbohydrates you ingest are broken down into glucose, unused blood sugar can be converted to "animal starch," which is a fast but finite supply of power. Muscle glycogen supercompensation, as carbing up is properly called, can increase endurance for long events up to 20 percent, although there is no benefit for short-duration events. But this technique is seldom practical for climbers since our main event doesn't always start at a set time on a specific day. To be effective, it takes at least three days with minimal activity and very high carb consumption (over 70 percent); much more complicated schemes involving depletion days provide slightly greater gains. Loading can also add five or more pounds of extra weight (mostly water) and may cause gastrointestinal problems, both of which can hinder your climbing. If you wish to try it, experiment with loading well before a major climb.

If you plan to start exercising within an hour or two of waking, it's best to just have a small (200-calorie), carbo-rich breakfast (bowl of bran cereal or bagel with jam, yogurt, and OJ) that will replenish liver glycogen lost during the night. If you don't eat anything, you may not think straight since the liver maintains blood sugar required by the brain. On the other hand, too many calories (big ol' stack of pancakes or an omelet with hash browns) will slow emptying from the stomach so the food may slosh around on the approach and not provide the energy when you need it. If you're a bit queasy, try a breakfast shake or meal replacement drink, since liquids empty faster from the stomach. Keep hydrating; drink a glass of water for each cup of coffee or tea.

POWER UP

No matter what you do, even with the most brutal training and carbo-loading regimens, your body can only hold enough glycogen for 90 to 120 minutes of vigorous exercise. The amount you stow away is roughly the same as your daily carbohydrate intake (depending on such factors as lean muscle mass and fitness). For example, a climber who consumes a 3,000-calorie diet that is 60 percent carb might store 1,800 calories: 1,400 as muscle glycogen, 320 as liver glycogen, and 80 in blood.

The meter starts running when you begin working hard and muscle glycogen is consumed. Once this supply is exhausted, you hit the infamous "wall" where suddenly everything seems much harder—your muscles are literally out of fuel. You can keep going a little longer because of the glycogen reserve in your liver. But it won't last long and then you "bonk": there's no fuel for the brain, and coordination and thinking suffer (irritability, indecisiveness, confusion, and lethargy are common). This is particularly dangerous in an alpine environment because low blood sugar impairs shivering so there is a greater risk of hypothermia.

To skirt the wall and prevent the bonk, you must consume about 40 to 65 grams of carbohydrates per hour while working at moderate intensity. If it will be a very intense day, such as carrying massive loads to a high camp in subzero temps, you may need to triple this intake to stay fueled. However, it takes practice to consume 200+ calories per hour while working hard; you must force yourself.

Climbers tend to be haphazard about their rest/fuel breaks and this leads to decreased performance. You can decidedly increase your energy level by getting a head start and sticking to a game plan. The only way to prevent fatigue is to start fueling at least a half hour before you feel tired. Rather than one big munchie break every hour or so at the belay, it's better to have small snacks three to four times an hour. This will prevent your muscles from having to compete with the digestive track for blood. Attach a pouch to your climbing harness or the hip belt of your pack so there is a ready supply of carbs (plus sunscreen, lip balm, etc.).

Bars and Gels. Despite the copious advertising hype, you really don't need any of the energy bars or gels. The only thing they offer is convenience—but that's a huge plus for many of us. There is minimal evidence that any of the sport products actually increase performance over thoughtfully selected normal food.

As you've probably discovered, some bars taste like sawdust-flavored shoe leather, others are sickeningly sweet, and several can solidify to jawbreakers in the cold. Many also contain questionable ingredients—such as vitamins, minerals, and herbs—added by the marketing department. Even if an ingredient has been shown to enhance performance, there is rarely enough to make a difference (for example, a product may have 25 to 50 mg of caffeine when it takes about 400 mg for a significant effect).

The best of the bars are about 70 percent carbohydrates (about 45 grams; the source doesn't matter that much) and low in fat (less than 5 grams) and protein (less than 10 grams). For optimal performance, avoid the low-carb bars that follow the 40-30-30 marketing scheme (such as Balance Bars and PR*Bars) because these are slow to digest (fat takes 2 to 4 hours) and do not promote fat burning. If you don't care about energy efficiency, you may as well enjoy a Snickers candy bar, which is 49 percent carbohydrate, 43 percent fat, and a heck of a lot cheaper and tastier.

If you find energy bars that you like and can get them cheap, great—but don't waste money on any that don't suit your tastes. Real food is every bit as effective at keeping your blood sugar up and far less expensive

BASIC CONVERSIONS AND WEIGHTS

When planning fluid intake and pack load, it's helpful to know some basic conversions and weights:

1 gallon = 4 quarts = 3.78 liters
1 quart = 2 pints = 4 cups = 32 ounces = 0.95 liter
1 liter = 1.06 quarts = 2.11 pints = 4.23 cups = 33.81 fluid ounces

1 gallon water at 39°F/4°C = 8.57 pounds = 3.89 kilograms
1 gallon water at 77°F/25°C = 8.32 pounds = 3.77 kilograms
1 quart water at 77°F/25°C = 2.08 pounds = 33.31 ounces = 0.94 kilograms
1 liter water at 77°F/25°C = 2.20 pounds = 35.27 ounces = 1 kilogram

than the fancy bars. If practical, try eating a variety of fruit (fresh or dried), fig bars, bagels, graham crackers, gorp (dried fruit, chocolate, and nuts), or hard candies.

Sport gels do have the advantage that they are absorbed faster, are easier to consume when you are puffing hard, and usually don't freeze. Gels also can be less irritating to the stomachs of runners because solids can jostle around a lot. Each packet contains about 25 grams of carbohydrate, so it's easy to monitor intake. But be sure to drink two cups of plain water with each gel for the fastest absorption and hydration.

DRINK UP

Water is our second most essential nutrient, after oxygen; even a small deficit has a significant effect on performance. Depending on size, gender, and leanness, your body holds about 30 to 60 liters of water. Men are composed of around 60 to 65 percent water

while women are 50 to 55 percent due to less muscle mass.

With a loss of only 1 percent of body weight (about two-thirds of a liter for a 150-pound person), your body temperature begins to rise, heart rate increases seven beats per minute, and performance can begin to slip. Losing an additional percent of body weight (3 pounds total for the same climber) will make you very thirsty, decrease your appetite, and slow you by about 5 percent. By the time you've lost 3 percent (2 liters for our victim-to-be), you'll have a dry mouth, your blood will be thicker (less oxygen to muscles and increased lactic acid), and your urine will be very dark (if you even pee at all). With a loss of 4 percent or more, things get very ugly: performance drops by 20 to 30 percent and you become a candidate for heat exhaustion or heatstroke (both serious medical conditions).

Sweat loss is highly variable among individuals and depends upon intensity of work, level of fitness (sweating increases with better conditioning), temperature, and humidity. Even though women have more sweat glands, men tend to sweat more. It's typical to lose about 1 liter per hour when playing hard but this can easily increase to 2 to 3 liters an hour (nearly 4 liters per hour has been documented) in extreme conditions, such as running on hot, muggy days in the South, basking on a Yosemite wall in July, or humping up a glacier in the sun. Cold weather and altitude compound the water loss due to heavy ventilation in the dry air; up to 1.5 liters a day may be lost just from breathing. Climbing on windy days, and speed sports like cycling or track skiing, can fool you because evaporation occurs so fast that you don't realize how much water you're losing.

Unfortunately, the thirst response in humans is not well tuned. By nature, we only consume two-thirds of water loss during exercise; this is even less refined in kids. If you don't start hydrating until you are thirsty, it's too late—you are already down 1 percent and it will be hard to catch up. At that point, if you are still exercising, you'll need to consume nearly 2 liters to get ahead; it will take an hour for that much fluid to be absorbed.

Drinking Strategy. The wise climber drinks early and drinks often. The day before a big climb, increase your normal fluid intake and consume a half liter of water before going to bed. When you wake, drink another half liter of fluid. Then top off the tank an hour before your workout. During the climb, try to consume a cup or more of fluid every 15 minutes (adds up to 1 liter per hour); drinking a lot quickly makes you pee more. On hot days, force yourself to drink more than you feel like. Plan ahead to ensure that you have adequate water; this

---

DO-IT-YOURSELF SPORT DRINK

> 4 cups hot water
> 2 tablespoons lemon juice or ¼ cup orange juice (7 grams carbohydrate)
> 4 tablespoons sugar (48 grams carbohydrate)
> ³⁄₁₆ teaspoon salt (440 mg sodium)

Dissolve the sugar and the salt (⅛ teaspoon plus half that makes ³⁄₁₆) in the hot water before adding the fruit juice, then refrigerate. This makes a solution with a carbohydrate concentration of 6 percent with an energy source consisting of about 45 percent glucose and 55 percent fructose. One cup provides 55 calories (14 grams carbohydrate), 110 mg sodium, and 30 mg potassium.

may require stopping to melt snow, hauling extra, or detouring to a stream.

Among the best inventions of the last decade is the hydration bladder, which encourages you to sip continuously from a hose running into your pack. While many companies now offer them, most of the bladders are poorly designed and result in frustration (but may be easily replaced). Be sure that it has a large-diameter hose with a high-flow nipple (that won't dribble) or you'll feel like you're sucking through a tiny straw.

Avoid putting anything but water in a bladder; sport drinks leave a permanent taste and breed nasty creepy crawlies. If you must, be sure to rinse it thoroughly afterwards. To prevent freezing, keep the bladder near your back and blow air back into the tube (the insulated tubes work poorly).

For any exercise bout lasting an hour or less, there is no advantage to sport drinks: imbibe water. Right from the faucet is fine in many locations, but some areas have "hard" water with a high mineral content that tastes lousy. A sink filter with activated carbon can improve flavor and guard against microorganisms like *giardia*. Bottled water is convenient and that's about all— the new "fitness waters" are just about taste and marketing, not performance.

When your climbs or workouts extend into the time where glycogen depletion becomes a factor, then you should consider your alternatives. Sport drinks can be a good choice if you are not consuming any other food. The ad hype never mentions that combining products, as most people do in the real world, can *decrease* performance.

The American College of Sports Medicine (ACSM) recommends a carbohydrate concentration of 4 to 8 percent for fastest hydration and energy replenishment (10 to 19 grams per 8 ounces water). More than this will slow gastric emptying, which means the fluid stays in your stomach where it sloshes around and is not absorbed. If you eat energy bars or gels and then wash them down with sport drink, the high carbohydrate concentration can increase dehydration because water is drawn into the small intestines. It's best to consume a sport drink on its own (without dilution) or to eat bars and gels with just water.

Most of the time, you don't need extra electrolytes (sodium and potassium) since there are plenty in your diet—the dash of salt in sport drinks improves taste, which helps you drink more. However, if you are sweating hard for more than 4 hours and only ingesting water, cramping is likely and there is a slight risk of hyponatremia, a potentially fatal condition involving a low sodium concentration in the blood.

Proper hydration means frequent urination: be sure that your clothing and climbing harness are designed to work together for this basic bodily function! Many of the outdoor companies choose fashion over function and make taking a piss difficult for men and women; zippers are often too short or difficult to operate. Women might consider using a pee funnel;

they can make your life easier but true woman-specific outdoors clothing is the best option.

RECOVERY FUELS

Following a good session of hard play, it normally takes at least 20 hours for glycogen to restore completely. If you intend to play again the next day, it's important to get a head start. Once your workout is over, there is a 30-minute window of opportunity to significantly speed recovery. During this time, when your muscles are still warm and circulation is enhanced, any carbohydrates that you ingest are readily sucked up by the muscle cells. It could also help to include about 20 percent protein to enhance muscle recovery; this 4:1 ratio may be slightly better than carbs alone, although the research is far from conclusive.

For the most part, it doesn't matter what kind of carbohydrate you eat or drink as long as you consume at least 50 grams in that first half hour. An exception is fructose, which does not replenish muscle glycogen as quickly, so avoid sodas, fruit juice, and drinks with high fructose corn syrup.

High-carb recovery drinks (20 to 25 percent carbohydrate; 48 to 60 grams per 8 ounces) offer convenience but there is nothing magical about them. You can recover just as effectively by eating real food such as a bagel sandwich with hummus or lean meat; fruit, cheese, and crackers; or a tray of sushi—all washed down with water or iced tea.

Don't stop grazing after your initial round of post-climb snacking. Over the next 2 hours, you should try to ingest another 50 to 100 grams of carbs, as well as 10 to 20 grams of protein, whether from engineered drinks or real food. If you don't maintain this carbohydrate influx, that climb the next morning is going to be a lot tougher!

The puritans assert that there is no value in the consumption of beer after a day of climbing. This defies a century of tradition and isn't completely true. Mass-produced beer that nutritionists and aficionados revile is made with rice, corn, coloring, flavorings, and enzymes; a 12-ounce can contains about 1 gram protein, 25 mg sodium, and only a trace of potassium or B vitamins. But a finely crafted beer is just made from barley, wheat, and hops; it contains about 2.2 grams protein, 75 mg sodium, 195 mg potassium, and 5 percent to 15 percent of the DRI for riboflavin, niacin, folic acid, and vitamin B6. Plus the high hops content contains nine flavonoids that you won't find in sport drinks.

Beer contains zero fat and zero cholesterol; moderate consumption may even raise your level of HDL (the good cholesterol). The typical 12-ounce serving of light beer has about 100 calories; a normal beer is around 150 calories, and a hefty stout can hold 250 or more calories. Although two-thirds of the carbohydrates in a beer come from alcohol, which does not convert to glycogen, you still get about 12 grams of restorative carbs per bottle.

No, beer isn't the ultimate recovery drink—but you could do worse. It's the french fries and nachos that really get you into calorie trouble. To offset the dehydrating effects of alcohol, it's a good idea to consume one glass of water for each beer consumed.

BIG-WALL FOOD

Life on a big wall is essentially vertical backpacking: the major difference is that you usually must haul all of your water. Frequently, climbers balk at the weight of the gear they have to schlep to the base of the route and, in an effort to cut back, they jettison fluids. There are countless stories of teams in Yosemite that ran out of water part way up: sometimes they tough it out, often they bail.

Most climbers who have run dry swear they will never make the mistake again. Even though the approach will suck, it's definitely better to take more water than you think you'll need; once you start hauling, the extra weight won't make that much difference and the load gets lighter as you get higher. If it looks like you'll have a surplus before you top out, you can be an unsung hero and leave a cache for unfortunates who have calculated poorly. Carry water in 2-liter plastic soda bottles wrapped with duct tape to attach a clip-in loop (or equivalent bombproof containers) in the bottom of several haul bags (read: don't put all your chickens in one basket).

In cool weather, as a bare minimum, you should carry 3 liters of water per person per day (6.6 pounds). If the route gets a lot of sun, add at least another liter (1 gallon total, 8.4 pounds) per person per day. For an El Cap wall in July, don't even think about going up with less than 6 liters of water (13.2 pounds) per person for each day. On alpine wall climbs, you may be able to melt snow but you'll also be toting a hanging stove and fuel, so the weight savings isn't as much as you'd wish.

These water rations assume you are also consuming hydrated foods such as cans of soups, stews, tuna, and fruit cocktail; possibly a daily tallboy, too. A day's ration of canned food weighs about 3 pounds per person; a team of two climbers should expect to haul about 17 pounds of food and water per day. Other popular wall entrées include premade burritos (tortilla, refried beans, rice, cheese, and salsa wrapped in foil, then stored in a resealable plastic bag such as Ziploc); Tasty Bites (prepackaged gourmet meals found at some groceries) with a baked potato; and bagels with sausage and cheese. You're only limited by your imagination, but it's best to select foods that are relatively crushproof and require no cooking.

Beware that some energy bars are virtually inedible without water to wash them down, so gels may be a better alternative for fast, convenient energy. Take some hard candies to combat dry mouth and, if possible, fresh oranges and apples—they will be unbelievably delicious after a few days on the big stone. For hygiene, bring premoistened towelettes or baby wipes to clean your hands after making a "wall burrito."

EXPEDITION NUTRITION

Anytime you are away from civilization for more than a few weeks, food becomes the number one topic of conversation. If you've done your homework and planned well, the banter is about how great the meals taste and getting fat. When you've gone with the low bidder for a trekking agency, the talk is about the first meal you'll get to enjoy back home and losing weight. At the base camps on big mountains, it's easy to spot the expeditions that skimped by the empty dining tents at mealtime.

Do not underestimate the importance of the cook. After your sirdar, who runs the show, he is the most important asset of the team; the expedition leader and liaison officer are less significant. You would do well to seek out recommendations for a cook from previous Western expeditions to the area (someone favored by Asians may not serve your particular taste). Both the cook and his staff must be well schooled on the importance of cleanliness (always washing hands and utensils, clean water sources, boiling water); don't assume they have already been taught.

The food for the trek and while in base camp are usually the domain of the trekking agency, though you should check their menus and make requests ahead of time. Be sure there is lots of variety and abundant quantities. It's also a good idea to bring some favorite treats for base camp (good coffee and a nonbreakable French press, hot chocolate, drink mixes, hot sauces, popcorn, Scotch whiskey, etc.) to enhance appetites and morale. For a successful expedition, base camp must be a place to look forward to when the weather deteriorates or when it's time to recoup before the summit bid.

Many climbers unwittingly set themselves up for disaster by not paying attention to their health before they reach the trailhead; once the trek starts, you're relatively safe. The moment your flight leaves home, if not a few days earlier from the last-minute packing frenzy, stress hormones in your blood rise significantly. Consider taking echinacea for a few days prior to a long flight to boost immune protection, since you'll be in a small box with a lot of other people.

After flying to the opposite side of the planet, it takes about five days to recuperate from jet lag (going north or south has minimal effect). The cities where you typically spend that time preparing for departure often have significant air pollution (carbon monoxide, nitrogen and sulfur oxides, and particulates) and noise that add to your stress. Be sure to get an air-conditioned hotel room (this is not a luxury) and take your antioxidants. If you must do a training run, do so early in the morning and try to find a park away from traffic.

Of course, be careful of what you eat and drink: before the expedition departs is not the time to sample the local street cuisine! You can indulge to your stomach's content upon your return. It's safest (but no guarantee) to dine at three- and four-star hotels, even if you don't stay there, or well-established restaurants frequented by many tourists. Stick with mainstream dishes that are sure to be made fresh daily; more exotic requests are likely many days old. No matter how bad your craving, do not eat salads, fruit you can't peel, or ice cream; it just isn't worth the risk. However, fresh yogurt can be a good, safe choice. Especially during monsoon season, be careful to avoid drinking the water when you shower; use bottled or treated water to brush your teeth.

Should you get a bout of diarrhea, it's best to knock it out early with a full course of antibiotics such as Cipro (consult your doctor). For the trek in, when the risk is highest, some climbers bring acidophilus tablets—the good bacteria found in yogurt—to help the digestive system recover after the antibiotics are finished. These tablets can be found at health food stores, but check the expiration date and avoid heat or freezing to keep the critters alive.

Mountain Fuel

Most of the food you'll eat above base camp must be brought from home. Do not count on finding edible mountain food in Katmandu or Islamabad; what's available is the stuff that nobody liked. Whether on a private or commercial expedition, do not assume that your tastes will be accounted for. Food is what gets you to the top. If you leave this critical element entirely up to somebody else, no matter how extensive the questionnaire you may have filled out, blame yourself for a growling stomach. Those with food allergies must pay extra-special attention to

what will go up on the mountain.

For high-altitude mountaineering, the climbers who eat and drink the most have the best chance to succeed. There are a lot of changes occurring within your body (see the section in chapter 3, "Altitude Basics") that conspire against adequate nutrition, but much of it is a question of willpower: you must force yourself to fuel even when you aren't hungry or feel sick. Simply living in below-freezing temperatures raises your basic energy requirement by about 1,000 food calories (more for lean people when clothing is inadequate). The extra weight, resistance to movement, and interlayer friction of clothing also increase caloric demand. Underfeeding yourself not only threatens your own chances but also that of your team—and possibly everyone's safety.

You will probably need 30 to 35 calories per day for each pound of body weight (a 180-pound climber will consume 5,400 to 6,300 calories a day); some days will be less, some more. Ideally, two-thirds of that intake should come from carbohydrates. Though the taste has improved in recent years, almost none of the freeze-dried meals on the market provide nearly enough calories; adding olive oil or margarine is a weight-efficient way to boost calories. Despite what some people claim to the contrary, many climbers crave nuts, sausages, and other fatty treats at high altitudes. Bring anything that sounds appealing—there are no bad calories above 6,000 meters—but accept that your tastes will change the higher you go.

Although they aren't ideal for optimal hydration, high-carbohydrate drink powders can be a good source of extra calories that are reasonably lightweight and compact. Some of these offer 150 to 200 calories of carbs per cup and they may also contain 30 to 50 calories of protein. There are at least a half dozen brands to choose from, but it's vital that everyone on the expedition test the candidates at home to see which tastes good and stays down. Beware sponsorship from a product that only one or two people can stomach! Consume these drinks in camp, not while climbing, and keep pumping down the fluids (tea, hot chocolate, soup).

CHAPTER 2

Mind and Body: Mental and Flexibility Training

It takes much more than good physical conditioning to be a successful climber. In truth, it's the power of the mind that separates the elite of the climbing world from the rest of us. When the crux is upon them, they can recruit a mental strength with immense energy. While flexibility seldom determines climbing prowess outright, a more supple body moves fluidly and may be more resistant to injury.

Fortunately you can train your mind as well as your body. Much of the teachings of any martial art or yoga form are centered around this point—indeed, many climbers practice them. While it is not necessary to become an Eastern adept, you can improve your climbing performance by stretching both your mind and body. Conveniently, you can often do both at the same time.

MIND FLEX

Few activities draw upon your mental powers like climbing on the sharp end. The complete concentration and focus required is what attract many people to the sport. Jobs, relationships, and everything else in life are quickly shoved aside for the business at hand. Yet if you examine the accidents you've suffered, the odds are that very few occurred when you were completely focused. It's the momentary lapse that fills the history of climbing with disasters; outside factors are but minor players in most of the dramas.

Veteran climbers who have developed their technique often find that the most difficult part about returning to the rock after an extended absence isn't a lack of strength. Recovering their "lead head," the ability to think when leading a pitch, can be more problematic. Without exercise, your mental muscle can also atrophy.

Walking a slack line—a length of webbing loosely strung between two trees, a foot or so off the ground—has long been a popular form of training for climbers. While many think of this as a balance exercise, for which it is useful, you will also find it requires a great deal of concentration. When your mind wanders, you're on the ground in the blink of an eye.

Although focus is critical to all aspects of climbing, you must learn to use it like a zoom lens. This only comes with practice. When performing at your highest standards on the relative safety of a sport climb, zoom in and isolate only that which gets you to the top: your movements and breathing, the features of the rock, and clipping the draws. Everything else—wind, heat, sounds, smells—is mentally blotted out.

However, this level of attention can get you killed in the more dangerous arenas of traditional and wall climbing, so you mentally zoom back to a "normal" perspective that includes the quality of gear placements, how the rope is running, the security of the belay.

When you enter the alpine environment, you must pull back even further to get the big picture. All of the above factors are still important, but to survive, your mind also is aware of the weather, the safety of the snowpack, the feel of the ice, the performance level of you and your partners. Your ultimate goal, grasshopper, is to master this mental zooming to the point that you can be focused and aware simultaneously.

GO WITH THE FLOW

Few drugs are as powerful and intoxicating—or as elusive—as "flow," the mental state where everything comes together. When you're in it, you know it. Once you've felt it, you'll want it again. It's that ecstatic feeling after you just floated up a pitch, ran with wings on your shoes, skied the perfect line. Psychologists define flow as the ideal performance state: movement is seemingly effortless and graceful, actions are automatic, attention is focused, fears are suppressed, you have a feeling of control, and time seems to slow.

Although there is no single path to the flow state, you can facilitate its arrival by training for relaxation, previsualizing, and establishing goals.

Learning to relax at will, even when your senses are screaming to do otherwise, is one of the most essential talents for a climber. This saves you valuable mental and physical energy, which are always in short supply. Athletes choke when they overanalyze themselves during performance.

Practicing relaxation in a nonstressful environment makes it easier to summon when under pressure. This is essentially a form of meditation, though you need not chant mantras, ring bells, or burn incense (unless desired). Normally we breathe shallow about fourteen times per minute—but taking deep inhalations only six times per minute synchronizes cardiovascular rhythms, calms the mind, and increases concentration. It's no coincidence that reciting prayers in many religions tends to create a relaxed mental state.

Find a comfortable place to sit or lie down where you will not be distracted. Begin by inhaling smooth, deep breaths through the nose and exhaling slowly through the mouth. Concentrate on the rhythm and fullness of each breath; actively think about pulling your diaphragm downward with each inspiration. When thoughts intrude, acknowledge them and return to focused breathing.

After a few minutes of meditative breathing, begin to notice any tension in your body—a clenched jaw, tight shoulder muscle, tense back—and release it. Practice relaxation by tensing a muscle very tightly for a few seconds, then quickly releasing it, and notice the smooth feeling that ensues. Learning to pay attention to your body for unnecessary tension, and teaching yourself to relax at a moment's notice with a few deep breaths, are essential for optimal performance in all sports.

Visualization is a well-proven method for improving performance; intensely thinking about an activity stimulates nerves in the associated muscles. When you visualize a climb, don't just study a topo or photo; imagine yourself there overcoming the obstacles. During this mental exercise, include full details: how you feel, rock texture, temperature, sound of the wind, light reflecting off a carabiner, reaching the top, the descent. This process helps eliminate self-doubt and calm fears because you have already rehearsed the route.

All aspects of your training become easier when you establish a major goal and a time frame. This goal needs to be specific, such as "do The Nose in a day next summer," "climb the Cassin Ridge in June," or "redpoint Just Do It this September." And your goal should be realistic, a good fit with your level of experience (the climbs just mentioned are only for veteran climbers), and meaningful.

Once you've picked your objective, write it down. Then divide it into necessary subgoals, along with definite measurements for your progress. Post this in a place where you will see it everyday—on the bathroom mirror or refrigerator door. Tell your friends and family your intentions and reap the benefits of their support: a little needling is sometimes good.

KNOW FEAR

Never climb with anyone who is fearless: it's just a matter of time until they become a statistic. The best climbers are intimately familiar with fear—it keeps them alive—but they do not let it control them. Fear becomes panic when it prevents action or causes critical thinking to falter. Learning to keep that knot in the stomach as a tight little ball comes from experience, but there are some guidelines that can help.

While it should be obvious, it's easy to overlook the fact that building a base of confidence makes fear more manageable. This means progressively increasing your expo-sure to fearful things, rather than jumping in over your head; that first rappel is a lot easier when it's on a slab and backed up with a belay instead of going off an overhang at night. This also includes preparing for emergencies by taking courses in self-rescue and advanced first aid; book knowledge doesn't cut it when the manure hits the fan. Learning from other people's mistakes is also an essential part of handling fear, since knowing what can go wrong is the first step in preventing calamity. Read *Accidents in North American Mountaineering* when it comes out every year, as well as accounts in articles and books; no form of climbing is completely safe.

Though you may have been working up to it for years, nothing quite prepares you for that initial glimpse of your first big wall or Himalayan peak. Nearly everyone wonders what they've gotten themselves into. But as a Lao-Tzu proverb goes, "a journey of a thousand miles begins with a single step." When you subdivide your goal into bite-size chunks, such as sections between bivis or camps, the overwhelming nature of the task becomes much less daunting.

Crises are inevitable if you climb long enough, and they come in all shapes and forms. You might be on a dicey lead when you look down to see your last piece has lifted out. Or a storm suddenly moves in while you are partway up a cliff. Or your partner might be severely injured in a fall. Handling your fears at these moments is essential—panic is not an option.

After the preliminary "oh shit," take a

couple of deep breaths and will your pulse to slow; this is when those relaxation exercises pay off. Cleanse your mind of negative waves and think positive thoughts. No matter how grim the situation, humor is an invaluable asset—smile—even a bad joke can be better than dour resolution. When you have a solid base of confidence, action becomes automatic. Only hesitate long enough to gather the required information that will help the circumstances. In most critical moments, time is the enemy.

ACCEPT FAILURE

When you talk with famous climbers about their achievements, most of them are quick to point out that they've had as many failures as successes. While these disappointments are often forgotten by admirers, the big names view them as essential elements of their careers. After all, if climbing were always a sure thing, few of us would even bother.

How you deal with failure will largely determine your climbing future. Temper tantrums, such as throwing shoes or loud cursing, do nobody any good—least of all those around you. It's important to put aside self-recrimination; shoulda-coulda-woulda doesn't help. While some climbers strive for perfection from themselves, this is an exercise in futility; it is more fruitful to aim for an optimal performance.

Step back and examine the entire scenario from an outsider's perspective, looking for correctable faults. Then address the problems with action. Revise your game plan and possibly adjust your goals. Anyone

reading this book will likely still be climbing years, perhaps decades, from now. Keep that long-term perspective when dealing with short-term failures.

BODY FLEX

It's easy to find excuses to not stretch, hence many climbers don't bother. Perhaps you've managed just fine for years without stretching as part of your normal routine. But sooner or later, age and injuries start to catch up with you. While many people simply consider stretching as a means to increase flexibility, which does benefit your performance, there is more to it than that.

Foremost among the reasons to make the time: you can play more. Stretching before and after climbing or other strenuous exercise can decrease your chance of injury because the elasticity of muscles and tendons is increased; with proper technique, muscle strains are significantly reduced. If a muscle becomes too tight from training, it can lead to misalignment of the joint or chronic tendon problems. Stretching after a hard workout can also reduce muscle soreness the following day.

There are subtle reasons to stretch as well. Prior to launching up a difficult climb, 5 to 10 minutes of gentle stretching gives you quiet time to clear your mind and prepare for the action ahead. As you concentrate on stretches, you become more kinesthetically aware of your body and learn how to relax muscles at will. And finally, stretching feels good—just ask any cat or dog.

STRETCHING BASICS

The most important rule is to never force a cold muscle; this does more harm than good. When stretching before a workout, you are just trying to loosen the muscles that will be required. This is not the time to work on flexibility. It's best to perform this stretching after 5 to 10 minutes of light aerobic warm-up that elevates muscle temperature and blood flow: fast walking, slow running, or easy cycling. These should be smooth, controlled stretches that are only held for a few seconds before you relax and repeat or move on to the next one.

Work on flexibility shortly after your cool-down session, which involves several minutes of light-intensity exercise that flushes the by-products of metabolism. Find a peaceful spot, perhaps with relaxing music, and put on some dry clothes so your muscles stay warm. A bouldering crash pad is ideal for stretching, but a closed-cell foam pad or yoga mat works well too.

Though there are several forms of stretching, the most practical involves slowly sinking into position and holding for 10 to 30 seconds (a passive, static stretch). This allows the muscle to relax without stimulating muscle spindles—length sensors that form a feedback loop telling the muscle to contract. To prevent this stretch reflex, do not bounce or use fast movements. (You'll get the idea if you press firmly below your patella, the kneecap. Nothing will happen. But tap quickly in that spot, and you get the familiar knee-jerk reaction.)

You can stimulate a muscle to relax even further by contracting it tightly for a few seconds, then suddenly releasing and then stretching. The contraction stimulates Golgi tendon organs, which are sensors in the junction of muscle and tendon that tell the muscle to relax.

This can also work to stretch the opposite (antagonist) muscle due to the phenomenon known as reciprocal inhibition. The body is wired so that flexing one muscle causes its antagonist to relax; for example, contracting the biceps enhances a triceps stretch by causing the triceps to relax.

STRETCHING ROUTINE

As with most aspects of conditioning, there is no single stretching routine that is ideal for everyone. The eighteen stretches offered here are a good foundation, but you may not need them all or may wish to modify or substitute some of your own. Depending on your level of flexibility and the types of training you enjoy, some stretches become more important while others take too much time and may not be as productive.

Allow about 20 to 30 minutes for a good routine so you don't feel rushed; two or three sessions per week is ideal. This is also a good time for contemplative mental training, relaxing mind and body. Alternatively, stretch for 10 minutes every day. Most stretches should be performed two or three times, though some problem areas may need more.

The order of the stretches is not particularly important, though you generally start first with major muscle groups that were recently used and progress toward smaller muscles. Start with the side that is tighter, since many people tend to rush the second stretch.

While you are stretching the muscle, breathe easily and deeply; identify any tension in your body. As you exhale, relax and sink deeper into the stretch, but stop short of the pain threshold. Never force a stretch beyond what feels natural; trying to impress someone in yoga class is begging for trouble.

Discussions of flexibility generally refer to the hip region. Because the muscles surrounding the hip joints are among the largest in the body, many athletes tend to become tight here. This not only detracts from climbing performance due to a limited range of motion, but can also lead to a variety of chronic complaints. A significant portion of your routine should concentrate on stretching the muscles and tendons connected to the hips.

Most upper-body stretches are performed to keep your body limber, not to dramatically increase range of movement. Be careful not to overdo stretches involving the shoulders; you don't want the ligaments too loose.

When climbing beyond the vertical, we sometimes contort ourselves into bizarre positions. Just as having a strong torso is essential for all sports, so too is good flexibility in this region. There are numerous possible stretches for the back that may benefit your climbing; a stretching or yoga class is recommended if you need work here. It is very important that you do not apply force to the spine when it is flexed.

STRETCHES

1 Chest Lift

Why

This stretches the chest (pectorals), front of the shoulders (anterior deltoids), and biceps.

How

- Interlace your fingers behind your back. Keep your elbows straight and lift your arms upward.
- May also be performed by placing your hands on either side of a doorway at shoulder height and leaning forward.

2 Behind the Back

Why

Gives a good stretch to the triceps, lats, and front part of the rotator cuff.

How

- Hold a towel in one hand and let it hang behind your head, with the elbow bent at a sharp angle.
- With the other hand, reach behind your waist and grab the towel.
- Pull down gently with the lower hand to stretch the upper triceps; raised arm should be straight up in the air.
- Then pull up on the towel until you feel a stretch in the front part of the opposite shoulder. Repeat on the other side.
- Once you have sufficient flexibility, you can eliminate the towel and interlock your fingers behind your back.

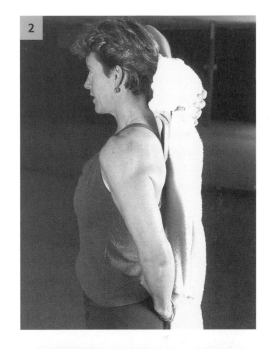

3 Crossed Arm

Why

This gets at the muscles between the shoulder blades (teres major and rhomboids) and the rear part of the rotator cuff.

How

- Either grab your upper arm just above the elbow or place one elbow in the crook of the other.
- Pull the arm across your body until you feel the stretch.
- For successive stretches, vary the angle of the arm (above parallel, parallel, below parallel) to reach different muscles. Repeat with the other arm.

4 Forearm Extension

Why

With all the gripping we do, the forearms get seriously worked. Regularly performing this stretch can prevent tennis elbow (lateral epicondylitis), which is pain on the outside when your palm is facing forward.

How

- Straighten one arm and bend your wrist downward at a right angle.
- With the other hand, pull gently until you feel the stretch on top of your forearm. Repeat on the other arm.
- May also be performed by pressing the backs of both hands into a pad.

5 Overhead Reach

Why

Another stretch for the triceps and shoulders that comes from a different angle.

How

- Stand facing a wall with your feet about two feet away.
- Place your palms overhead flat on the wall (like you're getting frisked).
- Bend from the hips, keeping your arms and spine straight.
- May also be performed one arm at a time to feel the subtleties or while kneeling and using the floor.

6 Forearm Flexion

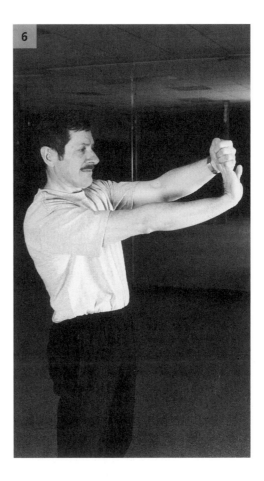

Why

When your forearms are about to explode, it's the flexors that are pumped. Stretching them can prevent golfer's elbow (medial epicondylitis), which is pain on the inside when your palm is facing forward. This can also stave off joint deformities (flexion contractures) that are often seen in the middle and ring fingers.

How

- Straighten your right arm and bend your wrist upward at a right angle.
- Place the fingers of the left hand at a right angle.
- Pull until you feel the stretch on the underside of your forearm. Press gently with your thumb to stretch the first joint of the fingers. Repeat on the other arm.
- May also be performed by pressing both hands into a pad, fingers pointed toward you. Keep the elbows straight.

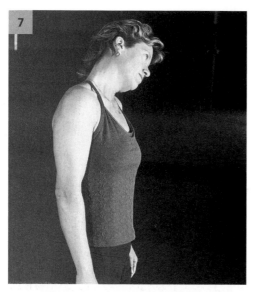

7   Neck Roll

Why

Due to the nature of the sport, climbers (and road cyclists and inline skaters in full tuck) spend a great deal of time with their necks fully craned upward. Stretching these muscles can prevent soreness.

How

- Start with your arms at your side, shoulders relaxed and chin pressed firmly to your chest.
- Slowly roll your head in a full, wide circle with your ear almost touching one shoulder, the back of the head trying to touch the back, the other ear reaching for the other shoulder and back to start.
- After several rotations, reverse the direction.

8   Shoulder Rolls

Why

Many of us unconsciously build up tension in our shoulders, whether from stress, work, or play. These rolls feel wonderful.

How

- Start with your arms at your side, shoulders relaxed and head facing straight forward.
- Slowly flex your shoulders forward as far as they will go, then roll them upward trying to touch your ears, then back squeezing your shoulder blades together, and back to neutral.
- After several forward rotations, reverse the direction.

9   Spinal Twist

Why

Making yourself into a pretzel helps stretch your side muscles (obliques), lower back (erector spinae), and hip abductors.

How

- Sit with your legs in front of you, then place the right foot outside of the left knee.
- Twist your torso to the right, placing the left elbow outside of the right knee and your right hand on the floor behind you.
- Push your elbow against the knee while trying to look far behind you. Repeat on the opposite side.
- Increase the stretch in the hips by bending the left leg so the foot is tucked underneath your right buttock.

10   Sitting Reach

Why

Both the lower back and the hamstrings get a good stretch.

How

- Sit with your legs out in front of you, knees slightly bent and pointing outward.
- Slowly bend from the waist and reach forward as far as possible. Exhale to increase the stretch.
- Keeping your legs straighter, but not locked, will increase the hamstring involvement and decrease that of the lower back.

11 Lying Twist

Why

Provides a good stretch to the lower back as well as the hip abductors.

How

- Lie flat on your back with arms outstretched.
- Raise up one leg so that the hip is at a right angle.
- While keeping your shoulders on the ground, allow the leg to slowly fall across your center line to the opposite side.
- Try to touch the knee to the ground without lifting a shoulder. Repeat on the other side.

12 Torso Side Bend

Why

A far reaching stretch that gets at many muscles of the torso. This variation includes the iliotibial band (ITB), which extends to the knee on the outside of the thigh and often causes knee pain when tight.

How

- Stand sideways an arm length from a wall. Take a step forward with your right foot, placing it a couple inches to the left of your left foot so your legs are crossed.
- Raise your arms.
- Slowly bend your torso to the right, keeping your weight on the rear leg with the foot flat on the ground and the right knee slightly bent. You should feel a stretch through your entire left side.
- Repeat on the opposite side with the left foot forward.

13 Lying Knee Flex

Why

Stretches the hip extensors (gluteus maximus and hamstrings) and the groin.

How

- Lie flat on your back with your legs extended.
- Bend one leg until the thigh reaches your chest.
- Use your hands to pull the thigh closer but keep the other leg straight.
- Repeat with the other leg.

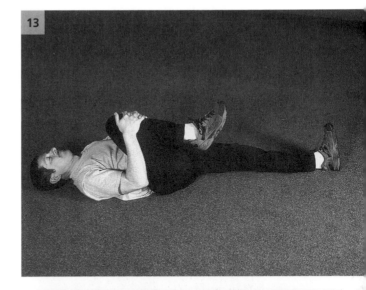

14 Forward Kneel

Why

Many people have tight hip flexors (iliopsoas, rectus femoris) thanks in part to lots of chair time.

How

- Kneel on one knee but extend it well behind you.
- Keeping your torso erect and spine neutral, press downward with your hips to achieve the stretch.
- Repeat with the other leg.

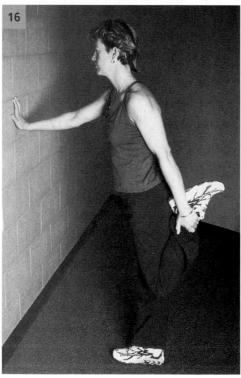

15 Butterfly

Why

An excellent stretch for the groin that will help you get your hips in closer to the rock. Men are often very tight here.

How

- Sit on the ground and bring your feet together so the soles are touching. Pull them to within a foot of your body using your hands.
- Keeping your spine neutral, lean forward and sink into the stretch.
- Also may be performed by lying on your back and pulling your knees to the ground with your hands.

16 Quad

Why

A long hiking or running descent really hammers the quads, as do many other aspects of fun. These large muscles can contribute to back and knee pains when overly tight.

How

- Standing on one leg with your spine erect and neutral, grasp the other ankle (not the foot). Use a table or chair for balance.
- Pull your foot toward the butt and point your bent knee straight down (thigh is vertical).
- For maximal stretch, rotate your hips forward slightly.
- Repeat with the other leg.

17 Hamstring

Why

Probably the tightest muscles and tendons in most of us, especially men. Since these are attached to the pelvis, lower back pains can originate here.

How

- Use a bench that is between knee and hip level to prop up one leg.
- Keeping your spine neutral and your toe pointed upward, bend from the hips to get the stretch.
- To increase the stretch, flatten the back rather than bend more from the waist.
- Repeat with the other leg.
- Also may be performed sitting by extending one leg forward and pulling the other in so the sole is against the knee and then bending forward.

18   Calf

Why

A climber's calves get a serious workout, especially on steep snow and ice. Tight calves are also the cause of many problems for runners.

How

- Brace your upper body against a wall and extend the right leg back several feet behind you while moderately bending the forward knee.
- Straighten the right knee while pressing your heel to the floor to feel a stretch in

the belly of the calf. Minimal weight is on the left leg.

- Bring your right foot forward so it is only a foot or so behind the left foot.
- Bend the right knee slightly and press your heel to the floor for a stretch of the Achilles tendon.
- Repeat with the other leg.

ALTERNATIVES

Many climbers are drawn to, or at least curious about, different methods of stretching and conditioning. Yoga in particular has much to offer, though it's important to realize that there are many forms of this five-thousand-year-old practice. Even if you are already in great shape, do not underestimate these workouts—they can kick your butt. However, despite claims about cardiovascular and strength gains, none of these are replacements for aerobic or resistance training.

Hatha Yoga

Hatha yoga, a mere two thousand years old, is the most popular form of yoga in the West. It has subdivided into many styles, but only a few are likely to help your climbing. Some positions can be injurious to joints, so use caution; a few instructors don't know what they're doing (there are no national certification standards) or push their students too hard. The purists interested in enlightenment may be contemptuous of Westernized yoga styles that lack the spiritual aspect, but it's just a matter of taste.

For climbers and other outdoor athletes,

three yoga styles are the most physical. Perhaps the most commonly taught classes involve the slow, balanced moves of Iyengar yoga, which emphasizes alignment and form using a variety of props (blocks and straps) to achieve positions. Ashtanga yoga, sometimes marketed as power yoga, is a fast-paced style with fluid movements that require strength and stamina. Bikram yoga is performed in humidified studios heated to at least 90°F, which makes it a demanding workout.

Pilates

Developed by Joseph Pilates in the early twentieth century for training ballet dancers, his methods have been adapted for a broader audience. Due to trademark issues, some variations go by other monikers such as The Method. But all blend stretches with light conditioning to get at the deep muscles we seldom think about.

Many of the exercises rely on exotic contraptions, with names like the Reformer (a spring-loaded sliding table), the Wunda Chair, and the Cadillac (looks like a kinky bondage device). Pilates mat classes are more akin to yoga (from which Pilates is derived, along with animal stretches) but still emphasize the inner musculature.

If you can find an instructor who is keyed into the needs of climbers, Pilates can be a good adjunct to your other training. However, beware that there is also a lot of hype about the advantages of Pilates. Those devices are very expensive and somebody has to pay for them. There is no evidence Pilates is superior to other forms of stretching and conditioning.

Tai Chi

This Chinese form of flowing movement and breathing can take an hour to learn and a lifetime to master. Like a dance performed in slow motion, tai chi (which translates to "supreme ultimate") is remarkably peaceful and invigorating. You may come away from a good class glowing, without ever breaking a sweat. Tai chi is a contemplative martial art that can benefit climbers by slowing them down in a hectic world; subtle but worth a try.

CHAPTER 3

Aerobic Conditioning

All climbers, no matter what aspect of the sport they are into, will benefit from improved fitness of heart and lungs. Those with the most to gain, obviously, are the alpinists and mountaineers who by definition breathe thin air while struggling uphill. Yet training for better utilization of oxygen—what aerobics is all about—will help other climbers improve overall stamina and control weight; you climb better when you aren't exhausted from the approach and aren't carrying excess baggage.

Aerobic training is any activity that gets your heart pumping between half speed and just short of full throttle for an extended duration. There are hundreds of ways to do this—a dozen are presented here—so you aren't just limited to running. However, unless you are doing continuous laps or circuits, gym climbing and resistance training have minimal aerobic benefit.

There are also long-term health benefits from superior cardiovascular function including decreased risk of heart attack, stroke, and diabetes. The well-known reduction in stress, release of endorphins, and improvement in sleep are all good reasons for regular aerobic exercise. Most of all, it can be a lot of fun!

AEROBIC FUN-DAMENTALS

When it comes to making a movement, everything boils down to a little molecule called adenosine triphosphate (ATP), which energizes muscle cells but must constantly be recharged. The easiest way for our body to juice up is with the aid of oxygen; though relatively slow, it's pretty much an infinite system.

When going full bore, we can't get enough oxygen and must rely on faster anaerobic processes to refresh that energy molecule. While these systems give you a quick turbo boost, they don't last long and tend to gunk up the works with a by-product called lactic acid (which soon converts to lactate). How much we can tolerate the presence of these leftovers is a major factor in athletic performance.

Among the many adaptations that result from an effective training program is increased aerobic capacity. This is the maximum volume of oxygen that you can utilize when working as hard as possible (VO_2max). By raising your VO_2max, you can do the same amount of work with less effort; your heart rate may be 20 to 40 beats lower per minute.

Depending upon the program, your current level of fitness, and inherent "trainability," VO_2max can be increased by about 10 to 15 percent. However, gains usually end after about eighteen months of training, and some people see no change. Nonetheless, VO_2max can be a good indicator of fitness and a benchmark for your own training. Since there are many variables that affect VO_2max, don't compare your result with someone else's unless the tests were done with the same lab protocol.

Although a high aerobic capacity is helpful when humping a pack up brutal hills, what matters even more in the mountains is your ability to sustain that output for a long time. When working very hard, you begin to breathe faster than your ability to consume oxygen (called the ventilatory breakpoint). At the same time, your body begins to switch from aerobic to anaerobic energy production (see chapter 4 for more details). Once you go anaerobic and are panting so hard you can't talk, you can only sustain a few minutes of output before you collapse, gasping for air.

One of the major goals of training is to raise the point at which your body transitions out of the aerobic realm. If you are out of shape, this may occur at about 50 percent of your VO_2max but it can rise to 80 percent or higher if you set your mind and body to it. Called the anaerobic threshold or lactate threshold (not the same thing but for practical purposes, the terms are interchangeable), a higher level allows a greater sustained peak output and faster recovery. In other words, you can go harder for longer. Even after you have maxed your VO$_2$max, you can still increase your lactate threshold and power output.

With training, your maximum cardiac output increases considerably, which means at full effort your heart pumps much more blood. The heart itself becomes larger due to bigger chambers and thicker muscle walls. Even the electrocardiogram (ECG) of the "sports heart" is altered and may resemble a heart attack on the printout if the doctor doesn't realize you're an athlete.

Your heart rate also recovers significantly faster once you stop exercising. As fitness improves, your resting heart rate can decrease about 10 beats per minute. Both of these adaptations are good signs that all that work is paying off.

Other changes include a greater volume of blood plasma (fluid), which improves oxygen delivery because your blood is less viscous. After training, your body also produces more red blood cells—each of which carries over a billion oxygen molecules.

Endurance training actually causes your body to grow more capillaries within the muscles and expand the existing ones. These minute blood vessels allow a greater exchange of nutrients while more effectively removing waste and heat. Enhanced circulation may also translate to warmer fingers and toes in winter conditions.

Within the muscle cells, myoglobin (a protein that stores and transports oxygen), mitochondria (the powerhouses that produce energy), and the activity of oxidative enzymes (which break down fuels for use) all increase dramatically. Trained muscles store more glycogen, your primary aerobic energy source from carbohydrates, and triglyceride, the fuel form of fat.

Of major significance for mountaineers and other long-duration athletes, aerobic training enhances your ability to use fat as a source of fuel. This effect, which can take years to fully develop, spares the limited amount of glycogen in the muscles and liver (only adequate for about 1.5 hours) by tapping into the nearly infinite reserves of fat.

Both tendon and ligament repair are enhanced due to increased collagen activity within these connective tissues from aerobic activity. These tissues have relatively poor circulation and are normally very slow to heal, but low- to moderate-intensity exercise can speed the process.

TRAINING PRINCIPLES

An effective training program is ruled by the aerobic triumvirate: frequency, duration, and intensity. If you don't go often enough, long enough, and hard enough, you will not get the desired results. Though not a complete waste of time—any exercise is better than none—haphazard workouts can leave you frustrated and out of breath. Train smart.

To make progress, you need to get out at least three days per week for 30 minutes or more. Your workouts don't have to be in a single session (for example, having three 10-minute periods is fine) but most people find that more convenient. The goal is to elevate your heart rate to roughly 70 percent of maximum; lower levels of intensity can have significant health benefits but do not improve aerobic capacity.

Forget about training in the "fat burning zone." This myth, which continues to be promulgated by airheaded aerobics instructors and the mass media, is based upon a poor understanding of physiology. Although it is true that exercising at low intensity burns a greater percentage of fat versus carbohydrates, this is a straw soldier. A higher level of intensity burns more total calories, including a greater amount of fat. Since few people have unlimited time or desire to train, make the most of every workout.

On the other hand, don't turn into a training junkie either. You can get health benefits with as little as 700 calories of aerobic exercise per week (roughly 5 to 8 miles of running). It takes more like 2,000 calories (15 to 25 miles) of effort to see significant fitness gains. Maximum aerobic results are achieved with 5,000 to 6,000 calories per week, which translates to 40 to 60 miles of running, although this depends upon body weight, intensity, and many other factors. Exceeding this volume may be necessary for long races (marathons and ultras) to prevent injury and train other components, but it won't enhance your lung power.

Many recreational athletes tend to train at a level of intensity that is too high for maximum gains. This is another case where more is not always better since some of the adaptations discussed previously only happen when you aren't going as hard. You also run a greater risk of injuries and overtraining, which can set you back more than training less.

In the grand scheme of things, it makes absolutely no difference whether you exercise in the morning, afternoon, or evening. While some argue the pros and cons of minute differences in calorie burning at different times of day, what counts is that you establish a pattern that works for your schedule. Don't allow some perceived advantage of a certain time prevent you from working out.

If you are an early riser and prefer to exercise before breakfast, that's fine. However, be aware that you may not get as high a quality workout due to lower energy levels and dehydration. Conversely, elevating your heart rate late in the evening may make it difficult to fall asleep; don't sacrifice this vital nutrient.

Give yourself time to see results; heaping on too much, too fast will lead to injury. Remember, too, that what worked when you were a twentysomething kid may not apply later in life. It takes about two weeks for your body to adjust to a change and a full two months to fully adapt to a program. Increase only one component of the aerobic triumvirate at a time by no more than 10 percent, and don't expect overnight miracles.

ON THE RUN (OR BIKE, OR SKI)

As with all other forms of exercise, to prevent injury and increase flexibility, it is vital that you warm up properly prior to a hard effort. Always start with 5 to 10 minutes of gentle exercise to warm the muscles, increase blood flow, and lubricate the joints. This also gets you in the proper mind-set for what is to come.

No matter your endurance sport, hills are your friend. Don't fear them. Seek hills out and embrace them. They will reward you with better physical and mental conditioning. If you are a flatlander, try running up and down highway overpasses, stadium steps, or office building stairwells.

When it is safe to do so (no traffic), listening to music can be an excellent motivator during your workouts. With a portable MP3 player, you can easily customize the tunes to start you out with a gentle warm-up, psych you through the tough sections, and relax you during the cool-down. Of course, if music bugs you, then listen to your own rhythm.

Be sure to warm down adequately following your play—don't stop cold! Active recovery removes lactate and other byproducts from muscles much faster, which will leave you less sore the next day.

FOLLOW YOUR HEART

Your heart rate is invaluable information for planning and carrying out an effective training program. There is a direct linear correlation between heart rate and training intensity. This fact allows us to monitor our level of exertion with greater accuracy than subjective interpretations of how we feel during a workout.

At rest, the heart rates of those who are out of shape is typically around 70 to 80 beats per minute, though this depends upon age (decreases as you get older) and gender (women's hearts are slightly faster at rest). Following an endurance training program, this can drop into the 40 to 60 range. Although elite athletes often have a resting heart rate (RHR) in the low 30s (some hearts may only beat 25 times a minute), a lower number does not necessarily indicate superior conditioning between competitors.

Your heart rate is lowest in the middle of the night, but taking your pulse first thing in the morning before crawling out of bed is fairly close (averaging three mornings in a row is best). This number is useful as an indication that your training is paying off (RHR can decrease 1 beat per week) and for planning your program. If you notice that your RHR has increased by 8 or more beats, it may be a warning sign of insufficient recovery, overtraining, or illness—time for a good rest. However, it could also mean you've just gone to a higher altitude, are jet lagged (west to east is harder), or are dehydrated.

Another method for tracking progress is to monitor how quickly your heart rate slows down once you finish a workout. You can either see what your heart rate is after a set amount of time, say 2 minutes, or you can measure the time it takes for your heart rate to drop to a certain point. In both cases, lower is better and ideally the trend should be downward.

Contrary to popular belief, a high maximum heart rate (MHR) does not indicate superior fitness. This value is genetically determined, so you must play the cards you are dealt. No amount of training will increase your MHR; indeed, it can actually decrease slightly as conditioning improves. However, maintaining a high level of fitness can slow the inevitable decrease of MHR that occurs with age.

If you are serious about improving fitness, it is very helpful to know your MHR with a high level of accuracy. This number serves as the basis for planning workouts at the proper intensity. Without this knowledge, you will be guessing—almost certainly incorrectly—and undermining your efforts. Don't waste time and energy; strive for quality.

The standard age-based formula for estimating MHR (subtracting your age from 220 for men or 226 for women) is a convenient method that is fraught with peril when it comes to developing a training program. For most people, the range of error is fairly high. The formula says a forty-year-old man should have an MHR of about 180, but about two-thirds of this age group will have an MHR between 168 and 192. This prediction is even less accurate for those over forty who have been athletic most of their life since their MHR declines more slowly.

The best method for finding MHR is via an all-out stress test using the American College of Sports Medicine (ACSM) guidelines and supervised by a doctor. If you are over forty, have a family history of heart disease, or are starting up an exercise program after years of inactivity, this should be performed on a treadmill while being monitored by an ECG to detect abnormalities (and have the paddles ready). Many sports medicine clinics offer this test combined with a test to determine your VO_2max to give athletes a benchmark.

Those who are certain of their health and have no reason to be worried about pushing their heart can find their MHR with the aid of a heart rate monitor. Following a good warm-up, gradually increase your running or cycling pace so that, after 4 to 5 minutes, you cannot go any harder. Record the highest reading on the monitor. Be sure to warm down afterward. For greater accuracy, take a rest day and then repeat the test to get an average.

CARDIO TRAINING

Heart rate monitors are routinely dismissed as toys by people who don't know how to use them. The feedback these devices offer can greatly enhance your training. But use a monitor intelligently and don't become a slave to the numbers.

One of the best aspects of a heart rate monitor is that it teaches you to listen to your body. With practice, you will more accurately learn the feeling of different levels of intensity—of working at different

ZONE PLAY

Zones 1 through 5 take you through increasingly tough aerobic training intensities at a target heart rate that is related to a desired percentage of your heart rate reserve (HRR). (See "Cardio Planning" and "Heart Sense" for details.) Remember that this is a continuum without hard-cut edges, that each of us is unique, and that our bodies are not static. Use this as a starting point and adjust accordingly.

Your Maximum Heart Rate (MHR): _____
Your Resting Heart Rate (RHR): _____
Your Heart Rate Reserve (HRR = MHR – RHR): _____
Your Target Heart Rate (THR) = HRR × desired percentage + RHR

Zone 1—Easy effort

Lower THR = HRR _____ × 0.5 + RHR _____ = _____
Upper THR = HRR _____ × 0.6 + RHR _____ = _____
Energy system: Extensive endurance zone; fully aerobic.
Feel: Can easily sing your favorite songs. Roughly 60 to 70 percent of MHR.
Typical activity: Recovery workouts in the days after major exertions; 30 to 90 minutes of power hiking or easy spinning.
Comments: Modest aerobic benefit. Starting zone for beginners—soon to be surpassed. Good training for the typical approach to sport climbs.

Zone 2—Light effort

Lower THR = HRR _____ × 0.6 + RHR _____ = _____
Upper THR = HRR _____ × 0.7 + RHR _____ = _____
Energy system: Extensive endurance zone; fully aerobic.
Feel: Can hold a long conversation. Roughly 70 to 80 percent of MHR.
Typical activity: Long, slow distance (LSD); 1 to 3 hours running or 2 to 6 hours cycling.
Comments: Seems too easy, but vital for building a base; many important aerobic adaptations occur in this zone. Good training for long uphill approaches and general mountaineering.

Zone 3—Moderate effort

Lower THR = HRR _____ × 0.7 + RHR _____ = _____
Upper THR = HRR _____ × 0.8 + RHR _____ = _____
Energy system: Intermediate endurance zone; both aerobic and anaerobic.
Feel: Can talk in short sentences. Roughly 80 to 87 percent of MHR.
Typical activity: Runs of 1 to 2 hours at typical marathon pace, or rides of 2 to 4 hours.
Comments: Without guidance, most athletes spend too much time here when other zones can offer greater benefit. Good training for breaking trail, carrying heavy loads, and high-altitude climbing.

Zone 4—Hard effort

Lower THR = HRR _____ × 0.8 + RHR _____ = _____
Upper THR = HRR _____ × 0.9 + RHR _____ = _____
Energy system: Intensive endurance zone; lactate threshold (LT) region.
Feel: Might be able to reply with a couple of words. Roughly 87 to 93 percent of MHR.
Typical activity: Intervals, fartleks, and hills, oh my; race pace for 5K to half-marathon runs.
Comments: Where the real gains in aerobic performance are made. Good training for summit pushes and trying to outrun a thunderstorm.

Zone 5—Maximum effort

Lower THR = HRR _____ × 0.9 + RHR _____ = _____
Upper THR = HRR _____ × 1.0 + RHR _____ = _____
Energy system: Fully anaerobic and downright painful; few climbers need go here.
Feel: All thoughts are on surviving, not talking. Roughly 93 to 100 percent of MHR.
Typical activity: 60-second or shorter intervals, followed by 4 to 5 minutes of no exercise.
Comments: Short, intense bursts of speed. Good training for trying to outrun an avalanche or a grizzly bear.

percentages of your maximum heart rate. In other words: the more you use a monitor, the less you need one. After a while, you may only want to strap it on every couple of months to confirm your gut instincts.

A midprice heart rate monitor is fine for all but hard-core athletes and nerds; the bells and whistles on the most sophisticated monitors often add unneeded complexity. Select a model that has a wireless chest strap and can record total duration of your aerobic activity, time spent within at least one range (or zone) of heart rates, and max heart rate. If it records a minimum (many don't), obtaining your resting heart rate is easy: just sleep with the strap on. Some heart rate monitors can approximate your VO_2max with a simple test; it's the trend over time that counts, not the actual number.

When using a monitor, realize that in a hot environment, dehydration reduces the volume of your blood supply. This results in an upward creep in heart rate, even though the level of exertion remains the same (termed cardiovascular drift). Since it isn't always possible to drink enough fluid, keep this phenomenon in mind when the heat is on.

CARDIO PLANNING

Determining proper ranges, or zones, in which to keep your heart rate during an aerobic activity is the basis of smart aerobic training. This need not be complicated, but the more you put into it, the better the results.

Basing training zones upon percentages of VO_2max is the most common method of prescribing intensities. A simple percentage of MHR can also be used, but leaves greater room for error at lower intensities; there is a straight-line relationship between MHR and VO_2max, but the slope varies with each individual and their level of conditioning.

Most recreational athletes do not care to visit a lab annually for VO_2max tests (low score on the fun meter). Fortunately, there is a good approximation available. Known as the Karvonen method, it uses what is called the heart rate reserve (HRR)—determined simply by subtracting resting heart rate from maximum heart rate (HRR = MHR - RHR).

Your target heart rate (THR) for training is then equal to your resting heart rate plus some desired percentage of HRR—the percentage depending on how hard you want to work (see Zone Play). (In formula form: THR = RHR + %HRR.)

For example: if your tested MHR is 180 and RHR is 50 (resulting in HRR of 130) and the desired percentage is 70, you'll want your heart pumping 141 beats per minute. You get this figure by adding your RHR (50) to 70 percent of your HRR (70 percent of 130 is 91) to arrive at 141. (In formula form: THR = 50 + 0.7 (180 - 50) = 50 + 91 = 141.)

HEART SENSE

With this heart rate information, you can determine your own training zones that allow progress in the most time-efficient manner. For specific training programs, see chapter 6, but here are some general considerations to keep in mind.

If you are just starting out with a conditioning program, take it easy at first and permit your body to get used to the new sensations. Depending on how long you've been on the couch and how much excess poundage you're carrying, this means 15 to 30 minutes at the low end of Zone 1 every other day for six to eight weeks. If even that intensity is too hard, relax and do what you can—just don't give up! Those with significant fat to lose should start with cycling, power hiking, or other low-impact activities; running is too hard on your joints. You'll be doing resistance training with weights, too, so it's important that you don't overdo it. Increase duration and intensity only 10 to 15 percent each week. Heck, if it takes twelve weeks, that's okay too—you're in it for the long haul.

When you can comfortably maintain 30 minutes at the low end of Zone 2, it's time to up the ante and build endurance. Despite the proclamations of fitness zealots, there is no need for more than four aerobic workouts per week; five to six days a week is overkill unless you plan to race. Just emphasize quality in each play session and you'll continue to make good progress. Keep extending the duration until most are about an hour long and one bout each week goes well beyond that.

During the endurance stage, spend most of your time in Zone 2 with occasional forays into Zone 3 and even Zone 4. It can be tough for those who feel they're in pretty good shape to rein back, but the long-term rewards are worth it. Fear not, several hours of Zone 2 will whip your butt. Allow three to four months to build a solid endurance base.

Even when you're ready to work on speed, you should still spend the majority of your time in Zone 2. But now, when you're chomping at the bit, you get to push harder and suss out the anaerobic edge. While you're only spending 10 percent of your time in Zone 4, it is important that you learn the feel of crossing over the threshold and intimately know the point just below it that can be maintained indefinitely. This phase of training lasts about two to three months.

For many climbers, this is a satisfactory end of the progression and they can enter a maintenance phase. This basically means go out and play hard aerobically a couple days a week for the rest of your life. When something major comes up, such as an alpine climbing vacation or expedition, then it's fairly easy to fine-tune yourself in a short period of time. Starting all over from scratch sucks, so keep playing.

MAXIMIZING PERFORMANCE

Using heart rate, or even just feel, to guide training is probably sufficient for the vast majority of recreational athletes. But when you desire to perform at the highest levels, there are more tools available to enhance training: your lactate threshold (LT) and intervals.

As exercise intensity increases into Zone 4 and we rely more upon anaerobic energy sources, lactate and hydrogen ions accumulate in the cells faster than they can be cleared. Eventually these by-products interfere so much that cells can no longer contract and the muscles stop working (ouch!); this corresponds to a particular heart rate, the LT.

Both the point of transition (it's actually a range) and our tolerance for lactate can be increased. For example, a person starting out may have a maximum heart rate of 180 with a lactate threshold down around 130.

INTERVALS

Here are some options for interval exercises, at various percentages of the heart rate that corresponds to your lactate threshold (LT). (See the accompanying section "Maximizing Performance" for details.)

Endurance Intervals
Interval: 8–15 minutes at 97%–98% LT (about 85%–90% MHR)
Recovery: 5 minutes at 70% LT (about 60% MHR)
Repetitions: 4–5
System: Aerobic

Lactate Threshold
Interval: 2–8 minutes at 98%–102% LT (about 90%–95% MHR)
Recovery: 4–6 minutes at 60% LT (about 55% MHR)
Repetitions: 5–6
System: Lactate/Aerobic

Lactate Tolerance
Interval: 1–3 minutes at 101%–105% LT (about 95% MHR)
Recovery: 1 minute at 75% LT (about 65% MHR)
Repetitions: 5–10
System: Lactate

Sprint Intervals
Interval: 10–30 seconds at 105%–108% LT (about 95%–100% MHR)
Recovery: 3–5 minutes at full rest
Repetitions: 5–20
System: Phosphate

But after a conditioning program, the LT might rise to 160. This greatly extends this person's aerobic range (140 is comfortable instead of painful), and it's now possible to hold out longer when at 165.

After a moderately high level of conditioning has been achieved (that LT of 160), climbers sincerely interested in the alpine world, or just playing really hard, will need to increase their LT even further (perhaps to 165 or higher). To be all that you can be without joining the Army, you'll need to find the heart rate corresponding to your LT and train accordingly.

Basing training upon your lactate threshold—versus your heart rate or your VO_2max—offers the advantage that it most accurately takes into account increasing (or decreasing) conditioning. Due to the complexity of the subject, an in-depth discussion of LT training plans is beyond the scope of this book. If you're in this sport for the money, consider hiring a coach. However, since the LT is the best benchmark of aerobic performance, it's a good way to track your progress even if you aren't that fanatical.

The ideal way to determine LT is from blood samples taken during a VO_2max test—and again, few of us want to go there. If you are well attuned to your body, you can recognize when you've crossed over the threshold by a queasy feeling, breathlessness, and a burning sensation—you hurt.

There are also several noninvasive tests that help you hone in on your LT (Conconi's is the most famous, but it's a hassle).

Instead, here's a simple self-test that can be performed while running or cycling, given a flat course and a calm day (variable wind messes with you):

Warm up for at least 10 minutes, then start the timer when your heart rate reaches 130. After 10 minutes, increase your speed until heart rate is 140. Continue to increase heart rate by 10 beats every 10 minutes. When you can't (or can just barely) last a full 10-minute segment, subtract 5 beats from that rate for an estimated LT heart rate. You can use this as a starting point to find the highest heart rate that you can maintain with little variation for 30 to 60 minutes: your maximal lactate steady state.

The standard approach for maximizing aerobic capacity is with intervals: alternating intense exercise bouts with recovery periods. There are numerous forms of intervals (see the Intervals sidebar for a few options at various percentages of your LT heart rate). Each form of interval is designed to elicit a different response from your body. The truly dedicated can follow precise interval workouts based upon times or heart rates, although fun is never an operative word.

Fortunately there are two good ways to get much of the gain from intervals without the anal-retentiveness: fartleks and hills. Fartlek is the Swedish word for "speed play" and basically means add some short bursts of high intensity into your light to moderate workouts. You don't need a watch or monitor for fartleks: just go hard till that tree, or surge up that hill. Mix it up; have fun.

Hill repeats are also unstructured intervals dictated by the personality of your favorite hill. Run up it hard, then cruise down easy; do it again and again. These are especially good for climbers since they target the same muscles and teach mental toughness.

Remember that all forms of intervals are very taxing to your entire system, which is why they work. Be sure to warm down thoroughly and make the next day an easy one.

CROSS-PLAY EXERCISES

Hard-body athletes have been been talking about cross-training for years—usually just referring to the triathlon sports: swimming, cycling, and running. Yet to many climbers, the term has onerous connotations that imply hard work with minimal benefit. The concept of cross-play, however, is to get 80 percent of the benefit while having 200 percent more fun.

Choosing your modes of aerobic play is largely a matter of personal preference, although some forms will be more directly applicable to climbing than others. The following selections are well-suited to climbers but are by no means the only options. While specificity is nice, of far greater importance is selecting sports that you enjoy. The more you emphasize fun, the easier it is to get out the door to train.

Don't just settle for one activity either.

Having several options in your quiver will prevent burnout and allow "active rest" from your primary games. Another major reason to develop skills at other sports is coping with the inevitable injury. Sooner or later, it's bound to happen and few things are worse than a grumpy climber who can't climb. These one-track people are not only boring but they rarely allow adequate time for recuperation, which leads to a vicious cycle of repetitive injury.

Now get out and have fun! That's an order.

TRAIL RUNNING

Pros. Arguably the king of aerobic exercises for climbers. It is the most physically demanding, and rewarding, form of running. Trails are lower impact than roads, and the irregular terrain offers greater variety for your joints and muscles. Trail running is also more mentally stimulating than running on roads, tracks, or treadmills. It provides an opportunity to recharge your batteries and connect with nature. If necessary, it is worth driving to a trail instead of pounding pavement.

Cons. Trail running can be addictive. Beginners, and those weaning from roads, run a greater risk of ankle or knee injuries. The progression to more rugged trails and longer distances is much like that to harder climbs—it takes time.

Form. The key to injury-free running is landing softly; you should move gently through the countryside, not plod along. Use either a midfoot or heel landing, depending on the terrain and your natural gait.

Keep your head upright, your shoulders relaxed, and your spine erect. Lean forward slightly from the ankles so that you need to place the next foot in front to prevent falling on your face: this momentum makes running smooth and effortless. Look at the trail well out in front of you, not down at your feet. Allow your arms to swing naturally back and forth, without crossing your midline, and keep your hands relaxed.

When running downhill, commit to the descent and, depending on the angle, either lean forward or remain upright; knees should be slightly bent, never extended, when landing. If you tense up or lose focus, disaster may be around the next corner.

Gear. When starting out on dirt roads and bridle paths, road-running shoes are more than adequate. But once you're ready for single-track trails in mountainous terrain, then real trail-running shoes make the sport safer and more enjoyable. These offer better traction, particularly on downhills, and more lateral support; both are needed for safe descents at speed. For sloppy winter runs, trail shoes with waterproof/breathable linings keep your feet dry (unless you have stream crossings) and encourage you to run through puddles, which is better for the trails.

Well-designed clothing is important in the mountains and on long runs. Avoid cotton like the plague; modern synthetics offer greater comfort and faster drying.

Wear a hydration fanny pack on longer

Photo by: James Martin

runs to carry clothes and accessories. Never wear ankle or hand weights when running (too much joint stress); increase intensity or add weight to the fanny pack if you want a harder workout.

ROAD RUNNING

Pros. The most readily accessible aerobic workout for many people: just head out the door. There are many clubs and countless races throughout the country that can help psych you to run and improve your technique. Comparing your race times is a good measure of fitness.

Cons. Inferior to trail running except for, perhaps, availability. Concrete is the hardest running surface, something you can feel in your body after a while. Asphalt is noticeably softer, but always running on one side of a cambered road can create imbalances in your body. The most challenging aspect of a marathon isn't the distance—average runners are only on the road for four to five hours—it's the boredom of such repetitive pounding.

Form. The same as with trail running. Run softly and land midfoot, weight over the bent knee at touchdown, followed by a quick bounce off the heel. Heel striking can be a symptom of overstriding, which slows you down and increases impact forces. As with cycling, a faster cadence is superior to long strides/lower gearing. There should be no vertical component to your movements; distant objects shouldn't bob up and down as you run. If you are new to midfoot landing, transition gradually to give your calves time to adjust; some people will find a gentle heel landing is preferable.

Try to vary your course frequently to avoid a rut. If possible, run in parks where you will breathe less air pollution and enjoy a modicum of nature. Running on a sandy beach, just above the water's edge, is a very demanding yet energizing workout (wear shoes unless you're sure there is no broken glass or sharp shells). Because of the cross-slope, it's best to run out and back to avoid imbalances.

Gear. Due to the very regular surface, good shoes with biomechanics suited to your feet are critical to prevent injury. Go to a specialty running store where the employees can give knowledgeable advice.

Photo by: James Martin

Look for a model with superior forefoot cushioning, but you probably don't need the fanciest models. Shoes with excessive heel cushioning encourage bad form.

Depending on your weight, among other factors, expect the cushioning to wear out after 300 to 500 miles—long before the uppers. Continuing to run on shoes that are worn out is the leading cause of injury in road runners. The change is subtle, so many runners keep two or more pairs of shoes (one a bit fresher) in rotation.

INDOOR RUNNING (TREADMILL, ELLIPTICAL TRAINER)

Pros. The lowest impact forms of running are also independent of weather and time of day—never miss an episode of Oprah. Elliptical trainers change their angle throughout the workout, and they also work in reverse so you get a more varied workout.

Cons. You're inside. Good treadmills and elliptical trainers can be very expensive but give a smooth ride; cheap ones ensure a lousy experience. The calories-burned estimations on most machines are worthless unless you input body weight (even then it's a guess) and some hype the "fat-burning zone" myth.

Form. On a treadmill, the angle needs to be about 1 degree to compensate for the lack of a headwind. Otherwise it's the same as road running.

When using an elliptical trainer, *never* rest your hands on the side rails. Set the program to vary the angles as you run to work muscles differently.

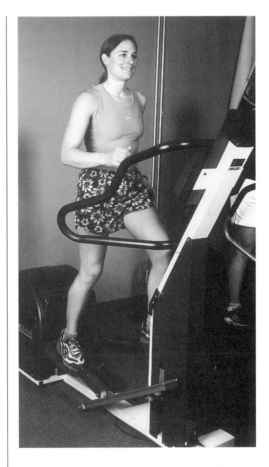

Gear. The cheapest home treadmills have a harsh ride and are noisy—little wonder they often can be found at garage sales for cheap. Better models, which start around $1,000, use higher-quality motors and more suspension points on the tread; they will last longer and are more likely to get used. Elliptical trainers are more complicated machines with a greater likelihood to require expensive maintenance. Cross-country ski machines are poor simulations of what is done on snow, and very different from running or hiking, but they do offer a serious workout.

POWER HIKING

Pros. This is the most specific form of training for mountaineering and a good all-around workout. Performed with trekking poles, this is basically aggressive hiking

Photo by: Dan A. Nelson

with the goal of keeping the heart rate up—it is not a walk in the park. Although hilly terrain is ideal, power hiking can be effective even on relatively flat ground. On long downhills, the use of poles can remove a huge amount of stress from your knees.

Cons. Almost none. You won't develop the speed that you can with running and may have trouble performing higher-intensity intervals. There also isn't the adrenaline rush of flying down a hill, but it's likely safer.

Form. Using trekking poles properly requires a bit of skill. Adjust the length so that your elbows form right angles. Use the straps as you would with cross-country, not alpine, poles; your hand enters the loop from below and the straps run between thumb and forefinger. Adjust the straps for a snug fit with the pivot point near the grip. The point of all this is that most of the weight from your arms is suspended by the strap—you shouldn't grasp the pole tightly.

When going uphill, raise the pole well in front of you and plant the tip near your feet. You are almost pulling your way upward, using significant upper body strength. On the descent, plant the pole below you and lower yourself downward. Throughout the entire workout, try to get a smooth, powerful rhythm going.

Gear. If you've never tried trekking poles, you can start off with some old alpine poles sans baskets. However, poles specifically made for hiking have a more comfortable grip (often made of rubberized cork) when used with sweaty bare hands.

The small baskets give flotation in sand without snagging on every bush, and the poles collapse for easier transport. The better trekking poles have shock absorbers built in to reduce elbow stress; some models allow this to be locked out, too.

Footwear is whatever is appropriate for the terrain; this is also an ideal way to break in mountaineering boots. To increase intensity, you can wear a pack. If you will be doing steep training climbs, consider weighting the pack with water and dumping some before descending to reduce knee strain.

A new form of power hiking, called Fittrek, is starting to appear in health clubs. The only real difference is that the classes are taught by an instructor, and 2-pound hand weights are worn with the poles to increase the upper body workout. These can be a time-efficient, highly motivated workout.

STAIRS/STAIR-STEPPER

Pros. Passable options for flatlanders preparing for the hills. Running up and walking down long flights of stairs is a good interval workout.

Cons. Not even close to the real thing. Stadium steps are usually concrete so there may be greater impact forces. Stair-steppers place a lot of stress behind the kneecap and they do nothing to simulate going downhill.

Form. Mix it up when running stairs: skip one or two steps, zigzag from side to side, bound upward—anything you can think of to vary the workout.

Photo by: James Martin

When using a stair-stepper, never rest your hands on the side rails—this bad habit reduces intensity by over 20 percent and won't improve your balance. Be sure to use a full range of motion while keeping your feet flat on the platforms (don't push with your toes).

Gear. Stadium steps are popular since

they tend to be long and have walkways that break up the repetitiveness. Old staircases in parks are often more uneven (a good thing) and offer better scenery. Those who live or work in a high-rise might investigate the stairwells, but they aren't exactly cheery places.

As with other inexpensive indoor equipment, you can often find stair-steppers collecting dust in basements or attics. The better commercial models have a smoother action and deeper range of motion.

ROAD BIKING

Pros. Cycling is superb aerobic training because you can go for 6 hours without feeling too beat up afterward. With good technique, road biking works nearly all the muscles below the sternum and is not stressful on the knees. In addition to a good physical workout, the mental aspect of road biking has much to offer. The mind-set of riding up a long, steep mountain is much the same as when slogging up a snow slope at high altitude. And the concentration

required while screaming downhill at 50 mph is much the same as what keeps you alive when climbing. A rich history permeates the racing world, with legends and heroes as great as any in mountaineering.

Cons. Traffic is a serious danger in many areas. Not an exact simulation of climbing. Less time-efficient than running. The upper body gets a minimal workout unless there are steep hills. Can be hard on your knees, back, and neck if the bike doesn't fit or you don't learn good form.

Form. Concentrate on smooth, fast pedaling (90 to 110 rpm) with a quiet upper body (no bobbing). Try to apply power throughout the pedal circle by pulling at the back of your stroke as well as pushing at the front; it's no faster, but balances the leg muscles.

On moderate hills, slide back in the saddle a bit and push more as you spin along. Stand up out of the saddle on steep hills and let the bike rock naturally back and forth beneath you (don't exaggerate the motion) but maintain a high rpm. Pull up on one side of the handlebar while pushing down with the opposite foot, directing your body weight directly into the pedal.

Unless you are in a full tuck (head to the bars, knees on top tube) on a steep grade, you should be pedaling hard down hills—this ain't no free ride! For a long, gradual descent off a pass or down a canyon, get in the drops of the handlebar and push down that hill.

Gear. Decent road bikes cost around $1,500, though you can easily blow many times that. Fortunately there are great deals available on the used market. The advantage of buying new at a specialty shop is that the bike will be tuned and properly fit to you. A poor-fitting bike is as painful as the wrong-size hiking boots! With a used bike, you may need to upgrade parts (handlebar, stem, seat post) and overhaul the components. However, with basic maintenance, a quality bike will last indefinitely, so a used high-end bike can be a better value than an inexpensive new one.

For your riding pleasure, spend top dollar on the contact points: anatomic handlebars with good, padded tape; bike gloves with shock-absorbing foam; comfortable saddle that fits your derrière; eight-panel bike shorts with contoured padding; totally rigid road shoes with floating cleats; comfortable helmet with good ventilation. It's advisable to get a triple crankset if you ride in the mountains.

A cyclo-cross bike is a fun alternative, or supplement, to a road bike. These resemble road frames with knobby tires but there are other differences that make them a blast for zooming along on dirt roads. Depending on where you live, a cyclo-cross bike can open up a new world on roads too rough for your road bike and too boring for a mountain bike.

MOUNTAIN BIKING

Pros. Where road biking offers great endurance workouts, mountain biking tends to give superb interval fun. The nature of the terrain dictates the workout—long and easy, short and fierce, or somewhere in between—but you often ride in spectacular country. Sometimes the rides include weight training (read: hike-a-bike).

Cons. Finding suitable trails can be difficult, depending on where you live. Long stretches of flat road are tedious at best; sections with sand are evil torture.

Probably draws more blood than any other sport offered in this book.

Form. As with road biking, a smooth and quiet riding style offers the best performance gains. There is a much greater emphasis on balance and body position; in many ways, mountain biking is akin to telemark skiing. On steep hills, standing out of the saddle requires more finesse than with a road bike; to maintain traction and prevent spinning out, lean forward sharply at the waist.

Good form also includes being polite to hikers and horseback riders by stopping to allow them to pass. Access is no less of a concern in the mountain-bike world than the climbing world—don't screw it up for others!

Gear. At the very least, you will want a mountain bike with front suspension. However, full suspension is the way to go if you plan to ride a lot. The current genera-tion of cross-country soft-tail bikes (3 to 4 inches of travel) climb well, descend great, and won't leave you feeling beat up at the end of a long, hard ride.

The best values are the midprice bikes (around $1,000 to $1,500) that you can upgrade later to reduce weight. The cheaper bikes rarely can be turned into good rides, while the more expensive machines often sport lots of jewelry but don't necessarily perform better. Sad to say, you should also consider how the bike carries over your shoulder; some designs look cool but are very awkward on long uphill hikes. Unfortunately, purchasing a used mountain bike is a risky proposition since, by definition, they get hammered and many early full-suspension designs were quite poor.

Comfortable shorts, well-padded gloves, and stiff shoes with aggressive treads for hiking are essential. Only idiots mountain bike without a helmet.

SPINNING

Pros. The best indoor aerobic workout around—high quality and time efficient. Spinning is somewhat of a cross between road and mountain biking, with an instructor who will push you hard. Although it is a group exercise, there is no peer pressure since nobody else knows how hard you are working. While emphasizing the lower body, there is substantial involvement of the upper body too.

Cons. Need to find a gym that offers spinning classes. The quality of the instructors varies and this greatly affects the workout. Trying to spin at home requires a lot of mental fortitude and will probably be less effective.

Form. Though it bears many similarities to outdoor cycling, there are significant differences. The hand positions are unlike that on either a road or mountain bike, which changes your form somewhat. On a normal bike, you generally strive for a quiet upper body and allow the bike to move underneath you. When spinning, however, the bike is fixed solidly to the ground, so you should emphasize upper body movement to release energy and avoid back problems.

As with other forms of cycling, a faster

cadence (over 90 rpm) is most efficient. When you apply power throughout the entire stroke, the bike offers positive feedback as a vibration you can feel.

Gear. Spinning bikes use a 45-pound flywheel that is fixed to the pedals; unlike normal bikes, coasting is not possible. The resistance is adjusted by turning a dial to squeeze the flywheel with felt pads. With

practice, you can dial in your heart rate to within a beat or two. Many classes require a heart rate monitor and it's a good idea to use one for all of them—you can learn a lot about yourself.

Plan on spending 40 to 60 minutes on the bike and sweating profusely. Cycling shorts and a synthetic top are a good idea. Bring a towel and a large water bottle. You can use running shoes, but it's best to wear stiff cycling shoes; many bikes have Shimano pedals.

If you have a road bike, you can use it to work out at home with an indoor trainer that uses magnetic resistance (best) or wind resistance (noisy). Rollers are another option but require more skill. You'll probably want a fan to cool you down and a drip guard if you have a nice bike. Since motivation is often a problem, you can even hook up to a computer for a virtual tour.

IN-LINE SKATING

Pros. A very good aerobic workout that also helps prepare you for ski season. Really works the legs, abdomen and lower back.

Cons. Not practical unless your city has a good bike trail system. If you go down, it's always painful.

Form. This is speed skating, not the trick stuff. The emphasis is on a strong push-off and a long glide on the opposite leg. As speed increases, you will crouch into a lower, more aerodynamic position. Arm swing may be used to help propel you forward until you reach cruising speed, then tuck them behind you. Keep your eyes

on the path well out in front of you, which means craning your neck.

Gear. Choose either four-wheel skates with a long wheelbase and no rocker or five-wheelers. Brakes are optional but recommended for beginners and those who have hilly bike trails; a drag stop is used

Photo by: James Martin

otherwise. The uppers should be comfortable (many aren't), well ventilated, and have decent ankle support. Hold off on the low-cut racing boots until you've been at it for a while.

When in-line skating at speed, always wear a bike helmet! You can be moving at 20 mph or more, with your head fairly close to the ground, and go down in a nanosecond if a stick, dog, or crack in the path suddenly appears. Wrist guards are another essential that can mean the difference between a minor mishap and weeks of infirmity. Beginners should consider elbow and knee pads as well.

CROSS-COUNTRY TRACK SKIING

Pros. The absolute top of the aerobic pyramid. Both skating and classic techniques will work your entire body like no other sport. Skating is particularly suited to climbers because the powerful upper body movements are similar to pulling down. The peaceful feeling of gliding quietly over the snow is like no other—Zen-like at times. An active racing scene, especially in Europe where some events resemble moving cities.

Cons. Requires groomed ski trails; these days it can be harder to find quality grooming for classic skiing. Both styles require a fair level of skill, though classic can take years to refine. You will also need to learn the fine art of waxing, though this is now greatly simplified. Can be difficult to stay sub-anaerobic, particularly when skating on hilly courses.

Corbis stock photo

Form. Herein lies a book. The smartest thing you can do is take lessons. For either style, work on full weight shift from the hips and emphasize gliding on one ski. Poling is intrinsically connected with breathing—track skiing is all about rhythm. As with rock climbing, where women who lack tremendous upper-body strength can often outclimb burly dudes, technique is more important than raw power.

Gear. If you are starting out, choose skating equipment and select the best that you can afford. You will get a better, more enjoyable workout with the lightest-weight gear that is designed for performance. A state-of-the-art nordic ski package (either style) costs less than a decent road bike and should last for years. Don't waste your money on "combo" gear; none of it is any good at either style. Used equipment is often a bad buy unless you really know what you're shopping for; the technology changes significantly every few years.

Dressing properly can be tricky. Even though it may be well below freezing, you will be working up a good sweat, so effective moisture management is important. Since you are moving fairly fast, the wind is also an issue. A lot of nordic clothing has wind panels on the front (men absolutely need windproof briefs!); however, quality multisport apparel also works well. Good gloves are important since your hands are often above heart level and may not receive the best circulation.

Due to the intense demands of this sport, staying well fueled and hydrated is vital. Many people bonk because the cold weather fools them into underestimating output. If your nordic center does not have trails that loop back to the lodge, you may want to use a winterized hydration pack.

BACKCOUNTRY SKIING

Pros. Excellent preparation for ski mountaineering. Whether on telemark or alpine touring equipment, breaking trail uphill with a pack on your back is a serious aerobic workout. The descent can be a supremely fun interval session. The early

days of climbing and skiing are closely related—great reading.

Cons. Requires a high level of skill and fitness, more so for free-heel, which is best acquired at downhill resorts (more vertical per day). Significant risk of avalanches. Rather expensive to assemble a complete package including the required accessories.

Form. On the ascents, there is no difference between the two forms of skiing; set the steepest track that your skins will climb. On flat or rolling terrain, telemark gear has a slight advantage since a more extended stride is possible—true kick-and-glide works best on packed trails with lighter gear. When it's time to go down, telemark and parallel techniques are very similar above the waist. Keep your upper body quiet and facing down the fall line with hands out in front of you. Your poling, breathing, and turns are all interrelated. Learn to fall properly; slow rearward, twisting falls are the knee killers.

Gear. The telemark is the most graceful of turns and modern gear has made it far easier. However, the lack of a fixed heel makes the equipment more tiring on long descents in difficult snow, and the boots are rather poor for climbing on snow and rock due to the square toe. For mountaineering, alpine touring equipment is more practical because it is less tiring when skiing in less than ideal snow or with a heavy pack. When the goal is climbing, most bindings will accept mountaineering boots, although they are quite poor for descents. You can also use alpine touring boots for pure skiing

fun; these are acceptable for moderate mountaineering and ice climbing.

With either setup, select the lightest gear that is practical for your needs. Used equipment is somewhat risky since older stuff is often heavy and breakage prone. You will also need ski poles, climbing skins, heel elevators (if not provided), a snow shovel, probe pole, and an avalanche beacon.

SNOWSHOEING

Pros. Good winter workout that requires almost no skill. Very low risk of injury.

More options for training grounds than with skiing. Less expensive, too.

Cons. Snowshoe running requires packed trails, though you can pack down your own course after a couple of laps. Arguably not as much fun as nordic skiing.

Form. For an aerobic workout, snowshoeing is more than just plodding along through the woods. Since this can be either power hiking or trail running with paddles on your feet, much of the concepts are the same. Pacing yourself requires attention to the terrain and snow conditions.

Photo by: Dan A. Nelson

Gear. Running snowshoes are quite different from those made for walking or mountaineering. They are lighter, smaller, and have an asymmetric design that allows for a more natural gait. The binding pivots on a strap so that the tail snaps back to your foot to keep it from dragging in the snow. These characteristics limit them to packed trails—they are lousy in the backcountry.

Most people wear running shoes or hiking boots, though they should be large enough to accommodate heavier socks for warmth. Shoes with waterproof/breathable uppers will keep your feet dry from melting snow.

Because running snowshoes kick up a rooster tail, your back side will be covered with snow. Therefore wear tops and bottoms with a smooth outer surface; fleece is a bad choice. Even in cold weather, the intensity can be quite high, so moisture management in your clothing is also important.

ALTITUDE BASICS

Altitude adds a whole new dimension to the climbing realm, one that armchair mountaineers seldom comprehend. Although it is impossible to predict how severely altitude will affect you, there are measures you can take to minimize its effect.

Planet-wide, the percentage of oxygen in the atmosphere remains a constant 20.93 percent. At sea level, the atmospheric pressure is 760 millimeters of mercury (mmHg), which means the oxygen content is 159 mmHg. However, at the summit of Everest, the oxygen content is just one-third of sea level; 53 mmHg in June (2.5 mm lower in January, a potentially critical difference). On the plus side, a 70 mph wind at that extreme altitude has only the force of a 40 mph wind at sea level.

Many climbers are cavalier with terminology in discussions concerning altitude, yet from a physiological viewpoint, the definitions are more specific. Elevations between

5,000 and 11,500 feet (1,500 to 3,500 meters) are considered *high altitude* and most people can adapt well given sufficient time. The range between 11,500 and 18,000 feet (5,500 meters) is termed *very high altitude* and is where individual factors determine performance; over 10 million people live here throughout the world.

Beyond 18,000 feet is considered *extreme altitude* where the lack of oxygen (less than half of sea level) is the major issue. Nobody can live at extreme altitude on a year-round basis, and performance is in a severe decline. The so-called "death zone," often claimed to start at 8,000 meters (26,000 feet), has no scientific basis.

CHANGE OF ALTITUDE

In as little as 3 hours after moving to a higher altitude, our bodies begin to adapt to the thinner air. But everyone's rate of change is different and it takes over a year to fully acclimatize.

Because we must suck in more air to make up for the reduction in oxygen, both the rate and depth of respirations increases. This hyperventilation messes with the blood chemistry, making it more alkaline until bicarbonate compensates. Even after eight weeks at 12,500 feet (3,800 meters), ventilation remains slightly elevated.

Another consequence of faster, deeper breathing is increased dehydration from the drier air, even when you're sitting around in camp. As if working hard in dry air weren't enough to dry you out, altitude induces diuresis (you pee more), and cold weather suppresses thirst. Thus few trekkers or climbers are adequately hydrated when in the high country.

This dehydration during the first two days reduces the volume of blood plasma, causing a sudden "false" increase in the percentage of oxygen-carrying red blood cells (a higher hematocrit). But as your hydration status improves, the hematocrit returns to the previous level and you are still easily winded since there aren't enough blood cells yet to compensate for the thinner air.

The reduced oxygen levels at higher altitudes triggers greater output of erythropoietin (EPO), the hormone that stimulates production of red blood cells (erythrocytes). It takes a week for an increase in EPO to have a noticeable effect on performance, from more oxygen reaching your muscles, but around a month to reach your maximum hematocrit and athletic potential.

Though it is sometimes used by elite endurance athletes, much to the chagrin of authorities, supplemental EPO would be a very bad idea for high-altitude climbers. Normally, the hematocrit of adults at low elevations is 36 to 46 percent (women are on the lower end). But after living in thinner air for several weeks, this can safely rise to about 54 percent; almost one-fourth of high-altitude natives are in this range. But a hematocrit that is too high decreases performance because the blood turns to thick sludge that perfuses muscles poorly.

To compensate for the temporary reduction in plasma volume, your heart rate at rest and submaximal efforts will dramatically elevate during the first week of exposure to altitude. As the plasma volume restores, these heart rates should soon return to normal; they may even go lower as red blood cells boost total blood volume. However, your maximum heart rate continues to decrease the higher you go and it won't improve until you drop lower. Even after six weeks at Everest base camp (17,600 feet; 5,400 meters), the average MHR is about 17 percent lower than at sea level.

VERY HIGH CONSIDERATIONS

Above 5,000 feet (about 1,500 meters), every additional 1,000 feet (about 300 meters) of elevation gain will decrease your VO_2max by about 3 percent, though this response is highly individual. The bad news is that those with the biggest aerobic capacity tend to experience the greatest losses. According to the physiologists, "altitude is the great equalizer."

On one Everest expedition, the average VO_2max of climbers declined from 62 ml/kg/min at sea level (way above average) to about 15 ml/kg/min near the summit. (VO_2max is expressed as the amount of oxygen utilized, in milliliters per kilogram of body weight per minute.) Considering that your resting oxygen requirement is about 5 ml/kg/min, that doesn't leave much room to perform without bottled gas. The good news is that Reinhold Messner, the only person to solo Everest without supplemental oxygen, had a sea-level VO_2max only on the high end of average.

Short-term (three- to five-week) studies at very high altitude indicate that VO_2max shows little, if any, improvement during this time. However, endurance (measured by time to exhaustion at submaximal levels) can improve by 40 to 60 percent. This is likely because you just can't go hard for long when up high, so the training that would improve maximal aerobic capacity is compromised, but not the intensity that helps endurance. For the first couple of weeks, you are pretty much reduced to light to moderate exercise, with lots of brief anaerobic episodes.

Just about everyone loses weight on expeditions to extreme altitude (men more so than women), sometimes dramatically, though a good portion of this is from chronic dehydration. Besides all the work you are doing, your basal metabolic rate (minimum energy requirement) increases by about 10 percent and fat utilization is lower. Plus your appetite changes; you feel full faster and turn from a gorger to a nibbler. Even without altitude sickness, forcing down enough food is difficult up high. Something that you love at base camp may be nauseating on the mountain.

Unfortunately, you aren't just losing water and fat. Muscle mass is also decreasing (cell diameter reduces) and you become weaker. This is due to less activity of enzymes within the muscles and a negative nitrogen balance. Plus much of the endurance work involved with high-altitude climbing is muscle-eating (catabolic).

Everybody has trouble sleeping at extreme altitude, especially above 23,000 feet (7,000 meters), and bizarre dreams are common. Even at much lower elevations, some people's breathing pattern really gets out of whack. While sleeping, they breathe faster and faster, then slower and slower—stopping for a scarily long time—then starting the cycle all over again. This phenomenon, called a Cheyne-Stokes pattern, is uncomfortable for the victim and distressing for their tent mates; sleeping pills can exacerbate the problem.

At very high altitude, many climbers exhibit slight bleeding in the retinas (back of the eyeball) and it's pretty much universal above 22,000 feet (6,700 meters), though this is generally considered harmless. Complications from eye surgery, such as LASIK, appear mostly related to incomplete healing; it's best to wait at least a year before going high.

Women should note that there is an increase in maternal and fetal complications at altitude. It's best to make babies at lower elevations. There does not appear to be any problem with the use of oral contraceptives at altitude. If you are on the pill, you can safely delay menstruation by not skipping a week.

To sum up, very high altitude ain't so great for living and extreme altitude is downright unhealthy—but those are great regions to visit!

GOING LOW

After acclimatization to high altitude, you will temporarily retain some benefits after returning to the lowlands. You can expect your best aerobic performances about seven to ten days after arrival. This should taper off gradually for over a month, since those mature red blood cells carrying extra oxygen last for about 120 days. However, some of this gain is offset by the noticeably thicker air and higher humidity.

Although you may still have an elevated red blood cell count, it appears that you lose your resistance to altitude sickness, pulmonary edema in particular, within days of going low. So flying from Everest Base Camp to Katmandu for a few days and then back again may not be a hot idea.

Training and sleeping high is not a formula for success because workout intensity is necessarily reduced. Athletes who both train and sleep high perform only marginally better than those who train and sleep low. The real winners are those who sleep high—about 9,000 feet (2,750 meters) is optimal—and train low.

IMPROVING ALTITUDE PERFORMANCE

Countless hours of training cannot prevent acute mountain sickness (AMS) or other altitude illnesses (pulmonary and cerebral edema). Indeed, superb conditioning may underlie some of the problems. Young, healthy men are the mostly likely to experience difficulties at altitude due to testosterone-induced stupidity; because they are very fit and think they're invincible, they push too hard too fast. Best advice: start slow and taper.

In addition to wisdom, age appears to confer other benefits for high-altitude travel, not the least of which is increased stamina. There is very little research on this, but old geezers routinely kick young pup's butts when mountaineering and in ultra-endurance events.

Still, going to the high mountains unprepared is foolish (see the chapter 6 section "High Mountain Expedition" for a training program). It's pretty much a given that you will be working hard for 6 to 8 hours a day, perhaps more, day after day. If you haven't worked up to this amount of stress beforehand, life is gonna suck.

Anticipate a lot of knee strain from carrying a heavy pack up and, especially, down hills that seem to last forever. You want to reach the mountains with a high lactate threshold and sufficient muscle mass that you won't wither away. Use the approach trek to help prepare for what is to come—if you have a choice between a short or long route (such as hiking from Jiri or Lukla to reach the Khumbu), take the longer option.

Those with a large disposable income can get a head start on the hills by purchasing an altitude tent or building an altitude room; currently in the $6,000 to $20,000 range. These are airtight sleeping enclosures with a molecular sieve, a sophisticated machine that removes oxygen to simulate higher altitudes. Used by many elite endurance athletes as a "natural" alternative to EPO injections, an altitude tent can also reduce acclimatization time for climbers by one to three weeks.

Some guides advocate "pressure breathing" at high altitude. The concept is that exhaling forcefully through pursed lips will increase pressure in the alveoli (air sacks in the lungs) and aid oxygen uptake. Mostly though, it serves to take clients' minds off how miserable they are from a fast ascent.

SUPPLEMENTS FOR ALTITUDE

Given sufficient water, nutrition, and time, there is rarely a need for any supplements or drugs to aid climbing at extreme altitude, let alone lower elevations. The problems start occurring only when you skimp on one or all of these key ingredients. It is infinitely better to avoid altitude illness than to rely on drugs.

Inadequate time for acclimatization is the primary evil when it comes to AMS. Keeping your ascents between camps to less than 2,000 feet (600 meters) per day is a well-proven tactic for fending off acute mountain sickness. Pushing too hard during the first days at altitude may also make things worse; stay at a light to moderate intensity.

It's also possible that some cases of AMS really are misdiagnosed cases of infection, because many symptoms are similar. Since your body is heavily stressed when climbing at altitude, it's probably wise to boost immune protection with antioxidants—particularly when traveling in foreign lands.

When mountaineering, the golden rule of hydration is to drink enough to pee "clear and copious." You should feel a need to pee almost hourly, and your urine should be a very pale yellow (barring mega doses of vitamins that you don't need). This means you need to drink at least 1 gallon (4 liters) on mellow days (cool temps, moderate exertion) and over 2 gallons (8 liters) on intense days (sweltering heat, mega work). Severe dehydration can shut down your summit bid faster than any snowstorm.

Emphasizing carbohydrates in the diet has numerous advantages when climbing at high altitudes. Although fat packs more calories per gram than carbohydrates, which makes it weight-efficient in your pack, it also requires more oxygen to burn. Furthermore, one study has shown that a diet of more than 70 percent carbohydrates decreased AMS after a fast ascent to 14,000 feet (4,300 meters) by 30 percent.

Here's a look at some of the supplements sometimes used in high-altitude mountaineering:

Multivitamins. Since diet is often out of your control once the trip starts, it's wise to continue taking your daily multivitamin/mineral supplement just to ensure your needs are covered. There is no justification for mega-doses (see the section "Supplements" in chapter 1).

Antioxidants. Due to the stress of exercise and altitude, antioxidants can help bolster your immune system for increased protection. One recent study of trekkers going to Everest base camp reported that supplementing the diet with 1,000 mg vitamin C, 400 IU vitamin E, and 600 mg alpha-lipoic acid (half with breakfast, the rest with dinner) gave a significant increase in blood oxygen saturation and a decrease in AMS. However, vitamin C combined with excess iron turns to a pro-oxidant, which can be dangerous—even fatal. Do not take high dosages of iron along with antioxidants.

Amino Acids. Both BCAAs and glutamine have been suggested as aids for acclimatization, and one study lends some credence to the theory. These amino acids are associated with improved recovery and immune protection, so supplementation might help, but more research is needed.

Garlic. Garlic has been used for millennia to help thin the blood. Four large cloves of raw garlic per day, or 2 grams of garlic powder, might improve blood flow in the lungs by reducing pulmonary vasoconstriction. It's been shown effective in rats, but no human studies have confirmed the results. Unfortunately, cooking deactivates the active ingredient (allicin), though other compounds are released that may also be beneficial.

Ginkgo Biloba. This is another folk remedy for AMS that has recently received scientific validation. This tree leaf has antioxidant properties, along with many other fanciful claims. Dosages of 160 to 240 mg per day of extract (more than many supplements contain) can significantly reduce the unpleasant symptoms of rushing upward. Numerous other herbs are marketed for preventing or treating AMS, yet none have proven themselves in good controlled studies.

Aspirin. For over a century, mountaineers have been taking aspirin to combat headaches at altitude. Other over-the-counter painkillers, such as ibuprofen and naproxen, work as well. However, aspirin also helps thin the blood, so it might help performance at very high altitude. Do not take aspirin with ginkgo biloba or high doses of garlic because they can increase the tendency to bleed.

Acetazolamide. When all else fails, you may need to resort to Diamox (acetazolamide), a prescription drug in many countries. This diuretic improves oxygenation at altitude by increasing your breathing rate. Diamox has proven very effective in speeding acclimatization and it greatly improves sleep (alleviates Cheyne-Stokes breathing). It will not, however, prevent AMS from worsening if the ascent continues—don't continue upward until symptoms subside!

Most people get substantial relief with two 125 mg doses (half a tablet) per day with minimal side effects. Start the course a day before a fast ascent is anticipated and discontinue after your second night at your high point. It's best to avoid taking aspirin and Diamox at the same time since complications may arise.

Diamox will cause frequent urination, therefore dehydration becomes an even bigger concern. It can also cause tingling in fingers, toes, and lips (paraesthesia), ruin the taste of carbonated beverages, and blur vision. Because this is a sulfa drug, people with allergies to those medications must refrain. If you've never tried Diamox before, do so before you get to a remote location to avoid any nasty surprise.

Dexamethasone. Some climbers also carry dexamethasone, a powerful steroid that reduces brain swelling. The oral form is used to treat AMS; however, it should only be used once severe symptoms have appeared, not prophylactically during the ascent. The treatment lasts three days, but AMS may rebound after it has been discontinued; some people report depression afterward too. Dexamethasone is also used to treat cerebral edema, given as an intermuscular injection.

Other Drugs. While it may sound like a joke, sildenafil (Viagra) may actually decrease the chance of getting high altitude pulmonary edema (HAPE) by suppressing the pulmonary artery pressure increase that normally occurs with hypoxia. However, it currently isn't available in low, long-acting dosages and much more research is needed. Another drug recently implicated in preventing HAPE is salmeterol (Serevent), a bronchodilator for asthmatics, but the jury is still out.

Nifedipine (Procardia) is often used in the treatment of HAPE because it dilates blood vessels by blocking calcium from entering them. For those susceptible to this condition, nifedipine may prevent recurrence. Whenever HAPE is suspected, descent is imperative; a Gamow bag can buy the victim some time. Be smart, ascend slowly; don't get sick in the first place.

Though it's use may stir an ethical debate over cheating, modafinil (Provigil) is a new drug that can keep you awake for several days without the nasty effects associated with amphetamines.

Supplementary Oxygen. The least

desirable supplement for mountaineering is oxygen. Due to physiological and logistical reasons, if you need supplemental oxygen for summits below 8,500 meters, you probably don't belong there. It is far better to acclimatize properly or attempt a peak within your capabilities. If you are concerned about possible brain damage (real but inconclusive whether it's significant), stick to lower peaks.

Even when a higher summit is the goal, you must seriously weigh the pros and cons of oxygen. When you rely on this gaseous crutch, you may be safer but you're also placing many other people at risk. The rich climbers using oxygen always need low-paid porters to make extra trips with the heavy cylinders through icefalls and avalanche terrain. Should the supply run out during the ascent or descent, you will turn to a useless blob and other climbers may be endangered by your mistake.

CHAPTER 4

Strength Conditioning

As the great philosopher Pogo eloquently stated, "We have met the enemy and he is us." In our case, climbers have been hampering themselves for decades with The Big Lie: climbing is the only training you need. This oft-repeated mantra sounds logical yet it ignores a realm of truth.

No matter the sport, if you practice it to the exclusion of everything else, muscle imbalances are created that can lead to decreased overall performance and even joint injury. In climbers, the muscles prone to underdevelopment include mid to lower trapezius, pectorals, deltoids, rotator cuff, triceps, and wrist extensors. A program of resistance training, often called weight lifting though there is a subtle distinction, is the most effective and efficient way of tuning the body.

Although climbing gyms have revolutionized the sport, most of us tend to work our strengths since that's more fun. Even with the use of campus and system boards, it can be difficult to target weaknesses because it's rarely possible to isolate muscles when climbing. It is also difficult to maximally train muscles because you fall off first.

STRENGTH BASICS

Lest there be any doubt: resistance training will *not* make you a better climber! It can make you stronger, safer, and more injury-free—hence increasing your performance—but technique can only be learned by climbing when the nervous system is trained and economy of movement is developed. Weight lifting is a supplement, not a substitute, for climbing. The proper balance depends upon you and your goals.

BENEFITS OF RESISTANCE TRAINING

For those who don't have unlimited time to work out, a primary advantage of resistance training is efficiency. With just 45 to 90 minutes of lifting weights, you can fully work every major muscle group in the body. Even if it were possible to get a total body workout while climbing, it would take many times longer to achieve the same results.

Although aerobic conditioning is invaluable for reducing excess body fat, it is only part of the solution since the calorie burning stops shortly after you do (couple of hours max). Building muscle is no less important if you want to lose weight and keep it off permanently. A pound of fat burns about 3 calories per day yet an equivalent amount of muscle burns 30 to 50 calories and it doesn't stop when you are sleeping. This increase in the resting metabolic rate adds up significantly in the long run.

Prevention of injuries is another major reason for systematic resistance training. Bone growth is stimulated by repeated mechanical loading beyond a minimal threshold. Without sufficient force, bone density and mass decrease: "use it or lose it" applies to bones as well as muscles. Both stress fractures (an overuse injury) and osteoporosis (a degenerative disease) may be prevented with training. And stronger bones will be less likely to break in a fall.

While aerobic endurance exercise increases the repair of connective tissue through increased collagen metabolism, high-intensity loading makes your tendons and ligaments thicker and stronger. Bone mass also increases where the tendons attach and injuries are less likely to occur here.

Should the unfortunate happen and an accident lay you up, resistance training (and physical therapy) is the shortest route back to the rock. Even when one limb is out of action, you can maintain the rest of your body and keep from going stir-crazy.

Yet another, more subtle, advantage of lifting weights is increased body awareness. When you isolate muscles, you learn their function (and names) and feel how they affect other parts of your body. The goal of resistance training is moving the muscles; for weight lifting, moving the mass is the emphasis and the body is secondary.

While resistance training will benefit people of all ages, seniors perhaps have the most to gain, or regain: vitality. Unless you are a dedicated masters athlete, you have probably lost significant muscle mass and bone density. Resistance training is unquestionably the best way to reverse the aging process. Besides, it's great fun to make the young'uns crack.

MYTHS ABOUT RESISTANCE TRAINING

The number one myth about weight lifting is that you will get "too big." Since climbing is a sport where the strength-to-mass ratio plays a significant role in performance, the fear is understandable albeit misguided.

This notion of overbulking is fostered by climbers who assiduously avoid the gym and have a poor understanding of physiology. They often point to the photos of the rather grotesque bodies in the muscle magazines as an example of what will happen if you heft a chunk of steel. Look further, beyond the pictures, and read the articles and advertisements. The extremes of training (15+ hours per week in the gym is common) and chemical supplementation (both legal and illegal) are scary: those people are desperate for anything that will make them more "ripped."

The truth is that over 80 percent of men and nearly all women are "hard-gainers." Without a volume of work far in excess of

what any climber would consider, we simply lack the genetic predisposition to look like the Incredible Hulk (or Hulkess). Although moderate intensity resistance training causes muscles to get bigger (hypertrophy), endurance training is catabolic (breaks down muscle). With a moderate amount of aerobic play and a normal diet, it is virtually impossible to gain excess muscle.

Another falsehood is that weight lifting creates "dumb" inflexible muscles; this can only result from dumb training. When done properly, resistance training actually increases flexibility. It is also easier to educate (recruit and coordinate) muscle cells that are developed than to raise them from infancy.

A related myth is that certain exercises can alter the shape of muscles, such as make them "short and bulky" or "long and lean." This was predetermined nine months before you were born and there is nothing you can do to change where tendons attach or the length of the muscle belly.

Many people claim that weight lifting is boring and, frankly, it is—if you approach it mindlessly. This boredom is most often the result of poor teaching that frequently occurs in school and commercial gyms; many coaches and trainers are not good educators. In reality, there is so much to think about while lifting that there rarely should be a dull moment—it is an intellectually stimulating, even fun, activity. When you are resistance training, your focus should be on your body, not the weight you are moving (or that cutie across the gym).

With all the exercises, intensities, and rest periods to choose from, there is no reason to fall into a rut.

The most blatant lie regarding resistance training is that abdominal exercises will give you a "six-pack" like those bulging abs on dehydrated fitness models (they cut way back on fluids for several days prior to a photo shoot). There is no such thing as spot reduction! Those damnable TV infomercials are scams: it is physiologically impossible to selectively remove fat from one area of the body (sans liposuction). Like it or not, men tend to put on fat in the upper body (apples) while women store it in the lower body (pears). Since this is the first place fat is laid down, it is also the last place that it comes off. While proper training does build the abdominal muscles, only after the excess fat is gone will they become visible.

Girls, what your mother and women's magazines may have told you is wrong: when it comes to training muscles, you are the same as boys. The structure and trainability of muscles is identical between the sexes. Both genders should use the same exercises and intensity. Since you have much lower levels of testosterone than men, lifting heavy will not turn you into a freak; gorgeous yes, overmuscular no. Feel free to argue with anyone who claims that women should only use light weights for "toning," "sculpting," or "shaping"; they need some sense knocked into them. These nonsensical programs and terms have been hampering women's athletic progress for over a decade. Women (and men) who want to climb hard need to *be* hard.

PHYSIOLOGY OF STRENGTH

When a muscle contracts (the agonist), its counterpart muscle (the antagonist) must actively relax to control and stabilize the movement; for example, the biceps are stabilized by the triceps. In addition to the prime moving muscles, other muscles like the brachioradialis are synergists that help refine the direction of motions. If the antagonists and synergists are underdeveloped, you will lose fine motor control as fatigue sets in.

Strength is simply the maximum force that your muscles can generate, no matter the velocity. If a movement can be performed more quickly, then greater power is generated: power = (force × distance) ÷ time. When training for power, you are increasing high-speed strength. The primary energy source for both maximal strength and power is the phosphocreatine (phosphate) system.

Endurance is the ability of muscles to either repeat an action many times or to sustain an action for a long time. Aerobic energy sources—the oxidation of carbohydrate, fat, and protein—provide most of the ATP (the cellular form of energy).

In between these two extremes of strength/power and endurance is a full continuum in which fast (anaerobic) glycolysis—the breakdown of blood glucose and muscle glycogen without oxygen—is a significant energy source. Since the end product of this process is lactic acid, which is in turn converted to a salt called lactate, it is also called the lactate system. Lactate can either be used as an energy source directly or converted back to glucose in the liver. Many people believe that lactic acid causes fatigue, but that is not accurate. During the conversion to lactate, a hydrogen ion is released that lowers muscle pH. This increased acidity impedes cellular function until buffers restore pH from a low of 6.4 to the normal 7.1.

While the high-intensity phosphate system will last 6 to 8 seconds, the moderate-intensity lactate system burns for about 2 to 3 minutes, and the low-intensity aerobic system is long-term (depends upon glycogen stores and fat utilization). However, it is never all-or-nothing—your body is always using all three energy systems, just in different proportions.

Attempts to describe this spectrum have led to a confusing array of terms that are sometimes used incorrectly (or imprecisely). Intensive power endurance, high-level power endurance, high-intensity endurance, and anaerobic endurance all mean that phosphate and lactate energy systems predominate. Extensive power endurance, low-level power endurance, and low-intensity endurance all imply that lactate and aerobic systems are the main energy sources. Local endurance, SACC (specific aerobic capacity and capillarity), and muscular endurance all refer to aerobic systems as the primary source. Finally, there are aerobic endurance and general endurance, which refer to the body's overall capacity of exercise, not certain muscle groups.

The practical aspect of this energy continuum comes when describing the intensity of training and even the character of a climb. The number of sets (a group of repetitions) of an exercise and the number of repetitions (reps) within a set determine the changes within the muscles. But again, there is no hard threshold where one aspect, such as strength, stops and another begins. The human body is far too complex for such simple distinctions.

Climbers have developed their own terminology not recognized by other sports, such as *contact strength* (ability to apply power to holds and sustain it) and *lock-off strength* (ability to pull into a high position for a long reach and hold); both are isometric (static) muscle actions. While we generally know what we mean, the definitions are rather vague since they really are describing strength and endurance simultaneously.

MUSCLE ADAPTATIONS

While it is universally accepted that resistance training increases muscle strength, the jury is still out on the mechanisms. Everyone agrees that the long, skinny muscle cells (fibers) become thicker in cross-section (hypertrophy). But a great way to start an argument with sport scientists is to ask whether heavy resistance training causes muscle fibers to split in two (hyperplasia); possible but unproven in humans.

We are all born with a predetermined percentage of Type I (red or slow-twitch) and Type II (white or fast-twitch) muscle fibers. The overall average is about 45 percent Type I and 55 percent Type II but this varies widely within the population.

Successful sprinters, for example, tend to have more Type II fibers, while marathoners have more Type I. However, the differences are not great enough to predict performance based on fiber composition alone. The distribution within your major muscles (the primary movers) is about equal, but postural and stability muscles tend to be higher in Type I; the soleus, a small calf muscle, has the most Type I fibers (88 percent) while the muscle that closes your eyelid has the least (13 percent).

You probably cannot change the ratio you were given, though debate continues. However, training can significantly increase the ability of fiber types to use oxygen; they can become more aerobic. There are two subcategories of Type I fibers and up to seven of Type II (these are usually lumped together as more oxidative As or less oxidative Bs) that can transform back and forth. Strength training turns those IIB fibers into oxygen-rich IIA—but the process can reverse when you lay off the weights.

ANATOMY 101

There is a lot of loose talk around gyms and in popular magazines about body parts that don't really exist. Likewise, gym talk frequently includes references to muscle groups that can be trained in sections when the evidence is to the contrary; EMG (electromyograph) studies show equal activation of fibers.

No such thing
- Inner and outer pecs
- Inner and outer delts
- Upper and lower biceps
- Upper and lower quads
- Upper and lower lats
- Upper and lower abs

For real
- Front, middle, and rear deltoids (anterior, medial, posterior)
- Upper and lower pectoralis major (clavicular and sternal)
- Upper, middle, and lower trapezius
- Inner and outer biceps (short and long heads)
- Inner and outer triceps (long and lateral heads)
- Inner and outer quadriceps (vastus medialis, vastus lateralis)
- Inner and outer abdominals (transversus and rectus abdominis)
- Abdominal segments (all sections contract but some more than others)
- Side abdominals (internal and external obliques)

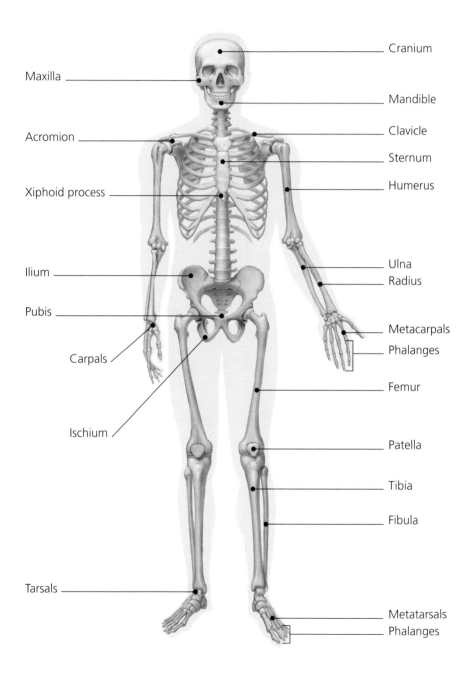

Cranium

Maxilla

Mandible

Clavicle

Acromion

Sternum

Humerus

Xiphoid process

Ilium

Ulna

Radius

Pubis

Metacarpals

Carpals

Phalanges

Femur

Ischium

Patella

Tibia

Fibula

Tarsals

Metatarsals

Phalanges

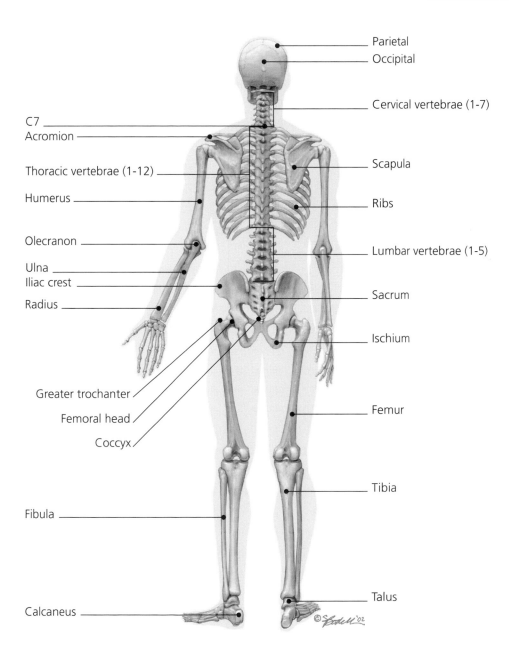

Parietal

Occipital

Cervical vertebrae (1-7)

C7

Acromion

Thoracic vertebrae (1-12)

Scapula

Humerus

Ribs

Olecranon

Ulna

Iliac crest

Lumbar vertebrae (1-5)

Radius

Sacrum

Ischium

Greater trochanter

Femoral head

Coccyx

Femur

Tibia

Fibula

Talus

Calcaneus

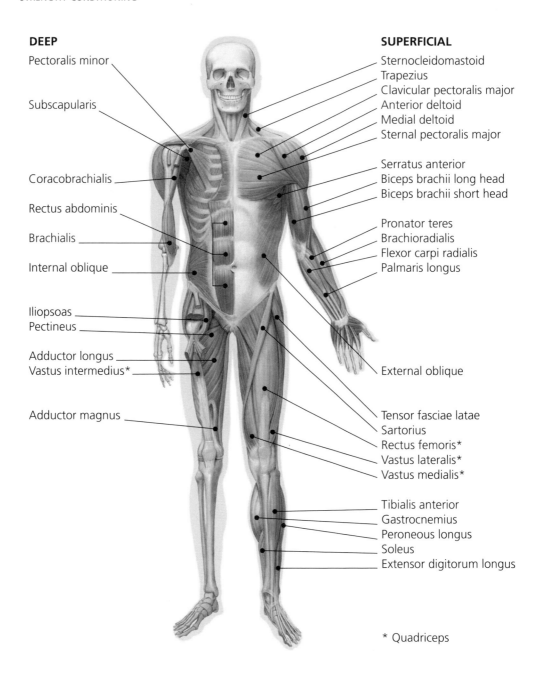

DEEP

Pectoralis minor

Subscapularis

Coracobrachialis

Rectus abdominis

Brachialis

Internal oblique

Iliopsoas
Pectineus

Adductor longus
Vastus intermedius*

Adductor magnus

SUPERFICIAL

Sternocleidomastoid
Trapezius
Clavicular pectoralis major
Anterior deltoid
Medial deltoid
Sternal pectoralis major

Serratus anterior
Biceps brachii long head
Biceps brachii short head

Pronator teres
Brachioradialis
Flexor carpi radialis
Palmaris longus

External oblique

Tensor fasciae latae
Sartorius
Rectus femoris*
Vastus lateralis*
Vastus medialis*

Tibialis anterior
Gastrocnemius
Peroneous longus
Soleus
Extensor digitorum longus

* Quadriceps

DEEP

SUPERFICIAL

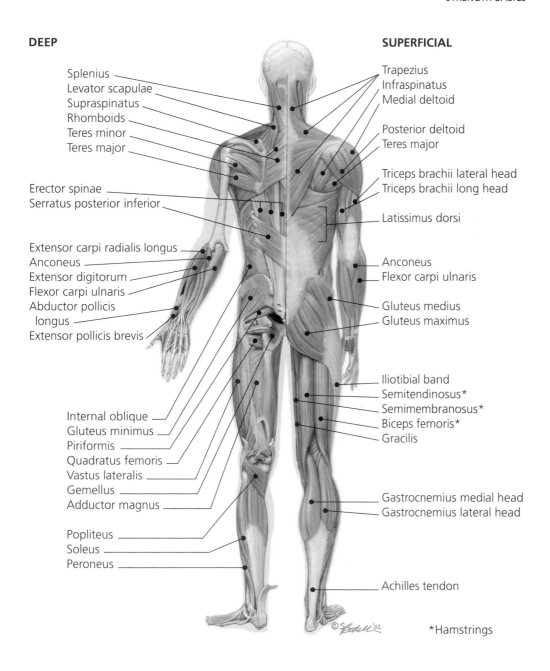

Splenius
Levator scapulae
Supraspinatus
Rhomboids
Teres minor
Teres major

Erector spinae
Serratus posterior inferior

Extensor carpi radialis longus
Anconeus
Extensor digitorum
Flexor carpi ulnaris
Abductor pollicis
  longus
Extensor pollicis brevis

Internal oblique
Gluteus minimus
Piriformis
Quadratus femoris
Vastus lateralis
Gemellus
Adductor magnus

Popliteus
Soleus
Peroneus

Trapezius
Infraspinatus
Medial deltoid

Posterior deltoid
Teres major

Triceps brachii lateral head
Triceps brachii long head

Latissimus dorsi

Anconeus
Flexor carpi ulnaris

Gluteus medius
Gluteus maximus

Iliotibial band
Semitendinosus*
Semimembranosus*
Biceps femoris*
Gracilis

Gastrocnemius medial head
Gastrocnemius lateral head

Achilles tendon

*Hamstrings

125

When exercising at low intensity, your body will use mostly Type I fibers. But as the intensity or speed increases, greater numbers of Type II fibers are called into action, termed recruitment. One of the major goals of strength training is to stimulate more of these Type II fibers so that they will get bigger. This can only be done with high intensity levels.

In addition to muscle fibers, we are also developing the nervous system that stimulates the muscles. During the first six to ten weeks of a program, neural training has a more significant effect on strength gains than muscle growth. Much of long-term training, and better climbing, is about enhancing neural factors.

Greater force can be applied at the origin or insertion of some muscles, which changes the recruitment pattern of the motor units (the nerve cell and the fibers it activates). Our muscles are also very particular about the movement pattern required to recruit different fibers. This is where specificity comes in and why it's important to train a muscle from different angles.

PRINCIPLES OF RESISTANCE TRAINING

All climbers need a combination of strength, power, and endurance; the ideal balance depends upon your goals. If your emphasis is on endurance climbing (multipitch and alpine routes), strength training will not harm your performance; indeed, it can help. However, if your climbing is strength-oriented (high-level bouldering or sport climbs), too much endurance training can make you weaker.

To increase strength or endurance, your muscles must be stressed to ever-increasing levels. This concept isn't exactly new: around 540 B.C., Milo of Croton trained for wrestling by carrying a newborn ox every day until it grew to full size (then he ate it in one day). Milo won five consecutive Olympics.

Termed progressive overload, this means that you should always strive for more weight, duration, or frequency; never be content with the status quo. More subtly, progress can also come from performing an exercise with better technique, control, or range of motion. Aim for perfection.

Resistance exercises consist of a concentric phase, in which the active muscles shorten, and an eccentric phase, where they lengthen. For climbing, both phases are important and should be trained equally; that is, it should take as long to lower the weight as to lift it.

Some training programs emphasize the eccentric phase (negative failure), such as doing a pull-up with two arms and lowering with one. The eccentric contraction generates higher force, so there is potential for greater strength gains; debate rages on this subject. However, it also results in greater delayed-onset muscular soreness (DOMS); those aches that set in two or three days later. Often used for rehabilitation, eccentric exercises may help you break out of a plateau or overcome a weakness. But climbers need to be well-rounded in their strengths and your training should reflect that concept.

In regard to climbing, the least effective

weight training is for muscular endurance because of the time involved. It is better to do this form of low-intensity workout in a climbing gym or on real rock where you will also improve technique and efficiency. If climbing is not an option, keep the endurance workouts to a couple of primary multijoint exercises, such as squats and lat pulls.

STARTING OUT

Those who are new to resistance training, even veteran climbers, are likely to make significant gains in the first six months. The results will be noticeable in the mirror and you'll feel better. If you've been thoughtful, you should be climbing better too. Enjoy it: never again will it be that easy to improve so much, so quickly.

Don't force the gains, either; it takes your tendons about twice as long to match the strength improvements of muscles. There is a fine line between training to failure—when you can just barely finish a movement with full control—and training till it hurts. While that last rep should strain the entire muscle, there should never be sharp pain; especially in a joint. Think: No pain, all gain.

Do not fear heavy weights: with good form, they are perfectly safe for healthy individuals. As you will see, lifting heavy potentially has the most to offer climbers. However, those who are new to lifting will need to work up to this level of stress, otherwise disaster (injury) is sure to follow. Due to spinal or knee problems, some of you will have to settle for lighter

KIDS AND TRAINING

Climbing is a great activity for kids! But they are susceptible to the same overuse injuries and muscle imbalances as adults. Starting at about age eight to ten, children can safely start resistance training with light weights. They can benefit from increased strength, enhanced bone development, fewer injuries, and better self-image. Prior to that age, let the monkeys scamper.

However, it is important that progress be slow and gradual—and form perfect—because the bones of children do not fully ossify until after puberty. Damage to growth cartilage in the joints or at the growth plate on bones, as well as the lumbar region of the spine, can have lasting consequences. Keep them at lower resistance and higher reps (no less than eight) and allow adequate time for rest.

Because kids grow so fast, a layoff from resistance training and climbing over summer break will basically nullify any gains. Boys aged twelve to fourteen and girls aged ten to thirteen (before the growth spurt) run a greater risk of bone fractures and need to be reined in somewhat. After about sixteen, they're good to go.

loads, but you can still make progress.

Every time you pick up a weight or sit at a machine, keep in mind that the ultimate purpose is to improve your climbing performance. With this focus, you won't waste time on things that have minimal benefit, such as the hip abductor and adductor machines that bulk thighs. Whenever possible, simulate movements made while climbing. For example, vary hand positions and lean back while doing lat pulls to mimic climbing an overhang. This will speed the recruitment of those muscles once you get on the rock, ice, or snow.

GYM CONSIDERATIONS

Among the top factors in a successful resistance training program are the accessibility and quality of your gym. The sad reality is that most people who start a program will end up dropping out after a few months, largely due to a lack of motivation. If your gym is inconvenient or depressing to visit, it becomes all that much harder to keep yourself psyched.

HOME GYM

Depending on where you live, a home gym can be an excellent option: you can't beat the convenience. If you have a spare room available, a decent gym can be created for only a couple hundred dollars. Much of the equipment at sporting-good stores is poor quality that will be uncomfortable to use and wear out quickly; try a fitness specialty store if you are serious.

The bare minimum consists of dumbbells—PowerBlocks are very fast to adjust and require little space—a multi-angle bench, a stability ball (large inflatable ball), a pull-up bar, and a fingerboard. As space and finances allow, add a dip station, lat pull station, a power rack, and an Olympic bar with weights.

Most of the exergadgets sold on TV and in department stores are junk. Some of the all-in-one systems (such as Bowflex and Total Gym, which are heavily advertised in the United States) are passable. However, since the basic models are inadequate for most climbers, these are fairly expensive systems—upward of $1,500. Despite the hype, none of them offers the number of exercises or benefits possible with free weights.

While a home gym is convenient, it can be difficult to block out a period of time without distractions (phone calls, kids, etc). For whatever reasons, some people have a harder time getting motivated to work out at home than going to a gym.

HOME WALL

A home climbing wall can provide an excellent, highly specific workout for the rock climber. Even if you join a rock gym, a home wall allows you to train when you don't feel like a drive across town to vie with the hordes for a pump. If you have lots of room and money, then go for it and build your own Fontainebleau!

However, a wall need not be elaborate to be effective. An 8-by-8-foot wall made from two sheets of half-inch marine plywood can provide sufficient variety that you won't become instantly bored. If possible, design it so the angle may be adjusted between 15 degrees and 45 degrees to work your muscles differently and allow for improvement. For a wall this size, plan on at least 250 climbing holds of all sizes and shapes, though you can get by with half that amount at first. You might start with a set of system holds or training strips that are intended for methodical workouts.

The key to success with a small home wall is a cheery atmosphere; otherwise it will have the appeal of a dungeon. Make sure the room is properly lit so you can see the footholds and the overhead light isn't shining in your eyes. Ensure a safe landing zone, adequate ventilation and, of course, good tunes. As your training progresses, you might consider a scuba diver's belt with the soft lead shot weights to increase resistance (distributes the load evenly around your waist).

COMMERCIAL GYM

In most cases, commercial gyms and fitness clubs offer far greater variety of equipment than what you might assemble at home. The atmosphere of like-minded people helps you stay psyched to work out. There are trainers available who can correct your form and show you new techniques. Many gyms at colleges, city recreation centers, and nonprofits (such as YMCA) have good facilities at reasonable prices.

Before signing a contract, some of which can be very difficult to break, it pays to shop around. The first consideration is distance.

Ideally your gym should be no more than 15 minutes from home or work. While taking a tour, try to get a sense of the friendliness of the staff and attention to maintenance. Beware the hard sell—some of these people, particularly at chains, are slimier than your stereotype used-car dealer.

When inspecting the facilities, be sure there are lots of free weights and benches, with at least two power cages (a steel-framed box with safety bars for lifting free weights). It should have plenty of floor space and mirrored walls for watching your form (not posing). Look for a good assortment of modern weight machines, but these are less important than the free weights. Gyms rarely have a fingerboard, but you may be able to convince the management that this inexpensive item is worthwhile.

Since aerobic areas tend to get clogged at peak times, be sure there are plenty of treadmills, elliptical trainers, bikes, and rowers. A spinning studio, with a full schedule of classes, is a real plus. Most gyms also offer yoga and stretching classes as part of the membership. The less froufrou stuff (juice bars, step classes, tae bo, etc.) the better, since they indicate a trendy social club instead of a serious place to work out.

Many rock gyms have an area with free weights that receives little traffic. Unfortunately this section is usually thrown in as an afterthought and is not conducive to a good workout, so it becomes a self-fulfilling prophecy. To be a viable alternative to a regular gym, the workout area requires a mirrored wall, rubber floor mats, good lighting (75 to 100 foot-candles), temperature regulation (72°F to 78°F), and ventilation (12 to 15 air exchanges per hour). There should be a number of well-maintained, good-quality aerobic machines, a full assortment of dumbbells and Olympic weight bars, several multi-angle benches, and at least one power cage.

The Gym Scene

If you've never been to a gym, or not since high school, it can be intimidating at first. There will likely be guys in there who could squash you like a bug and gals who might be supermodels. Relax. They don't bite, and half don't know what they're doing (but act like they do).

Your membership may include a free session with a personal trainer—be sure to use it. Have them show you how to operate all of the machines and the proper form with each. This is important because there will be times when a machine you want is occupied and it will be more expedient to simply use a different exercise for the same muscle group. Plus, variety is the spice of fitness.

Most gyms are packed on weekdays from 7:00 to 9:00 A.M. and even worse from 5:00 to 7:00 P.M. (except Friday). If you can arrange your schedule to avoid those peak times, you'll be able to finish your sessions faster. Try to establish a weekly routine and you'll soon recognize familiar faces.

Don't hesitate to ask one of the regulars how to use a machine, to check your form, or for a spot. If they aren't in the middle of a set, the vast majority will be happy to help (and the rest are just jerks). However, some posers who work out religiously have atrocious form, often accompanied by loud grunting and clanking of weights, and should be avoided. Be leery of anyone who lifts tiny weights a thousand times.

Some gyms enforce a time limit on aerobic machines during peak times. Even without a limit, it's a good idea to try a different motion after a while if you need a long workout. If the gym is crowded, it's okay to "work in" by asking to do a set while someone is resting. But don't disturb someone if a similar exercise is available elsewhere (usually the case). It's rude to hog a machine or bench by jabbering away unless you truly are resting between sets. Never use a power cage for anything but squats and other heavy lifts; performing bicep curls in a cage is proof positive of geekdom.

Although some people use the gym as a meat market and social club, especially at peak hours, most are there to get a workout without wasting time. Don't be perturbed if someone puts on a game face (or headphones) and is not interested in idle conversation; they may be more willing to talk after they're done. Holding a conversation during a heavy set isn't possible—it takes too much focus—so don't bother someone while they are lifting.

Not that it really matters, but the best way to earn respect from gym regulars is to keep showing up: attendance counts much more than appearance or how much you can lift. There is always an influx of soon-to-be-dropouts who clog the gym after New Year's and the start of school.

The worst breach of gym etiquette is

failure to rerack weights where they belong (10-pound plate on the 10-pound pin, etc.). Pick up after yourself! Avoid blocking someone else's view of the mirror; it's a tool. Many people sweat profusely during a hard workout and it's polite to wipe down the machine or bench when finished (rags and spray bottles are scattered around most gyms).

Wear clean workout clothes and deodorant (but not perfume); if you notice the gym clearing out around you, there's a reason. For liability reasons, many gyms require shoes (old running shoes are fine) and will not allow sandals. Leave your cell phone in the locker; don't let the outside world intrude upon your training or people nearby. To save time making trips to the water fountain, carry a water bottle as you move through the gym; drink a liter or more during your workout.

Do not wear a weight belt, because it will prevent strength gains in your abdomen and back—key muscles for climbing. It is better to work your way up to loads that you can safely handle. Similarly, gloves will prevent calluses and improve your grip but they reduce the training effect, so you are better off barehanded.

TRAINERS

From time to time, it can be an excellent idea to hire a personal trainer who will correct your form and push you harder, safely. Unfortunately, quite a few trainers are fountains of bad advice, giving information that is outdated or simply wrong. There are currently no state or federal requirements for calling oneself a personal trainer, so it's caveat emptor.

The lack of standards has resulted in an industry with more than 250 personal trainer organizations, some of which sell certifications with virtually no requirements. In the United States and Canada, among the most respected certifying agencies are the ACSM (American College of Sports Medicine) and NSCA (National Strength and Conditioning Association). With certification comes membership in a professional organization, continuing education, and liability protection.

No matter their certification, few trainers at fitness gyms understand the demands of climbing so you may need to educate them; they can still be of great help. While you are performing an exercise, the trainer may gently touch the active muscles to help you notice the contractions and improve technique. This "cueing" provides biofeedback and improves your self-awareness.

Many rock gyms have climbing coaches available, but there is no national standard or formalized training at all for this title (yet). Often these folks only know about sport climbing and have a limited understanding of physiology and nutrition. Which is not to say that all climbing coaches are bad, just that you have to be extra careful before hiring one.

With any trainer, your best bet is to watch them in action with other clients before committing your wallet and body. Make sure their style and knowledge match your needs. At the very least, get several references and talk to them. The hallmark of a good trainer is that they attempt to educate you about yourself by pointing out areas for improvement and correcting technique.

MACHINES VS. FREE WEIGHTS

Most gyms are very proud of their weight machines, largely because they cost huge amounts of money, and will often start beginners off using them. This isn't necessarily bad, because the newer machines do have their advantages, but there is still a lot going for free weights, no matter your training level.

Those who are new to resistance training are usually less intimidated by machines, in part because all those people with bulging muscles are over in the free-weight section of the gym. Machines also appear to be safer, since a weight won't come crashing down on you, but that is an illusion because they permit bad form at higher loads.

If you are of average height (5-foot-4 to 6-foot-2) with average proportions of arm, thigh, and torso length, you can get a good workout on machines fairly quickly. Not having to rack and derack your weights can save a significant amount of time. The resistance on most machines is adjusted by selecting a load from a weight stack or manually loading plates. Some new machines use pneumatic pressure or electric motors, which allows a computer to vary the resistance more accurately.

In general, machines fall into two categories: variable and constant resistance. Through the use of cams or air pressure, variable-resistance machines try to match the mechanics of the body by increasing resistance at strong points and decreasing resistance at weaker areas of the movement (isokinetic). While this sounds good in theory, the reality is that many people do not move with the velocity and movement pattern required by the machine.

The other style of machines use a round pivot point or pulley so they act more like free weights; the load being moved does not change (isotonic). With constant resistance, however, only the weakest portion of your range of motion is fully taxed because the angle of your limb changes.

The major drawback to either type of early-generation machines is that they lock you into a linear movement pattern. With free weights, you must draw upon many stabilizer muscles to control the weight. This provides a more effective workout (greater muscle recruitment) that promotes joint stability and is a better simulation of real life. Some of the exercises will also improve your balance. Another big advantage of free weights is they truly are one-size-fits-all. Although most barbells and dumbbells have a similar grip diameter ($1^1/_4$ inches), a recent study demonstrated significantly greater strength gains with a 2-inch grip.

The recent trend in resistance machines is to emulate free weights by allowing multi-axial and unilateral (left and right side don't assist each other) movement. While a step in the right directions, most climbers will be better served by free weights if time permits.

One device to avoid is the Smith Machine, which holds a barbell on a vertical track. A favorite of lazy personal trainers, the Smith offers the worst of both worlds—neither variable resistance nor activation of stabilizer muscles. The linear motion has value for rehabilitation of injuries and advanced bodybuilders, since very specific areas can be targeted. But multisport athletes are better off with free weights, even if lighter loads must be used.

WEIGHTY CONCEPTS

Whenever you are about to embark on a resistance workout, start with a 5- to 10-minute warm-up. Use any form of aerobic exercise you wish and go at a moderate pace until you just break a light sweat. The point is to increase circulation, warm the muscles, and lubricate the joints so that you can train harder and safer. If you choose a lower-body warm-up, such as running or cycling, then precede an upper-body workout with a light endurance set.

Some health professionals, physical therapists in particular, advocate "functional exercises" that combine balance and twisting motions. These are claimed to be superior since they more accurately simulate real-life movement patterns. While excellent for rehabilitation, these exercises require less resistance and do not optimally challenge the muscles because the direction of force changes relative to the orientation of fibers. For maximal climbing performance, keep your strength exercises pure, and use high resistance.

The golden mantra for every repetition of every exercise is: form, control, precision. It really helps to repeat this to yourself during a set. If possible, use a mirror to watch yourself while performing the movement to ensure that you are doing it exactly correct. Each repetition should work the full, biomechanically correct range of muscle movement. Use less resistance instead of partial reps.

For maximum muscle stimulus, a set should take about 30 to 90 seconds. This may be slower than what you'll see others doing at the gym, but it's a speed where the best gains are made for both slow- and fast-twitch fibers. Thus a full rep might include: 2 seconds pulling the weight toward you, 1-second pause, 2 seconds controlling the weight back, and a 1-second pause before starting again. A faster tempo, however, is more sport specific; training for power requires explosive bursts.

Never cheat a repetition by swinging the weight to gain momentum, springing at the bottom of a movement, or bouncing a barbell off your chest. This places greater peak forces upon your joints while reducing the training benefit for the muscles. When you can no longer maintain proper form, the set is over.

To prevent injury, always maintain a natural (lordotic) arch in the spine for upper and lower body exercises. You should not flatten your back against a bench or pad (tilts the pelvis), nor should you round your back (strains the lumbar region). Tighten your abdomen before lifting heavy to "block" your torso.

The neutral position is strongest when

you pull your shoulder blades together and slightly raise your chest, like a soldier standing at attention. Performing all heavy exercises in this retracted shoulder blade position will strengthen your core and improve posture. With lighter loads (over 15 reps), you can "unlock" the shoulder blades for more functional movement patterns.

When performing an exercise, your breathing is part of the rhythm. Inhale during the first half, exhale gradually during the second half, or vice versa; whatever comes naturally. The transition from the eccentric to the concentric part of the motion is often a sticking point, and it may help to exhale forcefully (for example, blow out as you are pushing up from the bottom position of a squat or bench press). Most of all, do not hold your breath during either phase as this spikes your blood pressure, which in turn makes your heart work harder (pushing the blood around becomes more difficult).

WEAK LINKS

Blindly jumping into a resistance program is a good way to ensure mediocre results. Climbers often state that they must "get stronger" to improve their performance. Yet you need to be specific in your goals or you will merely train your strengths. Your time will be much more productive by working on weaknesses.

In some cases, your body type may be indicative of a natural weakness. While there are plenty of exceptions, climbers who are long and lean tend to have relatively good finger strength and poor upper body strength. Conversely, those who are muscular and stocky will often have a powerful back and arms yet relatively weak fingers.

Relative to total body weight, women frequently have two-thirds the upper body strength and power of men (the disparity is less in the lower body). Part of this is because females have a higher body fat percentage and greater fat-free mass below the waist. Society, however, is also at fault for discouraging girls and women from proper training.

Since it can be difficult to honestly evaluate oneself, seeking comments from climbing partners is useful—assuming you can elicit more than, "Dude, you suck!" For those who are serious about maximizing their performance, good feedback is among the most valuable paybacks from hiring a coach or personal trainer.

If outside help isn't forthcoming, you may want to develop some self-tests for the aspects of strength that are important to your climbing; these could be either key exercises or climbs of a particular type. Many people find it useful to carry a small notebook and jot down details of their workouts. This information can be useful to monitor your progress, or lack thereof, and it can aid you, or a personal trainer, in developing a better program for you.

STRUCTURING THE WORKOUT

The emphasis of your training program should be on primary exercises that use multiple joints, instead of a single joint, in one plane of motion (no twisting or rotation). For example, a squat flexes the ankle, knee, and hip joints while a leg extension just bends the knee. "Compound" exercises tend to be more sport specific and they save time as well.

Use the "simple" single-joint exercises—such as the biceps curl and leg extension—for isolating and improving weak links. The spine and shoulder are considered single joints when training, though this is not literally the case.

In general, it is best to first exercise the big muscle groups most important to your climbing, then work your way to progressively smaller muscles. Thus you might start with the back, then work the arms and finish with the core (torso) and fingers. This way you are hitting the major muscles, and performing the exercises that require the most coordination, while you are fresh. Training smaller muscles at the end of a session also serves as a cool-down period.

After you are well-trained, you can try reversing the order to pre-exhaust the small stabilizing muscles before working the big muscles. However, it's more important to finish the session with easy aerobic activity to flush metabolites (such as lactate) from the muscles. There is also greater risk of injury since controlling the weight is more difficult.

A common routine involves doing all the sets of a pull exercise for one body part, followed by all the sets of a push exercise for the same body part. For example, three lat pull sets followed by two bench press sets. This way you are ensconced at one machine or station until you are done and, if you are doing another exercise on that muscle group, it gets a good rest before the next session. If this is too demanding when you are starting out, you can alternate upper- and lower-body exercises (say, lat pulls followed by leg presses) to increase the rests further.

When time is an issue, and the gym isn't crowded, you can perform supersets and get out of there in a hurry. This involves doing a set on the agonists and then, without taking a rest, doing a set on the antagonists of the same body part—for example, going straight from a set of lat pulls to a set of dips, or leg extensions to hamstring curls. Repeat this until the desired number of pushes and pulls are completed. Supersetting a routine can increase your endurance and will get your heart pumping since you don't stop the entire time.

Once you are ready to really tax a muscle group, you can start using compound sets. For these, you do two similar exercises in a row, alternating between sets with only a short rest. Try lat pulls followed by seated rows, going back and forth until the desired number of sets is complete, then moving on to the next body part. It hurts so good, but plan on a day off afterward.

The logical extension of this is a split routine, where you do upper-body exercises one day and lower-body the next, then repeat the cycle. Normally, splits are unwarranted for climbers but they may be used to make rapid progress for a major goal, such as an upcoming expedition. There are other variations of split routines, but they usually require more training time than most of us should consider.

FREQUENCY

How often you resistance train depends upon several factors, not the least of which is how much climbing you are doing. During the prime climbing season, if you have achieved a good level of fitness, you may want to suspend your gym membership for a couple of months. It's better, however, if you continue to get in one or two days a week of lifting to maintain the underutilized muscles that climbing doesn't hit.

For those who are starting a resistance program to build muscle, try for three days per week with a rest day in between (Monday, Wednesday, Friday works well for many). Two days is the bare minimum required by your body to make strength gains. You can, and should, climb on the days that you aren't lifting, but work on endurance and avoid very pumpy routes—this is "active rest" and you don't want to overdo it. Make one day per week a complete recovery day: no liftin', no climbin', no runnin', no nothin'.

After you have built a solid strength base, you can increase the frequency to four days per week if you are working toward a demanding goal. Before you do, read, mark, and inwardly digest chapter 5 on recovery. Climbers should only go to four days of lifting when their bodies are prepared for this level of stress and they

have a clearly defined reason for pushing so hard. Use a split routine to ensure adequate rest. Remember that you are also climbing and aerobic conditioning during this time: if you aren't careful, you may be sidelined by injury.

There is very rarely, if ever, a reason for climbers to resistance train five days per week. Six is right out. And seven will turn you into a bodybuilding gym freak. That much lifting places you at a high risk of overtraining and means that you aren't climbing enough—your performance *will* decrease.

INTENSITY

Selecting the proper intensity—the load lifted and number of repetitions—is at the very heart of resistance training. At first, it may be hard to decide how much you can handle, but it won't take long to get a good feel for what is appropriate. Never attempt lifts with more load than you can control; you should be able to stop at any point during the motion.

There are two methods for specifying the intensity of a set: the right way and the wrong way. The proper method is to state the maximum repetitions (RM) in which muscular failure occurs. When a set is 10 RM, there is little room for doubt: if you can only do 8 reps, the weight is too much, and if you can do 12, you need to add more. With a little practice, it becomes easy to dial in your load with a high degree of accuracy.

Unfortunately, the wrong way—basing the load on a percentage of your one repetition maximum—is still very common.

Based on meathead mentality, this method assumes that if you can lift 150 pounds one time, then you should be able to lift 90 percent of that (135 pounds) four times, and 80 percent of that (120 pounds) eight times. The problem is that all the charts assume a linear relationship between the load and reps, which is never the case. This also does not take into account your level of conditioning unless you actually test your 1 RM weekly—a rather dangerous and nonproductive procedure. Sometimes they test the 10 RM and then estimate the 1 RM from that, but this bassackwards approach still leaves a lot of room for error.

If you are new to resistance training, start out with 12 to 18 reps per set for the first couple of weeks to get used to the equipment and motions. Then work your way into the 8- to 12-rep range for a couple of months to build a solid foundation. If weight loss is one of your goals, this is where you will build the most muscle that eventually will burn off the fat. Once you are solid, then it's time to maximize your strength and power.

Because you must keep upping the ante if you want a bigger reward, the resistance must also increase over time. When you first start out at a particular load, you may be able to do 10 reps on the first set, 9 on the second set, and only 7 on the third set. After a couple of weeks, you should be able to max out on all three sets at 10 reps. When you can do this two training days in a row, it's time to add more weight.

The amount you increase the load will depend on your conditioning and the body part (err on the side of less with shoulder exercises). For the upper body, a beginner should add 2.5 pounds, an intermediate might add 5 pounds, and an advanced lifter could go up by 10 pounds For lower body exercises, a beginner can try adding 5 pounds, an intermediate will put on 10 pounds, and the burly can go for 15 pounds or more. Try the new load for a set and see how many reps you can bust out, then adjust accordingly. Don't overdo it or try to impress anyone!

VOLUME

Just as intensity affects the results of your training, so does the volume, which is the number of sets that a particular exercise is performed. When starting out, an untrained person can make significant gains by performing only a single set (but doing it really well). However, after a few months, this volume is often inadequate for continued improvement.

For most routines and intensity levels, a total of three sets per exercise provides superior stimulus for muscle development. This is a matter of rapidly diminishing returns: you get roughly 60 percent of the benefit from the first set, 20 percent more from the second, an extra 10 percent from the third, and even less in subsequent sets. So if time is short, it's generally better to do one set of all the exercises in a routine than to leave some out in favor of more sets.

When training in the hypertrophy range where most growth occurs (8 to 12 reps), most climbers should stick with two or three sets; rarely four if a particular muscle

MUSCLE MAGIC

Adjusting the intensity and rests for any exercise will yield different results. Higher intensity brings more muscle cells into play (greater recruitment) and emphasizes anaerobic energy sources. The "maximum load" is the amount of resistance required so that you cannot complete one more repetition with proper form.

Power

- 2–5 reps at moderate/high loads and maximum speed.
- 2- to 5-minute rest between each set.
- Fibers recruited: nearly all Type I, all IIA, all IIB.
- Maximum recruitment and neural training.
- No effect on muscle growth or endurance.
- Develops explosive power for short, intense problems, but greater risk of injury.

Strength

- 3–6 reps at maximum loads.
- 2- to 5-minute rest between each set.
- Fibers recruited: All Type I, all IIA, all IIB.
- Maximum recruitment and neural training.
- No effect on muscle growth or endurance.
- Develops raw strength for hard climbs without adding bulk.

Strength and High-Intensity Power Endurance

- 6–8 reps at maximum loads.
- 1- to 2-minute rest between each set.
- Fibers recruited: Nearly all Type I, nearly all IIA, many IIB.
- Moderate recruitment.
- Moderate muscle growth and power gains.
- Good gains, but training above or below this range may have more pronounced effects.

High-Intensity Power Endurance

- 8–12 reps at maximum loads.
- 45- to 90-second rest between each set.
- Fibers recruited: Most Type I, most IIA, some IIB.
- Maximum muscle growth.
- Significant strength, power, and low-intensity endurance gains.
- Good all-around training range when combined with aerobic conditioning.

High- and Low-Intensity Power Endurance

- 12–18 reps at maximum loads.
- 30- to 60-second rest between each set.
- Fibers recruited: Many Type I, some IIA, minimal IIB.
- Modest muscle growth gains.
- Minimal effect on strength and power.
- Best range to start a resistance program.

Low-Intensity Power Endurance

- 15–25 reps at maximum loads.
- 15- to 30-second rest between each set.
- Fibers recruited: Many Type I, some IIA, minimal IIB.
- No effect on strength, power, or muscle growth.
- Good range for warming up prior to hard sets.
- Useful but climbing is superior to this for training endurance of major muscles.

Muscular Endurance

- 20–30 reps at maximum loads.
- 15-second rest between each set.
- Fibers recruited: Less than half of Type I and very minor II.
- Improves capillarity and increases enzyme activity.
- Useful training for deep, minor muscles such as rotator cuff.
- Ineffective use of time for major muscles—go climb.

group is lagging. This won't bulk you up overnight but will prepare you for bigger strength gains.

Working on power and strength is a different matter. After a thorough warm-up of several lower-intensity sets (not counted), many athletes will go for five to six sets. Beware that these may not seem too taxing at the time, because it's just a few reps per set, but you'd better plan on taking the next day (or two) off.

Try to do your muscular endurance training on the rock (real or fake). If for some reason you can't climb, endurance routines are typically just two to three sets.

REST PERIODS

The period between sets is more important than many people realize since it determines lactate concentrations and how much phosphate energy recovery occurs. Don't just gab between sets; time the rest periods (an analog watch with a second hand is helpful) so they are neither too long nor too short.

For endurance sets, the rest break is only 15 to 30 seconds long to get the most gains. The greatest accumulation of lactate occurs in hypertrophy sets with short rest periods (30 to 90 seconds). By going with shorter breaks, you will eventually build your lactate tolerance and buffering ability.

Even though power and strength workouts are high intensity, the duration is fairly short so lactate remains at low levels. These sets normally call for 2- to 5-minute rests to allow sufficient recovery of the phosphate system for maximal efforts.

PERIODIZATION

Too much of the same thing leads to stagnation: you call this boring, your body calls it a plateau. The way to stay out of a rut and continue making gains is through cycles, or periods, where your training program varies in intensity, volume, and frequency over the course of weeks, months, or the year.

Many climbers do not need to schedule their training because the seasons do it for us: the shorter days and nastier weather of late fall and winter encourage strength training in the gyms; by spring, we are going stir-crazy and start getting out for aerobic play and early climbing, but variable weather still keeps us at the gyms a fair amount; when we finally get the long days and good weather of summer and early fall, we're out climbing and aerobic playing as much as possible, so the gyms are a matter of willpower.

However, those with a one-track mind—for example, preparing for a major climb or only interested in sport climbing and bouldering—should consider using periodization to maximize performance during a key period. This typically means subdividing three or four months into phases in which only one aspect of strength is trained. This level of structure does not suit everyone but can be effective for those who stick with the program. Although the peaks in performance can be higher, the valleys will also be deeper; without sufficient recovery, overtraining will result.

For intermediate to advanced athletes, a good way to break up the monotony of

EXERCISES TO AVOID

Many exercises performed in gyms are holdovers from the old days before biomechanical science: some myths die hard. Although these exercises don't guarantee injury, they offer greater risk with little additional muscle gain. We punish our joints enough while climbing; don't exacerbate problems while training.

- **Behind-the-neck exercises:** Both lat pulls and overhead presses in this position stress the shoulder joint in its weakest position. To make matters worse, and to the delight of chiropractors, the cervical spine is often strained as people crane their necks. Always keep your hands where you can see them.
- **Upright rows:** When your hands are close together, this barbell exercise creates a bone-on-bone arm position that can result in shoulder impingement problems. A wide grip is better, but still can overly stress the rotators.
- **Excessive shoulder range:** The Pec Deck is a common chest machine, where you squeeze two forearm pads together in front of you, that can place a lot of stress on the shoulder joints. Never let your arms move behind your centerline or allow your shoulder to rotate. Likewise, with a bench press, don't drop your elbows below chest level.
- **Excessive knee range:** Controversy rages over the safety of deep squats. Some cite greatly increased force on the patellar cruciate ligament and others point to the billions of people who squat deep every day without knee problems. When weight lifting, it's prudent to bend the knee no more than at a right angle unless you have strong reasons for going lower.
- **Excessive spine range:** Chronic back injuries are grim. Hyperextending (arching backward) or hyperflexing (curling forward) the spine places a great deal of force upon the ligaments, muscles, and discs between the vertebrae. Only for body core exercises do you flex your spine, and those are within a controlled range. Even when climbing, you should protect your spine from severe stress.
- **Bodyweight exercises:** Pull-ups, push-ups, and dips are free, but can be difficult to vary the resistance; they're often too heavy or too light. The direction of force is usually not at the optimal angle for the targeted muscle fibers. Certainly better than nothing, but less effective than resistance training.
- **Anything that causes sharp pain:** Either modify the exercise or avoid it. There are usually other ways to achieve a goal.
- **Any exercise in this book that isn't performed correctly.**

training is with one-week cycles. Thus you could make Monday a light day with lower weights so that you can do sets of 12 to 15 reps before reaching muscular fatigue (12 to 15 RM); Wednesday a heavy day (3 to 5 RM); and Friday a moderate day (8 to 10 RM). In addition to working different energy systems, this also protects against overtraining.

When doing a maintenance routine just one or two days per week, you might use a training pyramid for the primary exercises. This could start with a set of 15 RM, then increase the load for a set of 10 RM, then 5, then 10, then finish with 15. Or if time is short, you might do half a pyramid starting with 10 reps, then 8, then 6, then 4. Using machines makes pyramids and descending sets very time-effective since you only have to move a pin to adjust the resistance.

RESISTANCE EXERCISES

With all the options at your disposal—exercises, loads, sets, repetitions, cycles—there is no reason to ever get bored in a gym. Use your creativity and always maintain good form. Keep your eye on the prize: it's all about climbing more and better.

UPPER BODY EXERCISES

19 Lat Pull

Why

This multi-joint exercise is the next best thing to real climbing. Lat pulls are superior to pull-ups because you can lean back to simulate the angle of overhangs and better target the muscles. The lats originate at the spine and insert into the upper arm at several angles; a vertical orientation makes the resistance less efficient.

Muscles

Latissimus dorsi, teres major, middle and lower trapezius, rhomboids, posterior deltoid, biceps group.

Form

■ Position the seat and knee pad so that your hips and knees are at right angles, thighs are snug under the pad, and feet flat on the floor.

■ Stand up and grab the bar with your palms facing away and hands wider than your elbows. If the angled part of the bar is too wide, just grab where it's comfortable or select a different bar.

■ Sit down and tuck your knees under the pad. Elbows should be slightly bent.

■ Lean back at a 15- to 45-degree angle, keeping your spine and neck straight. Press your shoulder blades down and together and keep them in that position throughout the set.

■ In a smooth motion, pull the bar down to almost touch your chest.

■ Then control the speed of the bar as it rises. Don't just let it be lifted!

■ Back at the starting position, maintain the tension in your shoulder blades and pull down again. Don't let your elbows lock out straight. Repeat.

Tips

Concentrate on your back muscles, not your arms, and do not rock back and forth. Don't jerk the motion. Avoid overgripping with your hands; this isn't a forearm exercise.

Variations

- When the resistance is less than body weight, position the knee pad so that you can't use it. This requires more work from your core muscles.
- Vary your hand position: narrow, wide, palms facing you, parallel grip.
- Practice lock-offs at various angles by stopping the ascent of the bar for several seconds.

- Try one-arm pulls while sitting on a stability ball.
- The plate-loaded, unilateral machines allow a full range of motion to waist level.

Precautions

Do not perform lat pulls behind the neck; the motion has nothing to do with climbing, the direction is suboptimal for the muscles, and it places stress on your cervical spine and rotator cuff. Those with shoulder impingement problems or a torn rotator

cuff should be cautious with lat pulls. Try using a narrow, parallel grip instead (makes this a lat row).

20 Pull-up

Why

This multi-joint exercise has long been a favorite among climbers for barroom bragging rights even though it has little to do with climbing ability. Pull-ups require very little to no equipment—having a bar conveniently located at home or work allows you to pop off sets throughout the day.

Muscles

Latissimus dorsi, teres major, middle and lower trapezius, rhomboids, posterior deltoid, biceps group.

Form

- Use a bar approximately 1½ inches in diameter that is far enough off the floor for you to hang vertically. Bending your knees to fit is less desirable since you lose concentration.

- Grab the bar with your palms facing away and hands wider than your shoulders.
- Squeeze your shoulder blades down and together and keep them in that retracted position throughout the set.
- In a smooth motion, pull yourself up until your nose is at bar level. Exhale as you pull.
- Then lower yourself in a controlled movement. Repeat.

Tips

Try ascending 1:1 sets (do 1 rep, wait that time, do 2 reps, wait that time, do 3 . . . but stop 1 to 2 reps before your limit and start over) a couple times a day. If you have trouble with pull-ups, start with chin-ups (palms facing you). The assisted pull-up machines at gyms are excellent for those who lack the upper-body strength to perform many reps. At home, you can simulate these by attaching several quarter-inch elastic cords to the bar and standing in loops.

Variations

- Place a stool several feet forward of the bar and rest your heels on it while keeping your back straight; by varying the height and distance, you can change the angle of resistance.
- When you are ready, increase resistance by adding weights to a waist pack.
- While lowering, lock off at various angles and hold for as long as possible.

Precautions

Do not dead hang; keep some tension in shoulders and elbows between reps. Avoid pull-ups on a door molding; this is very stressful on finger joints and detracts from quality pull-ups. Those with shoulder impingement problems or a torn rotator cuff should be cautious with pull-ups.

21   Bent-over Row

Why

A multi-joint exercise that allows you to focus on each side of the back without straining the lumbar region. Rather like pulling in low to make a high reach with the other hand.

Muscles

Latissimus dorsi, teres major, middle trapezius, rhomboids, posterior deltoid, biceps group.

Form

- Prop yourself with one hand and one knee on a padded bench and the other leg standing on the floor, knee slightly bent; your back is horizontal. Also may be done standing with one hand resting on a table or chair.
- Grasp the dumbbell and allow your arm to hang straight down. The wrist is neutral, the elbow slightly bent, shoulder blades retracted, and your back is neutral.
- Starting with your back muscles, pull the weight toward your chest until your elbow is at a right angle. Your upper arm just brushes the ribs.
- Hold the contraction for a moment, then slowly lower the weight. Do not let gravity just pull it down. Repeat.

Tips

Emphasize the pull from your back, not the biceps. Keep your torso parallel to the floor;

don't rotate your chest to the ceiling or allow your shoulder to drop downward.

Variations

- Instead of a bench, kneel on a stability ball to discover some tiny muscles you didn't know were there.
- Vary the angle of your back from horizontal to as much as 45 degrees; this works well with a cable machine and a pulley near the floor.
- The barbell bent-over row is essentially the same, but you can't brace yourself so it requires more balance.

Precautions

An unsupported bent-over row places significant shear force on the lower back. Instead, do one side at a time or rest your chest on a bench or ball and use a pair of dumbbells.

22 Seated Row

Why

Since the back muscles are vital for all types of climbing, they need a good repertoire of exercises. This multi-joint exercise is excellent for improving posture and can be a good simulation of an undercling.

Muscles

Latissimus dorsi, teres major, middle trapezius, rhomboids, posterior deltoid, biceps group.

Form

- Sit at the machine with your feet firmly braced against the platform or floor. Knees are slightly bent.
- Bending at the hips, reach forward and grasp the handle. Then sit up until your back is vertical; this is the start and finish position.
- Pull your shoulder blades back and together and keep them in that retracted position throughout the set.
- Starting with your back muscles, pull the handle toward your abdomen. The elbows stay at your side and point behind you.
- Hold the contraction for a moment, then slowly reverse the motion. Do not let gravity just pull the handle back. Repeat.

Tips

Use a variety of grips and hand positions to mix up the stimulus.

Variations

- Most gyms have several machines that perform essentially the same operation—try them all.
- Use a straight bar and grasp it with an undercling (palms up).

Precautions

Rocking forward from your hips can strain your lower back; there are better ways to train and stretch these muscles. Don't allow your shoulders to be pulled forward or your elbows to hyperextend.

23   Straight-arm Pull-down

Why

This single-joint exercise, also called levers, is akin to dynoing for a hold. It works the back muscles with a different movement pattern than the standard exercises.

Muscles

Latissimus dorsi, teres major, posterior deltoid, middle trapezius, rhomboids.

Form

- Stand at arm's length from a lat pull or overhead cable machine. Knees and hips are slightly bent, back is neutral.
- Reach up and grasp the bar with your hands about shoulder-width and palms facing down. Your arms are straight and angled upward about 45 degrees; elbows slightly bent.
- Press your shoulder blades down and together and keep them in that position throughout the set.
- Press the handle toward the floor until it reaches your thighs.
- Hold the contraction for a moment, then slowly raise the handle while fighting gravity. Repeat.

Tips

Do this after other multi-joint back exercises if you still have some juice. Keep your elbows slightly bent to prevent excessive cross-loading of joints.

Variations

- Instead of the flat bar, attach a double-tailed, thick rope to allow a thumbs-up grasp.
- Seated levers, with your thighs under a

pad, allow you to lean back for a different angle but may strain your lower back.

Precautions

Pay attention for possible shoulder aggravation.

24 Bench Press

Why

This multi-joint exercise directly targets muscles that are often underdeveloped in climbers. A primary exercise in any well-rounded program—don't leave the gym without it. Sorry ladies, contrary to rumor, these chest exercises won't firm up breasts. However, apparent size can increase as muscle behind the mammary glands develop.

Muscles

Pectoralis major, anterior deltoid, triceps.

Form

- Sit on a flat bench with the dumbbells on either side of you and your feet planted flat on the floor.
- Pick the weights up and bend your elbows about 90 degrees. As you lean

back, push the weights straight up.

- Take a moment to get comfortable. Your arms are straight up, elbows out and slightly bent, thumbs pointed at each other. This is the start/finish position.
- Bending the elbows, slowly lower the weights in an arc until your upper arms are parallel to the floor—no lower!
- With a squeeze of the chest, straighten your arms. Do not lock out your elbows or bang the weights at the top. Repeat.

Tips

The jocks use a barbell bench press to impress chicks with their studliness. The bar makes the exercise easier since range of motion is limited and fewer stabilizer muscles are needed. Most of the machines are sorry imitations of the real thing (better ones follow an arc and allow a squeeze of the chest at the end).

Variations

- Raise the angle of the bench between 45 and 60 degrees to emphasize the upper pectorals and anterior deltoid (incline bench press).
- Lower the angle of the bench about 10 to 30 degrees to emphasize the lower portion of the pectoralis major (decline bench press).
- Use a stability ball instead of a bench for flat or inclined presses to involve more core muscles.

Precautions

Start off with lighter weights than macho-ness dictates. Increase the load only when you can fully control the weight. It's bad form to drop the dumbbells—but getting hurt is worse.

25 Fly

Why

This motion works the chest the way it is designed. It is a single-joint exercise that develops the anti-climbing muscles, those that our sport rarely hits.

Muscles

Pectoralis major, anterior deltoid.

Form

- Place a bench in the center of a cable crossover machine so that your shoulders will be aligned with the pulleys.
- Sit on the bench and grab one low handle and then the other.
- Lie back while raising your arms straight overhead.
- Take a moment to get comfortable. Your arms are straight up, elbows out and slightly bent, palms facing each other. This is the start/finish position.
- Keeping your arms straight, slowly lower the weights until your they are parallel to the floor—no lower!
- Contract the chest and bring your arms together. Repeat.

Tips

Be sure to get the last squeeze at the end for full benefit; there is no advantage to your arms crossing past midline. Dumbbell flies are less effective than cable flies since resistance decreases as your hands come together. The straight-arm fly machines allow you to superset with a reverse fly that works the midtrapezius and posterior deltoid.

Variations

- Substitute a stability ball for the bench to work your core muscles.
- Incline the bench to target the upper pecs.
- Instead of a bench, stand at the cross-over machine with a 30-degree bend at the waist and use the high grips; this targets the lower pecs.

Precautions

A potentially dangerous exercise when performed with heavy resistance; stick to lighter weights or bench press instead. Never let your arms reach behind your body. Fly machines that bend your elbow 90 degrees, a "pec deck," may cause elbow and shoulder pain yet are no better for chest development.

26 Dip

Why

A multi-joint exercise that can help on those mantle moves. This also balances the major climbing muscles. Dip machines reduce your body weight to allow more weight than might otherwise be possible.

Muscles

Pectoralis major, triceps.

Form

- Set the handles on the narrower width if the machine has that option.
- Stand on the foot bar and lean forward at the waist slightly. Elbows are slightly bent, back straight.
- Lower yourself until your upper arms are parallel to the floor—no lower!
- Contracting your chest, push back to the top. Repeat.

Tips

A vertical body alignment emphasizes the triceps, while leaning forward emphasizes the pecs (but stresses the front of the shoulder joint). Treat assisted dips as a hypertrophy or endurance exercise with sets that are a minimum 8 RM. Because these machines often double for assisted pull-ups, this makes a great superset.

Variations

- You can use two parallel chair backs for assisted dips at home or when traveling. Face them away from each other and just over shoulder-width apart and balance on your toes.

Precautions

Dips can be very stressful on the elbows and shoulders—some people just shouldn't do them. Avoid going lower than a right-angle bend of the elbow or using heavy loads. Beware of pain on top of the shoulder when you are in the start position.

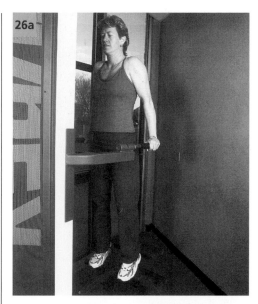

27 Shoulder Press

Why

This multi-joint exercise is the opposite of just about everything you do while climbing—a good reason to do it.

Muscles

Anterior deltoid, medial deltoid, triceps.

Form

- Sit on a stability ball or bench; knees and hips are at 90-degree angles and the spine is erect the entire time.
- Hold a dumbbell in each hand at shoulder level, elbows bent and pointed down, palms facing forward.
- Press the dumbbells upward in a natural arc until your arms are almost straight.
- Lower the weights to the starting position. Repeat.

Tips

Keep the dumbbells in the same plane throughout the motion. For higher resistance, use an incline bench set about 15 degrees back from vertical to target the muscles without stressing the shoulder joints.

Variations

- Called a military press when performed with a barbell; you can lift more but don't get as much benefit (fewer stabilizers are used).
- Many machines replicate the shoulder press, but look for ones with multiple joints and hand positions.

Precautions

Many machines can create problems with shoulder impingement. Avoid the behind-the-neck barbell press unless you enjoy shoulder problems. If you want to target the posterior deltoid, some of the machines are a safer choice.

28 Rear Delt Row

Why

This multi-joint exercise develops shoulder and arm muscles that are often used when climbing. It's similar to a bent-over row except your elbows are away from your side.

Muscles

Posterior deltoid, mid and upper trapezius, rhomboids, biceps.

Form

- Prop yourself with one hand and one knee on a padded bench and the other leg standing on the floor, knee slightly bent; your back is nearly horizontal. Also may be done standing with one hand resting on a table or chair.
- Hold the dumbbell perpendicular to your body and allow your arm to hang straight down. The wrist is neutral, the elbow slightly bent, and your shoulder blades are retracted.
- Starting with your back muscles, pull the weight upward until your elbow is at a right angle. Your upper arm is extended straight out to the side.
- Hold the contraction for a moment, then slowly lower the weight. Do not let gravity just pull it down. Repeat.

Tips

Don't let your shoulder be pulled all the way to the floor at the bottom of the movement; keep a flat back.

Variations

- Instead of a bench, kneel on a stability ball to improve balance.
- Use a split rope with a cable machine, either sitting or standing.

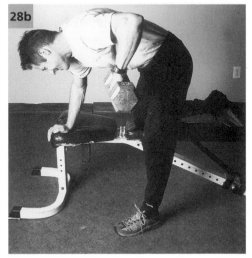

Precautions

An unsupported rear delt row places significant shear force on the lower back. Instead, rest your chest on a bench or ball and use a pair of dumbbells.

29 Arm Side Raise

Why

A single-joint exercise that targets the top of the shoulders. As with the other shoulder exercises, this is about injury prevention—not showing off.

Muscles

Medial deltoid, anterior deltoid, supraspinatus.

Form

- Pick up a pair of lightweight dumbbells and stand with feet shoulder-width apart, knees and elbows slightly bent, palms facing each other.
- To give the middle deltoids maximum resistance, you can bend at the waist slightly, keeping your spine straight.
- In a smooth motion, raise your arms to the sides until they are parallel to the floor. Elbows remain slightly bent.
- Hold the contraction for a moment, then slowly return your arms to vertical. Repeat.

Tips

Your shoulders are not built for significant stress in this manner. If you need heavier loads, it may be safer on a variable resistance machine.

Variations

- May also be performed on a cable crossover machine using the low pulleys; stand sideways and grasp the handle with the opposite hand.

Precautions

Don't raise your arms above shoulder height with resistance—it won't help and can damage the rotators.

30 Internal Shoulder Rotation

Why

Those who have been through shoulder rehabilitation will recognize this as a standard exercise. It's better done before, rather than after, you've torn a rotator cuff.

29a

29b

Muscles

Subscapularis.

Form

- Attach a therapy band (stretchy rubber tube available in different flexes) to a solid post at elbow height.
- Stand sideways next to the post and put your hand in a loop of the band. Your elbow is next to your side and bent at a right angle.
- Adjust your position so that your forearm is partially rotated toward the post—don't force it—just to one o'clock.
- Without allowing the elbow to move, in a smooth motion, pull your hand across your body as far as it will go.
- Hold the contraction for a moment, then return to the start position. Repeat for a full set, then do the other side.

Tips

Do not rotate your torso. Some people attempt this exercise while standing with dumbbells; however, the resistance is not optimal for the muscles so it's less effective. Occasionally perform sets with less resistance and higher reps for greater endurance.

Variations

- The best alignment is with the elbow slightly farther away from your body than the shoulder. Reach across with your other hand and tuck it between the upper arm and chest or use a folded towel.

- Lie on your side and hold a dumbbell in the hand next to the floor, then raise and lower the weight.

- May also be performed on a cable machine with the pulley at waist level. Some gyms have a machine designed for rotator cuff rotations at various angles: use it.

Precautions

You may be sorry if you don't do this one regularly.

31 External Shoulder Rotation

Why

The counterpart to the internal rotator rotation to promote shoulder stability. The two exercises aren't "either-or"—they're "both or suffer."

Muscles

Infraspinatus, teres minor.

Form

- Attach a therapy band to a solid post at elbow height.

- Stand sideways next to the post and put your hand on the opposite side in a loop of the band. Your elbow is next to your side and bent at a right angle.

- Adjust your position so that your forearm is rotated toward the post as far as it will go while keeping your elbow in position.

- Without allowing the elbow to move, pull your hand across your body and smoothly rotate outward as far as it comfortably will go.

- Hold the contraction for a moment, then

31a

return to the start position. Repeat for a full set, then do the other side.

Tips

Keep your body from twisting. Occasionally perform sets with less resistance and higher reps for greater endurance.

Variations

- Lie on your side and hold a dumbbell in the hand opposite the floor, then raise and lower the weight.

- Kneel next to a weight bench so that you are face down and your back is parallel to the floor. Place your upper arm across the bench, straight out from your side, with

exercise options available at most gyms. While important, biceps strength is just one link in the chain. Don't get carried away.

Muscles

Biceps brachii, brachialis, brachioradialis.

Form

- Stand erect with knees slightly flexed.
- Hold a dumbbell in each hand with your upper arms pressed to your sides, elbows slightly bent and palms facing outward.
- Without allowing your elbows to move, raise your forearms as far as possible.
- Hold the contraction, then slowly lower your arms to the starting position. Repeat.

Tips

When the palms are up, the large biceps brachii does most of the work. When the forearm is neutral and thumbs up (hammer curl), the weaker brachioradialis is emphasized. The brachialis is used equally for all hand positions. Maximum muscle activity occurs when the wrists are not rotated during the curl. A cable machine is a good alternative to dumbbells: superset by using the low pulley for biceps curls and the high pulley for triceps extensions.

Variations

- Varying the angle of the upper arms by resting them on an angled pad will alter the resistance somewhat.
- When lowering, lock off at different angles and hold for a few seconds before continuing the motion.
- Few of the gadgets come close to the effectiveness of properly performed dumbbell or cable curls. Using barbells allows the stronger arm to compensate for the weaker one—not good.

your elbow bent at a right angle. Start with the forearm hanging straight down and rotate it up to parallel with the floor.

Precautions

Rotator cuff exercises should not be forced beyond a comfortable range of motion.

32   Biceps Curl

Why

A single-joint motion to isolate and build the big guns for climbing greatness. Since males subconsciously associate biceps girth with penis size, there are numerous

When resting the upper arms on your thigh or an angled pad, be careful not to hyperextend the elbows. If you insist on using a barbell, select one that matches the angle of your wrists; a straight bar is not always a good option.

33   Triceps Press

Why

It is vital to balance the muscles of the upper arm, both for better climbing performance and the prevention of injury. There are several single-joint exercises that work the triceps. Varying the angle of the upper arms changes the emphasis to different heads of the triceps muscle, but hand position matters little.

Muscles

Triceps long, medial, and lateral heads; anconeus.

Form

- Lie on your back on a stability ball (or bench) with feet on the floor.
- Hold a dumbbell in each hand and extend your arms straight up in the air, elbows slightly bent, palms facing each other.
- Keeping your upper arms vertical, bend your elbows to lower your forearms to parallel with the floor.
- Hold the contraction, then straighten your arms to vertical. Repeat.

Tips

Avoid bending your elbows significantly more than 90 degrees. Performed with a barbell (or a single dumbbell) in both hands, this is called a skull crusher—not recommended for obvious reasons. The triceps kickback (performed with the opposite knee and hand on a bench) is identical in motion to this lying version but you can only do one arm at a time.

Variations

- When doing a standing triceps press, use a double-tailed rope handle. This allows your hands to move farther at the

33a

33b

bottom of the motion and increases the contraction of the lateral head.

- Try a standing overhead triceps extension (upper arms are just above parallel to the floor, hands reach behind your head).

Precautions

Do not lock out your elbows at the end of the motion.

34   Wrist Curl

Why

Better than nothing if you can't climb or use a fingerboard. About 15 percent of the population is missing a small wrist flexor muscle (palmaris longus) on one or both arms; sometimes the muscle is there but in the "wrong" location. Flex your wrist with resistance and check for a prominent tendon in the center (another is next to it but closer to the thumb).

Muscles

Wrist flexors.

Form

- Stand with a barbell in your hands, palms facing out.
- Allow your fingers to relax and let the bar roll till you can just hold it.
- Curl your fingers up, raising the bar as far as possible. Repeat.

Tips

Climbing is more fun.

Variations

- Possible with dumbbells but trickier to coordinate: watch your toes.
- When rehabbing an elbow, you may use a therapy band by standing on the opposite end.

34a

34b

Precautions

Do not hyperextend your wrists backward with forearms propped on your thighs or a bench.

35 Reverse Wrist Curl

Why

These muscles are little used when climbing so they are often underdeveloped—the underlying source of many elbow pains. An ounce of prevention. . . .

Muscles

Wrist extensors.

Form

- Grab some light dumbbells and sit with your forearms resting on your thighs.
- Your wrists should be straight and unsupported, palms facing downward.
- Raise your wrists as far as possible, then lower until straight. Repeat.

Tips

May also be performed with your arms extended in front of you, thus overcoming the temptation to use weights that are too heavy. A therapy band is a good alternative to dumbbells since you can easily adjust the resistance.

Variations

- Attach a weight to one end of a 4-foot piece of 5 mm cord. Fix the other end of the cord to the center of an 18-inch-long, 1-inch-diameter wooden dowel. Wind the weight up and then down, using your hands to alternate on the dowel.

Precautions

Do not lower your wrists below your forearm; it's an unnecessary strain.

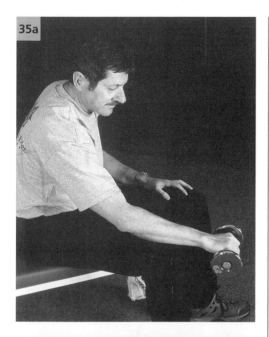

35a

35b

36 Finger Hangs

Why

Short of actual climbing, there is no better training for finger strength than short hangs on a fingerboard. Novice climbers should only use large holds and longer hangs—you need to strengthen the ligaments and tendons before working on the forearm muscles (there are no muscles in the fingers). For a multitude of reasons, no matter your conditioning, fingerboards are a bad choice for endurance training and pull-ups.

Muscles

Finger flexors.

Form

- Do hangs at the end of a workout or after a thorough warm-up. Prepare your muscles by hanging with both hands on large- to mid-size edges for about 30 to 60 seconds. Keep your elbows slightly bent and some tension in your shoulders (don't dead hang). Rest for a minute, then repeat.

- Move to your "problem" holds while you are still fresh. Hang for 3 to 8 seconds with an open grip, then rest for 5 seconds. If you can do one-arm hangs, then it's just a matter of moving from hand to hand. Avoid pockets unless you are an advanced climber.

- Perform 6 of these high-intensity reps, then rest for 2 to 5 minutes until fully recovered.

- Move to larger holds, preferably slopers, or decrease resistance. Hang for 25 to 40 seconds until you fail, then rest for about a minute. Repeat.

■ Move to even larger holds or decrease resistance again. Hang for 45 to 60 seconds until you fail, then rest for about a minute. Repeat.

Tips

Place a clock with second hands directly in front of you to time the hangs. Decrease resistance with elastic cord or by using a stool to rest your legs. If you still need to increase resistance after progressing to one-arm hangs, hold a weight in the opposite hand or wear a waist pack. Do not use holds smaller than first joint; they have no training benefit but do stress the knuckles. Many fingerboards are too abrasive; either file the holds down or clog them with chalk.

Variations

■ Many different routines are possible on a fingerboard. You can focus an entire set on one aspect of strength or a particular type of hold. All of the basic resistance training principles apply—including knowing when to quit.

Precautions

Never crimp or dead hang when training! Crimping increases the leverage on joints and places three times more force on the A2 pulley that holds the tendons near the bone than on the fingertips. A dead hang, when the elbow and shoulder are fully relaxed, places nasty strain on the connective tissues—it's a good rest position when climbing, not when training.

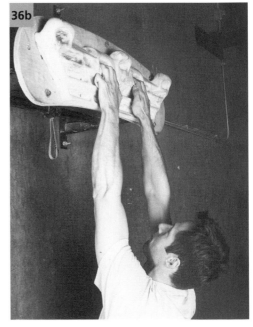

BODY CORE EXERCISES

37 **Back Extension**

Why

The muscles of the lower back are no less important than your abs for climbing. Without this core strength to unite the upper and lower body, all of your sports— and much of life—will be more difficult.

Muscles

Erector spinae, deep spinal rotators.

Form

- Lie face down across a stability ball with your legs spread wide for balance. There should be a slight forward flex in your back and your neck is neutral.
- Cross your hands behind your back.
- Slowly raise your torso off the ball until you feel a strong tension in your lower back. Your head will only raise a couple of inches.
- Hold the contraction for a moment, then reverse the motion. Repeat.

Tips

To increase resistance, place your hands behind your neck, but do not apply pressure! To decrease resistance, lie on the floor or a bench to limit the range of motion.

Variations

- Lie face down across the ball. Now raise your right arm and left leg until they are straight. Hold the contraction, then return and repeat with the opposite arm and leg.
- Lie face down across the ball and, keeping your body and arms straight, use your hands to walk forward until only your feet are supported (cross them

37a

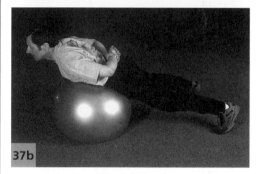

37b

to make it even more challenging). Then walk back until your stomach is supported, and repeat.

- The back extension platform is another alternative. Adjust the pad so that the top is just below your hip joint, then hook your heels under the lip on the foot platform. Cross your arms in front of you and hinge forward from the hips, keeping your back straight. Continue until your torso is vertical or you feel a stretch in the hamstrings. Then raise up until you are straight again. Hold a weight plate in your arms to increase resistance.
- Stiff-leg dead lifts also work these back

muscles, plus the glutes and hamstrings, but this exercise requires perfect form. Consult a trainer if you need more options.

Precautions

Desist if you feel sharp pain in your back.

38 Crunch

Why

The abs are central to all outdoor sports. Climbers especially need strong abs on overhanging terrain to hold our feet into the rock. Of course, there is also something to be said for a nice "six-pack" that isn't hidden beneath a layer of fat. The rectus abdominis is a long sheet of muscle (about 54 percent Type II fibers) that contracts together, though individual segments can contract harder than the others (hence the mistaken reference to upper and lower abs).

Muscles

Rectus abdominis, internal and external obliques.

Form

- Sit on a stability ball and walk your feet out until you are on your back. Knees should be bent at a right angle, shoulders higher than the hips, and neck straight.
- Cross your hands behind your head.
- Slowly pull your rib cage toward your pelvis, raising your torso off the ball, until you feel a strong tension in your abs. There should be no pressure against your head; hands just lightly touch.
- Hold the contraction for a moment, then reverse the motion. Repeat. Feel the burn.

Tips

For any abs exercise, if you can do 15 reps, you need to add resistance—three sets of 8 to 12 reps is best. Neither hundreds of crunches nor working abs every day will do any good. Don't be fooled: Torso raises and leg raises train the hip flexors (iliopsoas, rectus femoris) and cause a burn in the abs from isometric contraction. However, there is very little training effect on the abs unless the spine curls.

Variations

- Doing crunches on a bench or the floor is easier because of smaller range of motion and lesser demand on the obliques.

- To decrease resistance, cross your hands in front of your chest. Rolling farther out on the ball, so there is less support for your upper torso, will increase resistance, but do not allow your shoulders to drop below your hips (excessive spine flexion).
- Crunch machines allow you to easily fine-tune the resistance for a good workout. According to an EMG study, very few of the ab gadgets are worth a damn compared to ball crunches, though the wheels are passable.
- Lie on your back, place your arms at your side, and grab the ball by squeezing it between your upper and lower legs. Slowly raise the ball and pull it toward your head (reverse crunch).

Precautions

Do not hyperextend your back! Too much flexion can aggravate disks between the vertebrae.

39   Torso Side Raise

Why

For most climbers, there is no such thing as a core that is too strong. In addition to the front and back, you can train the sides of the "box" to achieve balance.

Muscles

Internal and external obliques, rectus abdominis, erector spinae, quadratus lumborum.

Form

- Lie sideways across a stability ball with your legs spread to create a tripod—top leg forward; bottom leg back. Use your

lower arm to brace against the ball; the other hand can go on your abdomen, if you wish, to feel the tension.
- Slowly contract the obliques to raise your torso upward (bottom of rib cage moves toward pelvis).
- Hold the contraction for a moment, then reverse the motion. Repeat.

Tips

Keep your ears even with your shoulders. Increase resistance by putting your upper hand behind your head and by placing the ball farther under your hips.

Variations

- May also be performed on a back

extension platform by turning sideways. Increase resistance by holding a weight in the lower hand.

Precautions

Don't attempt this until your core strength is already developed.

40 Twist Crunch

Why

The external obliques come into action on twist-lock moves and when skiing steep lines. Better abs make better lovers.

Muscles

External and internal obliques, rectus abdominis.

Form

- Sit on a stability ball and walk your feet out until you are on your back. Knees should be bent at a right angle, shoulders higher than the hips, and neck straight.
- Cross your hands in front of your chest.
- Slowly pull your rib cage toward your opposite pelvis, raising your torso off the ball, until you feel a strong tension in your side abs.
- Hold the contraction for a moment, then reverse the motion. Repeat to the opposite side.

Tips

Keep your neck straight throughout the exercise. Don't use momentum to cheat; always maintain control and precision. The diameter and air pressure in the ball will affect the resistance—experiment.

Variations

- Use a flat bench for less resistance or a decline bench to increase resistance.

- Rotary torso machines are effective for this muscle group but may not be appropriate for those with spinal issues.

Precautions

Be cautious if you have lower back problems.

LOWER BODY EXERCISES

41 Squat

Why

The ultimate multi-joint exercise, the squat works many large muscle groups simultaneously and increases joint stability. Useful for all climbers, it is invaluable for alpinists and mountaineers. If time is short, this one exercise can replace all others for the lower body.

Muscles

Gluteus maximus, semimembranosus, semitendinosus, biceps femoris, vastus lateralis, vastus intermedius, vastus medialis, rectus femoris.

Form

- Adjust the power rack by moving the pins so the bar is just below shoulder level and the safety crossbars are just above the knees.
- Load the bar with plates and secure with spring collars.
- Place your hands on the bar several inches wider than your shoulders and tuck your head under to position the bar across the trapezius (above your shoulder blades and below the big spinal bump, C7).
- Bend your knees slightly to get directly under the bar and stand up.
- Take a step back and position your feet slightly wider than your shoulders, with your toes straight ahead or angled slightly outward (doesn't matter). Varying foot width can slightly alter muscle activation and knee forces.
- Slowly descend by flexing at the hips, knees, and ankles in a smooth motion. Keep your spine neutral and look straight ahead, watching your form in the mirror.

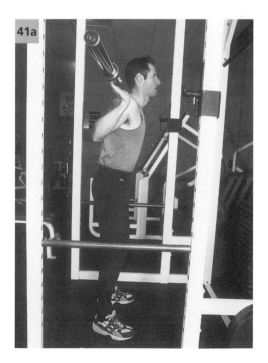

41a

41b

Knees should track directly over the toes and your heels remain flat on the floor.

- When the top of your thighs are parallel to the floor (or as low as possible while maintaining the natural arch in your spine), stand up by reversing the motion and exhaling. Do not pause at the bottom. Repeat.

Tips

Start with an empty bar until you've mastered the form. Don't hold your breath: you might throw up or pass out. Never place a board under the heels; it is safer to increase flexibility naturally. Going deeper than parallel, even with perfect form, probably isn't worth the risk of knee aggravation.

Variations

- Use a single dumbbell held between the legs to work up to barbell squats; this is more functional than two dumbbells and removes some strain from the spine.

Precautions

Do not use a Smith Machine—we *want* to hit all those stabilizers. Those with a lower-back or posterior cruciate knee injury should be careful to use lighter weights and only go part-way down; you may have to avoid squats altogether. The front squat (bar held before you) places more torque on the knees; best to avoid or reduce weight.

42 Leg Press

Why

An easier, though less effective, alternative to barbell squats that removes forces from your spine. With care, the leg press is the safest exercise for heavy resistance.

Muscles

Gluteus maximus, semimembranosus, semitendinosus, biceps femoris, vastus lateralis, vastus intermedius, vastus medialis, rectus femoris.

Form

- Adjust the angle of the back pad.
- Sit with your back fully in contact with the pad (do not flatten the arch) and your feet hip-width apart, toes angled outward. Rest your head on the pad or tilt slightly forward.
- Push a bit with your legs, release the safety stops, and grab the handles.
- Control the descent of the sled by bending your hips and knees. The base of your spine should remain in contact with the pad and your knees track over your feet.
- When your knees are bent at a right angle, hold for a moment, then push the sled uphill. The weight is evenly distributed between toes and heels (feet stay in full contact throughout). Your knees should not wobble or lock out at the top. Repeat.

Tips

Think about pushing with your heels to emphasize the glutes. Vary the width of feet placement and their vertical location on the platform. Some machines allow you to steepen the angle of the backrest to emphasize the quads or decrease the angle for greater hamstring involvement.

Variations

- Many gyms have several leg press machines that offer subtle differences in the movement. Try them all but

42a

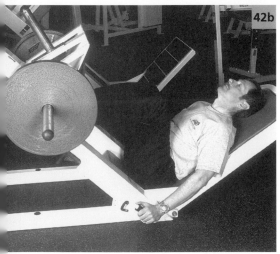

42b

experiment cautiously with lighter weights.

Precautions

Avoid the hack squat machine or reduce the load significantly; it emphasizes the quads but increases torque on the knee.

43 Static Lunge

Why

This variation of the forward (traveling) lunge is less stressful on the knees, yet equally taxing on the muscles and better for improving balance. Also called a split squat, it's a good strength exercise for all backcountry sports because of the asymmetric position—ideal for telemark skiers.

Muscles

Gluteus maximus, semimembranosus, semitendinosus, biceps femoris, vastus lateralis, vastus intermedius, vastus medialis, rectus femoris.

Form

- Holding a barbell across the shoulders, as in a normal squat, stand upright and take a long stride forward (about twice the distance of a normal step) with one leg. The knees of both legs are slightly bent.
- Position the forward foot with heel and toe in line with your leg and flat on the floor; the rear foot will be on bent toes; feet are about hip-width apart (not aligned) for stability. Center your hips and pelvis, watching yourself in a mirror. This is the start position.
- Slowly descend until your forward thigh is almost parallel to the floor (adjust foot position if necessary). The rear knee will be a few inches above the floor. Keep most of the weight over the forward leg.
- Hold the contraction momentarily, then return to start position. Repeat. The up-down movement is only a foot or so—burn, baby, burn.

- After the desired number of reps, explode back to a standing position. Then repeat with the opposite leg forward.

Tips

The front of your knee should not move forward of the toes or to either side. Pay attention that your shoulders and hips remain squared and level; look straight ahead. Raising the rear foot up on a 6- to 18-inch platform can reduce strain in that knee and increase the quad's resistance.

Variations

- Using a dumbbell in each hand is slightly easier since it requires less balance.
- Forward lunges are the same but you return to standing after each knee drop;

another version, the farmer's walk, just keeps going forward. Both are more permissive of sloppy technique that stresses the knee. Reverse lunges are the best dynamic option.

Precautions

Especially when doing the forward lunge, be leery of sharp knee pains.

44 Quad Extension

Why

This single-joint exercise isolates the quads when additional development is required. The sitting position reduces involvement of rectus femoris so the vastus muscles (important for patellar tracking) get more training effect. Because it applies a significant shearing force to the knees, this should be done after squats or leg presses so less resistance is needed.

Muscles
Vastus medialis, vastus lateralis, vastus intermedius, rectus femoris.

Form
- Adjust the back pad so that the center of your knees line up with the pivot on the machine and position the lower pad to just above the ankles.
- Sit in the machine with your spine erect and right-angle bends of the hips and knees. Hold the handles lightly.
- Contract the quads until your legs are not quite straight (about 10-degree knee bend). Do not lock out your knees.
- Hold, then slowly return to the start position. Repeat.

Tips
Keep your toes pointed upward and pull them back to stretch the calves. Occasionally do one-leg extensions to ensure there is no left-right imbalance; if there is, work that weaker leg.

Variations
- Use both the variable (cam) and constant (pivot) resistance machines to work the muscles at their strong and weak points.

Precautions
Do not use very heavy loads—no more than 8 to 10 RM!

45 Hamstring Curl

Why
If you do quad extensions, balance them with hamstring curls. These also strain the

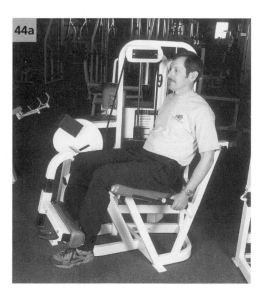

just above the ankles. Set the angle so that your knees are slightly bent.

■ Sit in the machine with your spine erect and pressed against the pad. Lower the knee brace and hold the handles lightly.

■ Contract your hamstrings until the knees are bent about 90 degrees.

■ Hold, then slowly return to the start position. Repeat.

Tips

Don't allow your hips to rise off the pad or your back to arch. Pull your toes back to keep a right-angle bend in your ankle; point your toes straight up. If you have tight hamstrings, use the machine where you lie on your stomach until you solve the real problem.

Variations

■ Use both the variable (cam) and constant (pivot) resistance machines to work the muscles at their strong and weak points.

Precautions

Don't allow the machine to hyperextend your knees.

46 Calf Raise

Why

Strong calves are essential for all climbers— we spend a lot of time on our toes. If you ever climb at Devil's Tower, you're going to wish you'd done more of these. And front-pointing up a long couloir with a pack is like doing calf raises for hours!

Muscles

Gastrocnemius, soleus.

Form

■ Adjust the height of the shoulder pads so

knee joint and should not be done with high-loads, low-reps.

Muscles

Biceps femoris, semitendinosus, semimembranosus.

Form

■ Adjust the back pad so that the center of your knees line up with the pivot on the machine and position the lower pad to you need to push up slightly to enter the machine.

- Place the balls of your feet on the platform, hip-width apart, with your toes pointed straight ahead. Your knees should be straight but not locked out.
- Start with your heels just below the toes and contract your calves to raise up your heel as high as possible.
- Hold, then slowly lower down until level.

Tips

As flexibility increases, allow your heels to drop lower. However, do not force a stretch; allow this to come naturally. Varying foot angle has minimal affect, don't bother.

Variations

- When your legs are straight, the gastrocs (major calf muscle) do most of the work. When in a sitting position with your knees bent at a right angle, the soleus muscles take more of the load. Be sure to use both machines.

Precautions

The biggest danger is not training your calves enough. Be sure to include stretching in your training program. Excessive calf and Achilles tightness is a common problem in athletes.

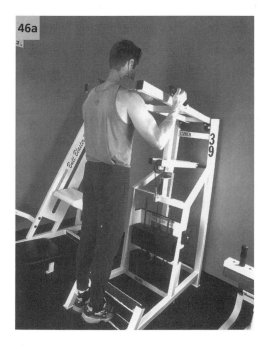

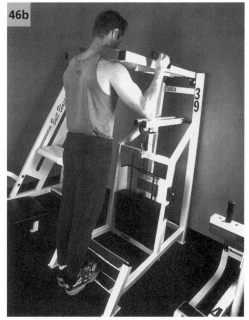

CHAPTER 5

Recovery: Rest and Rehab

Would that it were otherwise, but odds are you will get hurt one day. Much of this book has emphasized training as a means for the prevention, or at least reducing the severity, of injuries. Yet recovery is no less important: ignore at your own peril.

REST UP

Climbers are notorious for their fanaticism, often climbing day after day with nary a break. When you're in your teens and early twenties, you can get away with this devotion—for a while. But even in the prime of your youth, the body needs time to recover for optimal performance.

After a hard day's play, it's common to experience muscle soreness from by-products of exercise (such as lactic acid) and edema (swelling of muscle tissue by fluid borrowed from blood plasma). Normally, if you cool down and refuel properly, this goes away within a couple hours of stopping. Recall, however, that it takes about 20 hours to replenish muscle glycogen stores. So even when soreness abates, you may not be fully recovered.

If your pleasure included a lot of eccentric motion, such as descending a steep trail or lowering yourself down on holds, then you are likely to feel it over the next couple of days. This delayed onset muscular soreness (DOMS) results from edema and actual damage to the muscle fiber. While DOMS is uncomfortable, it isn't necessarily bad (assuming it goes away) and may be required for maximum strength gains. However, the affected muscles cannot generate as much force until recovered and do not replenish glycogen reserves during the repair process.

Many athletes underestimate the value of rest. Taking time off is not an option! Your body gets stronger only during recovery, not when you are actually training: more, more, more is not better, just dumber. If you don't listen to your body, you will start the downward spiral of overtraining syndrome, which can take months out of your schedule.

A rest day doesn't mean lying on the couch eating popcorn (passive rest), though sometimes that's a good thing. Following a very intense workout, such as a long alpine climb or running a marathon, give yourself two full days off; you deserve it and your body needs it. After a hard day of climbing very pumpy routes, use the next two days for easy endurance climbs and aerobic play (active rest). When you look at the training schedules in the next chapter, you will see that both active and passive rest are built into even the most challenging programs. If you prefer to create your own conditioning program, be sure it deposits adequate rest into your account.

Along with gray hairs, or the lack thereof, there are some other unfortunate truths about aging. It isn't your imagination that it takes longer to recover after a hard workout. If you've stayed in shape, you can still climb as hard as the young punks but you won't be able to do it several days in a row. Be smart and anticipate the need for additional rest.

SLEEP TIGHT

Because it's so natural, many of us take sleep for granted, which can be a mistake. Sleep is an essential nutrient; without sufficient quantity and quality, performance suffers. While you already know this from the extreme—most everyone is familiar with the bleary-eyed feeling of too little sleep—minor disturbance has subtle effects on mental and physical performance.

While 7 to 8 hours is the standard prescription for adults, we each have different requirements and, yes, there really are morning people and night owls.

Don't fight your own nature; give your body what it needs. Another benefit of increased fitness is a higher resting metabolic rate that improves your quality of sleep, which is as important as quantity.

You should avoid eating a large meal less than 4 hours before bedtime since the digestion process revs up your engine. And try to eliminate those late-night snacks; while they won't make you fatter (unless you exceed your calorie balance), the sugar buzz doesn't help you sleep. Since it takes stimulants (caffeine, nicotine) and alcohol (both a depressant and stimulant) about 4 to 6 hours to clear your system, be kind to yourself and hold back. And because increased body temp lowers sleep quality, don't engage in a strenuous workout (other than sex) less than 4 hours prior to bed.

Although the mattress infomercials are hokey, they do have a point: you spend about a third of your life in bed so it behooves you to make it a good one. It's worth the time and money to shop around for a quality mattress and pillows that suit you and your significant other. Also try to make your bedroom a dark, quiet place with good air exchange. All of these factors contribute to better, more restful sleep.

When possible, go to bed and wake up the same time everyday, even on weekends. This regularity prevents "blue Monday"

JET LAG

Traveling east or west by more than one time zone messes with your body clock; going from west to east is particularly rough because daylight hours are reduced. Traveling north or south has little effect since the external cues about time remain the same. In general, it takes a full day to adapt for each 2 hours of time difference.

- If you are about to make a long flight, you can get a head start on jet lag by slowly adjusting your sleep period at home.
- During the flight, especially ones heading east, try to rest up. Bring an inflatable pillow, sleep mask, and earplugs and request a blanket if one isn't provided.
- Stay hydrated (avoid too much alcohol) and keep moving your legs to prevent blood clots; take a walk.
- Upon arrival, get used to the new time zone quickly; make sure your hotel room has a window and do not take a nap.
- Avoid heavy exercise until your resting heart rate returns to normal.
- The hormone melatonin may help reset your body clock faster, but it has a number of contra-indications and potential side effects (requires a prescription in the UK). A standard course is 1 mg before bedtime for the first couple of nights. Avoid high dosages or the bedbugs might bite.

because it takes 24 hours to reset your body clock after sleeping late one hour. If you're dragging a little during the day, a 10- to 30-minute nap can be blissfully restorative. However, don't nap after 3:00 P.M., because it may interfere with that night's sleep.

MASSAGE

The harder you train, the more you will benefit from a good massage. Aside from feeling wonderful and reducing stress, body work can break up adhesions that occur when muscle fibers bind to each other. Sometimes called trigger points, these spots prevent full muscle function and don't usually go away on their own. Following a very hard workout, a light massage can flush lactic acid and metabolism by-products from your muscles to speed recovery. If you complete a race that offers sport massage to participants, it's often worth standing in line.

Therapists are usually schooled in several types of body work (certifications take 700 to 1,000 hours), but climbers will probably get the best results from either Swedish or sport massage (a blend of styles). This is much deeper than post-race massage; they should take you just to the edge of pain tolerance. While massage isn't cheap, upwards of fifty dollars per hour is common, your body should feel noticeably more fluid and relaxed. Once you find a good therapist, it's best to stick with him or her as they will learn your body and concentrate on areas that ail you; more bang for the buck.

Another expensive form of massage that may improve climbing performance is called Rolfing. This specifically targets muscle fascia, the sheath that covers each muscle like plastic wrap, and involves very deep, sometimes painful, body work. A complete course of Rolfing consists of ten sessions and often results in improved posture and sometimes unexpected emotional release. Not for everyone but worth considering if your body is really out of whack.

It's also possible to perform self-massage that can be quite effective. This may simply involve rubbing sore muscles, both laterally and longitudinally. There are also a number of inexpensive tools, available from stores and Internet sites offering massage products, that help you get at tough spots. Among the better ones: The Stick (a wonderful rolling pin for calves and other muscles); TheraCane (a U-shaped rod that reaches back muscles); and knobby foot rollers (just 'cause they feel great). The better electric massagers (percussive with a 20-watt or larger motor) can be a nice luxury but are rather expensive; the cheap ones are just annoying. So far, there is no convincing evidence that massage therapy using magnets has any real benefits.

REHABILITATION

Now ya gone'n done it—messed up and hurt yo'self. Quit your moping and be proactive about healing. With an appropriate amount of self-love, you can get back on the rock sooner and reduce the chance of re-injury. On the other hand, not paying attention to your bodily needs will result in far more downtime.

Obviously, anytime pain is severe or a broken bone is suspected, you need to see a doctor as soon as possible; the longer you wait, the worse the potential outcome. Less painful injuries involving joints should also be examined since there is a greater risk of unpleasant complications. Note that a ligament can completely rupture with minimal pain (the joint will feel unstable); these will never heal on their own; surgery is required.

If the ache is tolerable, you may be able to heal thyself. When the onset of pain is sudden, either from accident or overload, you are dealing with macrotrauma, and there is typically significant tissue damage. Acute injuries to muscles and skin, if not too severe, will heal relatively fast, while ligaments and tendons require much longer because they have less blood circulation.

The more insidious problems involve pain that may not be felt until after you stop climbing and continues for several hours, recurring in the same place; this is an early harbinger of an overuse injury (microtrauma). As the damage intensifies, the pain will start earlier and last longer. These nasties can begin as minute tears of the tendon structure (muscle origin or insertion, musculotendinous junction, or the tendon itself) and be complicated by inflammation of the tendon (tendinitis or tendonitis, same thing) or the sheath surrounding it (tenosynovitis). Stress fractures of bone are another form of microtrauma; while rare in climbers, they are fairly common in road runners and gymnasts.

Beware that it's easy to keep aggravating an overuse injury before it fully heals, thus setting yourself up for very long layoffs (a year in some cases). Many troublesome injuries once diagnosed as tendinitis (fairly rare) now appear to be cases of tendinosis in which the collagen structure has degenerated (common). This is bad news because of the longer recovery time and possible re-injury. Tendinitis can heal in several days to two weeks, with a low re-injury rate, but tendinosis can take six to ten weeks to heal, with a 20 percent chance of chronic problems. Another possible cause of problems is neuropathy in which the nerves are damaged; consult a physical therapist for stretches that may help.

REPAIR SCHEDULE

All soft-tissue injuries follow the same course of events, though the time period varies depending upon severity and circulation. At first, the area around the site becomes swollen as blood and fluid leaks into tissues. This inflammation combined with increased pain serves to limit movement for two or three days.

Then the repair phase begins, during which new capillaries grow and collagen fibers are randomly laid down to form a matrix. By the end of this stage, pain will have mostly subsided, but the scar tissue is relatively weak. The most dangerous and frustrating period for climbers is the remodeling phase, when the collagen aligns in the direction of loading and thickens for greater strength.

Once the swelling is gone and range of motion is almost back to normal, you can cautiously start working out again. Begin with a volume only one-tenth of where you were prior to injury. Then every other workout you can increase your efforts by 10 percent. Allow a full month to get back to where you were.

Starting back too soon and too hard is the biggest mistake an athlete can make! You can turn an inconvenient acute injury into a debilitating chronic injury that will ultimately reduce how much you climb. Use cross-play to preserve your sanity; resistance and aerobic training for limbs that are unaffected will speed recovery.

MINOR TREATMENT

The standard treatment for soft-tissue injuries, even those that require a visit to the doctor, starts with RICE—rest, ice, compression, and elevation. During the first 48 hours, before the repair process begins, the injured area is very susceptible to further internal damage. Any movement or rubbing will delay healing, not to mention that it will hurt.

Cooling the injury will contract blood vessels, thus significantly reducing bleeding and swelling; blood is toxic outside the circulatory system and edema can hold the damaged tissues apart. The sooner you soak in a creek or apply a cold pack, the better. Whichever method you use, the objective is to thoroughly numb the area: 15 minutes on, 15 off, as often as possible during the first 24 to 36 hours. No matter what, do not take a long soak in a hot tub after trauma.

Compressing the injury with an elastic bandage will also help minimize swelling. However, this can be tricky; start wrapping well above the injury and continue well below it. The pressure should be firm but not so tight that it impedes circulation (several attempts may be necessary to get it right). By elevating the limb higher than your trunk, gravity will assist the draining of fluids; standing around on a sprained ankle is a bad idea.

Taking a non-steroidal anti-inflammatory drug (NSAID; see "Rehab Aids") can also speed healing by reducing the swelling. After the initial pain and swelling are gone, discontinue the NSAIDs so you don't risk long-term problems.

COLD TIP

As a cold pack, crushed ice inside a resealable plastic bag and wrapped in a towel will work in a pinch, as will a bag of frozen vegetables (peas or corn). But you can make a better cold pack by mixing 1½ cups (375 ml) of water with half a cup (125 ml) of rubbing alcohol in a plastic bag. Store this in a freezer; it makes a slush that molds easily. But if you're no stranger to injury, the commercial cold packs are more comfortable and are easier to secure.

After two or three days of RICE, see a doctor if the injury does not improve since you may have done more damage than you thought. However, if the pain and swelling are mostly gone, you can apply heat either with a hot water bottle or an electric heat pack; despite the ad hype, warming creams do not penetrate deep enough to be effective. At this point in healing, the heat is soothing and will help disperse swelling. Carefully start to move the limb, but only within the range of pain-free motion. Then you can begin exercising the injured area with isometric contractions (simply tighten the muscle and hold the contraction) and the joint at different angles.

Once you are back to nearly a full range of motion, you can slowly and carefully increase resistance training. This is when a gym is especially valuable because you have a wide variety of workout options that allow small increments of progress (many gyms also have trainers who specialize in rehab). When dealing with tendon injuries, either acute or from overuse, emphasize eccentric exercises; perform the motion slowly and gradually increase speed, only

REHAB AIDS

While pain relief is nice, getting the swelling down quickly is the main reason to take non-steroidal anti-inflammatory drugs (NSAIDs) following soft-tissue trauma. Everyone is different, so none of these medications is clearly superior to the others; you'll need to experiment to find what's best for you. To build up the anti-inflammatories in the blood-stream, don't skip a dosage when it's due; intermittent usage is significantly less effective.

NSAIDs work by suppressing the production of prostaglandins after cells have been traumatized. They do this by inhibiting an enzyme, COX-2, that is needed for production. Unfortunately, they also inhibit COX-1 that is found in the stomach lining. Newer prescription drugs only inhibit COX-2 (Celebrex and Vioxx are both heavily advertised in the United States), for daily users with gastric complaints. For sports injuries lasting a few days, COX-2 inhibitors offer no real advantage to most people.

Adverse reactions (such as ulcers, exacerbated bleeding, ringing in the ears, liver and kidney malfunction) are possible with any NSAID, so use these only when necessary and in the proper dosage. There's no reason not to buy generic. Children should avoid aspirin and naproxen sodium. Sorry, even though you may wish to drown your misery, you really should limit booze intake to two drinks per day while on any of these medications.

Aspirin has been a popular pain, fever, and anti-inflammation medication for over a century; it also appears to offer heart protection. Once derived from willow bark, which has been used for at least 2,500 years, the synthetic form is more effective and cheaper.

increasing the load after you can do the move quickly.

It bears repeating: don't push yourself too hard! At first, pain will be your guide. But after a while, when you are in the remodeling stage, you need to be smart. Resistance training gives you a clear indicator it's safe to climb hard again when the injured area is back to full strength (compared to the other limb or prior performance). Unfortunately, climbing itself doesn't offer this precise feedback so the tendency is to start too soon—and get hurt all over again.

COMMON CLIMBING INJURIES

With proper education and caution, climbing is far safer than the general public thinks. But as with any sport, if you do it often enough, there are certain problems that tend to arise. Knowing what they are ahead of time allows you to take preventive action.

Skin

Scratches and abrasions are certainly the most frequent damage we inflict upon ourselves. These are little concern when small; perhaps apply a dab of chalk to the wound while midpitch to stop the bleeding. Larger

Sometimes referred to as ASA, for acetasalicylic acid, it is still the standard against which others are judged. Unfortunately, many people cannot tolerate aspirin. Do not take aspirin if you are on Diamox or on other NSAIDs.

Analgesic creams containing 10 percent trolamine salicylate have been shown to delay the onset of muscle soreness, reduce the severity of pain, and speed the demise of pain without the stomach irritation of aspirin taken orally. Unlike warming creams, these have direct action on the injury site.

Acetaminophen (known as paracetamol in the UK) is an analgesic (painkiller) but does nothing to reduce swelling, no matter the dosage, so it isn't an NSAID. Use it for headaches, back pain, or fever if the other options bug your stomach; used properly, there are few side effects. But do not exceed the recommended dose or drink alcohol: severe liver damage is possible.

Ibuprofen is an effective alternative to aspirin, with fewer side effects. This drug has become widely overused in our society. Do not take with aspirin since they interfere with each other.

Naproxen sodium is also effective for reducing inflammation as well as pain and fever. This lasts longer in the body than other NSAIDS, so it requires fewer dosages throughout the day.

gashes should be cleaned and protected by a flexible bandage. If it's a big abrasion (palm-size or larger, a.k.a. road rash), then you need to be aggressive about cleaning out debris and then apply a topical disinfectant. Keeping skin wounds airtight will speed healing and make the scar tissue more pliable. The new high tech bandages, such as Liquid Band-Aid, stay on better and promote faster healing than old-fashioned strips.

Calluses often form on the fingers. If these become too thick, they may tear off, creating a painful "flapper." Since calluses are merely dead skin, you can trim them with flat nail clippers. Washing dishes the old-fashioned way (in a sink) is also effective for getting rid of calluses. The drying effects of chalk is hard on the skin, so it's a good idea to regularly use hand lotion.

Many climbers worship the sun and are convinced that they, personally, are immune to melanoma. Yet skin cancer is still on the rise throughout the world, despite better awareness and skin care products. There is no such thing as a "safe" tan, and that bronze skin you flaunt in your invincible teens and twenties may very well come back to haunt you decades later. Even if you luck out on the cancer front, there is still the undeniable aging effect from sun overdose that wrinkles and dries skin. Anymore, a deep tan is an indication of foolishness not sexiness.

Hands

Since climbing is a hands-on sport, it should be little surprise that's where most of the injuries occur. The most common injuries in experienced climbers involve either tears of the finger's flexor tendons ("climber's finger") or the second annular (A2) pulley, a fibrous ring that holds the tendons near the bone. These are primarily caused by overstressing the joints on small holds (or one-finger pull-ups) and usually affect the middle and ring fingers—often with a loud pop.

With a torn tendon, pain will occur near the site on the palm side of the finger and is increased by movement. Damage to the A2 pulley is accompanied by pain and swelling at the base of the finger. If it's fully blown, the tendon will pull away from the bone on the palm side, called *bowstringing,* as the finger is flexed against resistance. With either injury, you are facing two to six months without climbing.

Contrary to popular belief, wrapping tape around a finger offers minimal protection against pulley rupture, absorbing only 12 percent of the force when done properly (many don't achieve this). Taping may be useful as a reminder against crimping, but that's about all. Don't let this practice make you overconfident or pretend it will allow you back on the rock faster after injury.

Another common injury among climbers is a tweaked knuckle, which is damage to the collateral ligaments that run on either side of the joint. This usually occurs from sharp sideways pressure on the knuckle, as in overcranking or falling on a finger jam. For minor cases, you can follow the standard therapy and can prevent re-injury by taping the finger to another. If the joint feels very loose, but there isn't much pain, you may have really messed up and need surgery.

Overuse injuries of the fingers are relatively rare but can be especially difficult to treat. Pay attention to pain that begins after you stop climbing; it may be time to switch sports for a while. More frequent is inflammation of the sheath around the wrist tendons, which is indicated by swelling and a creaking feeling that you may even hear. This tenosynovitis may be brought on by lots of ascending fixed lines since most mechanical ascenders place the wrist in a nonergonomic position.

Purposely or accidentally cracking your joints, while obnoxious, increases range of motion but does not appear to cause arthritis. When the joint is manipulated, dissolved gases (about 15 percent of the joint's volume, and made of 80 percent carbon dioxide) are suddenly released from the synovial fluid, causing the noise. While not as bad for you as it sounds, there is a correlation between popping your knuckles and a temporary reduction in grip strength followed by swelling.

Elbows

Nearly all elbow aches among climbers can be traced to overuse and muscle imbalances. With your arm at your side, palm facing forward: if the pain is on the outside (thumb side), then you may have lateral epicondylitis (tennis elbow); pain on the inside may indicate medial epicondylitis (golfer's elbow); and pain in the middle could be anterior epicondylitis (climber's elbow).

In mild cases, the treatment will involve reducing inflammation, if present, and taking time off to heal. Reverse wrist curls with a therapy band may help balance muscles once the swelling is down. If you didn't heed the warnings and allowed the condition to progress, more aggressive therapy will be required. This may consist of ultrasound and painful cross-friction massage, which will *really* make you wish you'd listened to your body (and hate your physical therapist). If this still doesn't help, you may need steroid injections or even surgery.

Shoulders

The shoulders of climbers are at high risk of trauma due to the odd positions and torques we sometimes apply. The shoulder socket (glenoid) of the scapula is very shallow, which gives this complex of joints (it's actually made up of four joints) greater range of motion than any other, with more than 1,600 positions. While large, superficial muscles do most of the work, relatively small, deep muscles—collectively known as the rotator cuff—keep the head of the upper arm bone (humerus) in position.

The rotators are most vulnerable when your arm is raised overhead to the side and rotated forward (thumb down, elbow moving upward); do this now so you know what it feels like. Be especially careful to avoid loading your shoulder in any manner while reaching up and back! Likewise, never do an arm bar with your thumb pointed down: a slip could be disastrous. No move or climb is worth a partial dislocation or full dislocation; the latter can be near the top of the pain scale.

Once you've torn the tendons or ligaments of the shoulder, you are facing a long rehab; several months of no climbing, if you're smart. Assuming the damage wasn't too severe, you'll need to work on strengthening all the muscles of the shoulder region. Should your shoulder go out a second or third time, surgery is probably your best option; doctors have a lot of practice, so the success rate is good.

A common overuse injury among climbers shows up as impingement of tendons (or nerves) that run across the top of the shoulder joint. These tendons run through a tunnel between the clavicle and scapula, and irritation from repeated overhead stress can cause swelling that further aggravates the problem. This may start as minor soreness at the front of the shoulder, especially when the arm is raised, and continue to worsen without adequate rest.

Somewhat less common, but still prevalent (particularly in the over-forty crowd), is damage of the tendon used to raise the arm to the side (supraspinatus tendinosis. Again, these microtraumas are often the result of muscle imbalances, overuse, and improper training so pay attention to yourself. Avoid sleeping with your hand behind your head; the additional shoulder strain can slow recovery.

Back

Many climbers suffer from lower back pain, though this is often more life-related than the result of climbing. By some estimates, over 80 percent of the adult population will experience back pain that interferes with activity; half of those sufferers will experience a flare-up within three years. There are numerous causes, including weak back and abdominal muscles; tight muscles of the upper legs and buttocks; poor posture when sitting or standing; and obesity. All those little stresses add up over time until the proverbial straw breaks the camel's back.

Proper training and stretching can solve the majority of back pains and prevent future episodes. This is a far better option than spinal manipulations that don't solve the underlying problem—a weak core. However, bad lifting technique can result in a stress fracture of the spine (spondylolysis) or ruptured disk.

If you work at a desk, be sure your desk and computer screen are set up at an optimal height and that you have a high-quality chair; sitting on a stability ball is an excellent alternative. For those who spend a lot of time on their feet, pay careful attention to your footwear (good cushioning, no elevated heels). Preventive action is far superior to follow-up care for back injuries.

Climbers should pay attention to their sit harness; the more you weigh, the greater the lumbar support (wide, firm back) it should offer. Many sport harnesses are woefully designed considering that ropes in rock gyms are notoriously worn out and have lost much of their elasticity (though they won't break) and belays are often fairly static—a double whammy for more impact on your spine. Also be sure that your internal frame pack is properly fitted; minor tweaks can make a big improvement.

Legs

Rock climbers seldom suffer from overuse injuries in the legs. However, mountaineers may experience "trekker's knee" from long descents with a heavy pack; use trekking poles to prevent this. If you also cycle or run a lot, beware of a tight ITB (iliotibial band), which can cause knee pains if you don't stretch. Another common complaint is patellofemoral syndrome (chondromalacia), which results from muscle imbalances that prevent the kneecap from tracking properly in its groove. Runners should also watch out for Achilles tendinitis and the more insidious tendinosis, resulting from too many miles and inadequate calf stretching.

Due to extreme contortions, climbers are subject to various traumas. Groin pulls are possible from very wide stemming; this is another injury that can become quite nasty if not allowed to heal. Heel hooking can result in a strain of the hamstrings, often near the back of the knee. The most significant problems come from applying a twisting force while attempting a drop-knee or high rock-over; these positions place a great deal of pressure on the ligaments in their weakest position, when the knee is severely bent.

Women in general have more problems with torn ACLs (anterior cruciate ligaments) in the knees than men; possible reasons include less training, greater angle of the thigh bone (due to wider pelvis), and hormone influences. One large study showed that female alpinists run the same risk of knee injury as downhill skiers and basketball players. No matter your gender, learn to fall safely when skiing. Among the most knee-damaging are slow, backward, twisting falls when the ski tail cannot move; this can even pop an ACL when you're stopped.

Ankles

The main risk to a climber's ankles is landing wrong while bouldering, or swinging into the rock after a fall on lead or top-rope. Crash pads have certainly made bouldering safer, though some of them have cheap foam, which does little to absorb impacts, or gaps to allow folding that can turn an ankle. Always try to land on the balls of your feet so your ankle acts as a crumple zone; heel landings can result in a broken heel bone (calcaneous).

Sprained ankles are fairly common among runners, especially those making the transition from road to trail, but climbers turn their share on talus approaches and descents. Rehab is the same as with other connective tissue injuries. To increase range of movement, write the alphabet with your toes. Once recovered, trail running in proper shoes is among the best strengthening options.

Feet

Climbing ranks with ballet for unkindness to feet. Years of cramming feet into shoes, especially if you start early in life, can lead to significant problems such as bunions (a painful swelling of the first toe joint leading to displacement of the toe) and neuroma (tumorous mass of nerve tissue). Fortunately rock shoes have improved anatomically so an ultratight fit is no longer necessary; indeed it can decrease performance since you lose sensitivity.

Spend the time to shop around for the shoes that best fit *your* feet and ignore the recommendations of anyone else. What some hot-shot climber wears is immaterial unless he or she happens to have a foot shaped identically to yours. Most dedicated climbers have several pairs of rock shoes: snug, sensitive shoes or slippers for sport and gym climbing; stiffer shoes for edging and crack climbing; perhaps a looser all-around shoe for long traditional climbs.

Rock shoes are perfect breeding grounds for all manner of microorganisms that emit vile, toxic odors. Be certain to remove shoes from your pack after a day of climbing so they can dry out. Occasionally sprinkle the insides with foot powder; washing with soap and warm water will help in more extreme cases.

Toenail fungus (onchomycosis) is ugly, highly contagious (about 7 percent of the population has it), and persistent, so it's a good idea to avoid walking barefoot in damp, public areas, such as showers and rock gyms. Prescription drugs are expensive, might not work, and can be harsh. If you have a mild case, you might try painting on tea tree oil or grapefruit seed extract for several months.

Mountaineering boots can be a source of blisters or black toenails if you do not shop carefully. Be sure your heel lifts no more than an eighth-inch inside the boot when you walk and that your toes do not hit the front when you kick a solid object. Generally, boots for high-altitude mountaineering are purchased a full size larger than those for technical alpine or ice climbing; it's a matter of circulation versus precision.

Select high-quality wool-blend socks and wear them during the testing and break-in period; your feet will be happier. Vapor-barrier socks (and inner boots) can result in clammy feet and even trenchfoot unless you are religious about changing liner socks; avoid neoprene socks for mountaineering. Dry your socks and boots at every opportunity on an expedition; some climbers apply antiperspirant to their feet (your tent mate will appreciate it).

Most boots come with chintzy foot beds that offer poor support and break down quickly. Excess foot movement in stiff boots is tiring and can lead to heel spurs (bony lumps). While often unnecessary in softer shoes and boots, custom foot beds can improve comfort and performance because mountaineering boots are often worn for long walks and hours of frontpointing; the custom foot beds also may be helpful in rigid cycling shoes.

If you are also a serious runner, beware of plantar fasciitis, a very painful and difficult-to-treat condition resulting from excessive tightness (or looseness) in the feet. This typically starts as a small pain under the heel when you wake in the morning and becomes progressively worse if you don't heed the warning for rest. A new shock-wave therapy machine offers sufferers potential relief without surgery.

LEARN TO FALL

'Tis a far, far better thing to avoid getting hurt in the first place. The mental training discussed in chapter 2 is an important first step: stay focused. But climbers also need to learn how to fall—something rarely taught.

- Whenever you are leading, top-roping, or bouldering, watch your drop zone. This means constantly being aware of your impact area, whether it's the ground below or a wall that you might vector into because of the rope. While you don't want negative thoughts to interfere with your ascent, somewhere in the back of your mind should be a contingency plan.
- Though you shouldn't give up prematurely, once you're off, completely free yourself from the rock or ice in that instant. Allowing a body part to linger can result in tweaked fingers, torn shoulder or knee joints, or a nasty head injury from being flipped upside down.
- As with a cat in midflight, you must contort your body to anticipate the landing—then go soft in that last split second. Tensing your muscles leads to greater injury, which is why drunks often walk away from car crashes that kill others.
- Those on the ground must stay sharp as well. When belaying a leader on an overhanging route, it's often best to pay out some slack should they come off. If you lock off the rope or try to take in, they will swing violently into the rock instead of dropping straight down.
- Bouldering has become a much safer sport now that the macho era is over and most people are using crash pads. But spotters still play a vital roll of directing the falling climber and protecting the head and neck.
- Wear a helmet; the advantages far outweigh the disadvantages.

COLDS AND FLUS

It's always hard to know when it's safe to play again after suffering through a cold or the flu. First you need to decide which virus you have. If you have a slow onset of sore throat, runny nose, and congestion—but no fever—then it's likely a cold. With the flu, you tend to suddenly get a fever, chills, and body aches but your sinuses and lungs are okay. Neither illness is associated with stomach problems; if you are vomiting or have diarrhea, it's likely something else.

New prescription drugs can shorten the length of the flu if taken soon after the bug bites, although there is no cure. Over-the-counter medications can relieve flu and cold symptoms but nothing has been shown to cure the problem; antibiotics have no effect. Standardized extract of echinacea (250 to 500 mg per day of 5:1 extract) has proven effective for boosting your immune system and shortening the duration of cold- and flu-related blahs. Though echinacea is often combined with goldenseal, so far, no human studies have verified the efficacy of the latter. Zinc lozenges have been shown to help shorten the duration of a cold, but not the flu.

Once you start coming down with a cold or flu, you are contagious for up to four days. Do not go to a gym during this time! You can spread the virus to others who use the same holds or equipment. With the flu, don't try to work out until the fever is completely gone; that will just make the bug linger. Even though you're antsy to get back on the rock, you're better off giving yourself some extra time to recover.

ALTERNATIVE MEDICINE

If your injury hasn't responded well to standard treatment, and surgery has been ruled out, alternative medicine or faith healing—much the same in some cases— may be acceptable choices. Promoters of alternative medicine seldom support their claims with hard evidence. Just because it's "natural" or a thousand years old doesn't mean it's safe or works.

There are certainly good aspects to alternative practices, and traditional medicine doesn't have all the answers. Some procedures used in acupuncture and chiropractics have scientifically proven effective for treatment of specific ailments.

Unfortunately, practitioners are often big on show and light on credibility; the tests some chiropractors use to diagnose maladies belong in a grade school science fair. Don't rely solely on the diagnosis of a chiropractor for a serious problem; go to a medical doctor too. Avoid chiropractors who try to sell routine manipulations or treat anything beyond neuromusculoskeletal problems of mechanical origin. Ideally, they should do all manipulations by hand and be a member of the National Association for Chiropractic Medicine, the only chiro organization grounded in science.

While the advocates may seem sincere and will be quick to deny it, many of the "cures" are likely related to the placebo effect and the patient giving their bodies much-needed rest. Little to no credible evidence supports homeopathy, crystal healing, magnet therapy, healing hands, aromatherapy, applied kinesiology, energy balancing, hair analysis, iridology, phrenology, or reflexology.

If you have the disposable income, alternative medicine in most cases will do no harm and might help if standard medicine has been ineffective. However, serious problems can arise if a patient delays seeking an M.D.'s opinion at the onset of an injury or illness. Even more foolish is the patient who combines standard and alternative medicine without informing caregivers; drug interactions with herbal medicines can be fatal.

AFTER MAJOR INJURY

Broken bones and completely torn ligaments or tendons are a bad deal, no doubt. But in most cases, they don't spell the end of your climbing career—just a long vacation. Consider your experience a lesson in mental fortitude.

When dealing with the medical establishment, understand that most doctors already think that climbers are nuts (or worse), though professionalism prevents them from saying so. Thus you often run into a wall of resistance if you even mention that you still want to hang by your fingernails over oblivion (your doctor's concept of all forms of climbing). While it's important to disclose all vital information relevant to your case, they don't need to know the rest of what you do (same goes for your parents).

After the initial go-round in the emergency room, you will need to consult with a specialist; check with your insurance provider to see who is on their list. If at all possible, seek out a sports medicine doctor, because this specialist will better understand your needs. Since all doctors are not created equal, you might get recommendations from several physical therapists in your area; they see the results of various doctors' handiwork.

The more you know about your condition, the greater the odds of a superior outcome since you can ask the right questions and know your options. Once a diagnosis has been made, and before you commit to the knife (assuming time permits), try to learn all you can, including the precise medical terminology. You can find a wealth of information on the Internet and in libraries; however, be very skeptical and check medical-studies references on MEDLINEplus (*www.medlineplus.gov*).

Even if they seem innocuous, be sure to inform your anesthesiologist before surgery of any medications, herbs, or megadoses of vitamins you are taking. For example, excess vitamin C can cause anesthesia to wear off faster than normal (so a heavier dose is needed and recovery delayed), while vitamin E or ginkgo biloba can interfere with blood clotting.

For broken bones, in many cases full immobilization has thankfully given way to minimal casting, which reduces muscle atrophy. Do yourself a favor and request a waterproof cast or removable splint, even if it costs extra. Although it may seem logical, drinking extra milk or taking calcium supplements will not speed healing.

Following surgery or nonsurgical severe trauma, your best friend—and worst enemy—is the P.T. (a.k.a. physical therapist, physiotherapist, or painful terrorist). He or she is absolutely critical for faster recovery and minimizing aftereffects. While you typically only follow up with your doctor a couple of times, you may visit the P.T. a few times a week for a month or more. Unlike doctors, many P.T.'s do understand the desires of climbers and outdoor athletes and will encourage your goals.

In addition to the therapy, you should start some form of aerobic conditioning as soon as possible. The increased circulation will aid the repairs, and the stress relief will preserve your sanity. With a bit of ingenuity and pluck, you may be able to resistance-train your unaffected limbs as well; consult with your P.T. first. Use your downtime for intellectual and philosophical pursuits you wouldn't have time for when healthy; don't get "TV remote thumb."

CHAPTER 6

Synergy: Coalescing and Planning

If you have read everything up to this point, you should have a good understanding of *what* to do for improving your climbing performance, as well as *where* and *when*. Equally important, you'll know *why* you're doing some things and not others. Now it's time to synthesize this knowledge into a time-efficient plan of action. In other words, here's *how* to do it. Don't forget to have fun!

PUTTING IT ALL TOGETHER

Once you decide to get serious about improving your climbing, you must make some hard decisions. Not the least of which is what you mean by *climbing*. While many tend to think only of difficult rock routes, this is a narrow-minded view of the sport. A skier can choose from many very different aspects of snow sliding, each with its own set of gear: giant slalom, all-mountain, randonée, telemark, backcountry touring,

general touring, light touring, classic track, skate. Our sport is no less diversified—from bouldering at Hueco to summiting Everest—and you need to adjust your training to your goals.

Just as no one in modern times will win a gold medal in both alpine and nordic skiing, no climber can truly excel at all aspects of the sport. So you must decide if you are going to be a specialist or a generalist. And if the latter, whether you want to focus more at one end of the climbing spectrum—from rock to alpine—or can accept being equally mediocre at everything. Of course, those who make climbing their lifestyle (guiding, bumming, etc.) can attain a fairly high level of proficiency at many different things. However, these folks are the minority and everyone else must fit climbing into everyday life.

No matter how dedicated you are to climbing, choose at least two other sports for aerobic cross-play. In fact, the more specialized your interest, the more important these outlets become for recovery and recuperation. The cross-play options in chapter 3 are well-suited to climbers, but if swimming, rowing, or whatever turns you on, then go for it. The key is to embrace the activity: learn proper technique, acquire good equipment, play often.

If you really want to improve, keep track of your progress with a training journal. Without this reference, everything becomes guesswork and it's difficult to pinpoint weaknesses. This can be a full diary entry every day, if you wish, or simply a few benchmarks jotted down in a notebook every couple of weeks.

Whether you are climbing, lifting weights, stretching, or cross-playing, every workout is an opportunity to improve. A half-assed attitude gives half-assed results.

MAKING THE TIME

Yeah, yeah . . . you're busy. So who isn't? After the excuse scrolls are recited, you must say the magic words: "I want to climb better." Problem solved. Passion takes over. Once you commit to the major goal—create a more specific mantra if it helps—the time will appear. Perhaps it means getting up an hour earlier, making your lunch break a workout, or getting to the gym after dinner.

There will be days when you have to drag yourself out the door for a run or a trip to the gym. And if you manage that, you spend the first 10 minutes of the workout asking, "why am I doing this?" But if you repeat the magic words and stick with it, everything gets better. Really.

Ever so rarely, too many other life-pressures intrude and you just can't get psyched—in this case, call it a day. Missing a workout here and there will not ruin your conditioning, and a rest may very well help.

Don't expect overnight miracles! In fact, they should be avoided; they indicate a problem with what you're doing. Sudden dramatic weight loss, such as 10 pounds in a week, is absolutely not sustainable and will come back to haunt you. Similarly, massive strength gains in a short time mean you likely have muscle imbalances and your tendons are relatively weak; overuse injuries are just around the corner.

When you are training smart, significant results take time. Since you have realistic expectations, this doesn't disappoint. Knowing that it may take three or four months for your body to fully adapt to a substantial program change, you take the long view. This is what gets you to the top of major climbs, too. But the ultimate goal is to put young climbers to shame when you're sixty-five, and still be climbing when you're ninety-five.

TRAINING FOR ROCK

If you've decided that your interests lay more toward the rock end of the climbing spectrum, you can adjust your training accordingly. Of course, within the general term *rock climbing* there are subspecialties: sport climbing and bouldering, which are mostly about power; trad, which is about power and endurance; and big wall, which is mostly about endurance—plus the distant relatives, canyoneering and caving. Each of these has its own training requirements, though there may be considerable overlap and they are by no means exclusionary.

For all forms of the sport, the overriding rule is: Climb first, train second. Strength and aerobic conditioning are for naught without technique, which can only be learned by doing. The first corollary is: Climb at as many areas as possible. For the best technique, it is essential to encounter different types of rock and styles of climbing. It's a dirty job, but ya gotta travel and have fun to be a better climber. The second corollary is: Don't train on the sharp end. Training should be a separate activity from leading, with different goals. When you are leading, put all of your mental and physical energy into reaching the top.

So given this Prime Directive, the rest of your conditioning adjusts to forays that are often determined by time of year, climbing partners, and job realities. Plan your training to accomplish major goals and tweak it to hone weaknesses.

This emphasis on climbing must also be tempered by a dose of reality. If you have a good fitness gym that is ten minutes from home while the nearest rock gym or crag is two hours away, then resistance training may need to form the bulk of your weekday workouts. It will be incumbent upon you to train smarter, build a home wall if possible, and get out on real rock at every opportunity. Perhaps you and a few others in the same boat can pool your resources to create a deluxe garage rock gym.

While resistance training is an important part of any program, it is only one component that will vary in significance over the course of a year. Used thoughtfully, not just as a playground, rock gyms can be fantastic training tools. Integrating the two forms of gym training can yield greater results than either alone. Neither, however, prepares you fully for the real world; for example, learning crack or slab technique requires getting outside.

For the best results, isolate areas of weakness and concentrate on improving them. If your arms routinely give out on climbs, determine which aspect of strength suffers most. Then do lat pulls, pull-ups, and other arm exercises at the appropriate intensity. But do not attempt to train your arms on a fingerboard or while bouldering, since quality will suffer. On the other hand, if finger strength is a weakness (which is common), then focus on those exercises without combining arm work.

Endurance

Though climbers often feel they need to get stronger, muscular endurance is frequently their major limiting factor. This aspect of strength is emphasized on trad climbs where you hang on while placing protection (sport climbing is just clip-and-go) and when there are multiple sustained pitches. Big-wall climbing also requires muscular endurance for a day of nailing overhead, hauling the "pig," and jugging fixed lines.

As discussed in chapter 4, training for muscular endurance requires low resistance and high numbers of repetitions. Because endurance training is fairly time consuming, this is best performed by actual climbing, rather than with weights, so that technique also becomes ingrained. The exception is for specific small muscles— shoulder rotators and wrist extensors—that do not get worked by climbing.

Rock gyms are ideal for training endurance because there are often several routes of desired difficulty. Warm up on some fun, easy climbs in preparation for your workout. If possible, select a moderate yet long climb that you can top-rope. With a cooperative belayer, do as many laps as possible—climbing up and down—without stopping for at least 10 minutes.

When downclimbing, use slow, controlled movements and do not drop down onto holds (bad for the joints). Some climbers will climb up, then lower off, and climb again, but this neglects an important skill—retreat—and emphasizes concentric movements to the exclusion of the eccentric. Use big holds on the way down to rest your fingers. If you can stay on your course for over 20 minutes, then either increase the level of difficulty or start wearing a fanny pack with weights.

When endurance training, focus on steady breathing; if necessary, have your belayer remind you not to hold your breath. Long bouldering traverses are an acceptable substitute for enduro-roping if a patient belayer is unavailable. However, other people often get in the way, so you may need to hop off, then find a free section of wall with minimal rest.

Power Endurance

When you go to the rock gym without a plan, chances are most of your time will be spent unsystematically working power endurance, the transition stage that uses both aerobic and anaerobic energy systems. In general, if you can walk up to a route you've never seen and flash up it (an onsight ascent), you will mostly be using low-intensity power endurance. Working a harder route for an eventual no-falls climb (redpoint ascent) calls upon high-intensity power endurance.

Likewise, the power endurance zone is

where many people routinely train at a fitness gym since this is where maximum muscle gain is attained. While this is certainly an important aspect of strength, and a good starting point for a conditioning program, you don't want to spend too much time here either.

If you find that you have trouble with onsighting routes that should be within your capabilities, then you may need to work on your ability to sustain an extended pump (raise your lactate threshold). Since few rock gyms have routes long enough, this means climbing a route near your onsight level, then lowering off and climbing it again without a rest. Overall, you want to spend about 5 to 10 minutes in action before you flame out, so it may take two or three laps. Take a good long rest while belaying your partner, then repeat the pumpfest on a slightly harder route. If there is time, go through the cycle again, but be sure to warm down afterward.

Improving your redpoint ability, if you are falling because of the pump, may require increasing your lactate tolerance. This calls for high-intensity interval workouts lasting 1 to 3 minutes followed by brief rests of about half that duration. Relating this to a climb, it means selecting a pumpy route right at your limit and climbing until you fall. Then lower a few moves, and after a short hang, start climbing again and try to get higher. Should you reach the top, lower and repeat until you've managed 5 to 10 intervals. Needless to say, this is a painful workout and thorough recovery is essential.

Power

Many climbers can do quite well with general fitness and finesse; these may be sufficient for everything you wish to do. But as you progress to more difficult climbs, greater power is required. At the highest levels, technique will only get you so far. Raw strength alone is also insufficient since the ability to generate maximal force has limited practical value. Climbers often need to create the most force early in a move to counteract gravity; this high-speed strength reaches a maximum in the explosive thrust of dynoing for a hold.

Although strength is not the primary goal, you must be strong before you can start to train for power. The number of reps and rest intervals for strength and power are very similar (see the sidebar "Muscle Magic" in chapter 4.) The major difference is that strength sets are performed at maximum resistance so that you can just barely complete the last rep with good form. When training for power, the resistance is significantly decreased, but you are completing each rep as fast as possible. Although you are not drained by the end of power sets, these are very taxing workouts that require thorough rest afterward.

Bouldering is a great way to train power, though you can also use a campus board or system wall. The goal is to link a few very hard moves into a problem that takes 10 to 40 seconds to complete, then do nothing (complete rest) for 3 to 5 minutes before doing another problem. A full power session will involve from 6 to 10 of these intervals, but you should never get a pump;

this is targeting the phosphocreatine system and should not give you that lactate burn.

When fully committing to high-end sport climbing (roughly 5.12c and above, UK 7a) and bouldering (V5 and higher), a major change in training may be required. The shorter and harder the climb, the more power is required. However, muscular endurance training has a negative effect on power (fortunately for everyone else, the converse is not true: power training does not harm endurance). Thus sport climbers have less need for aerobic conditioning but should find some outlet that suits their tastes. Since excess muscle mass below the waist seldom enhances climbing performance on overhanging routes, legs may not need as much resistance training.

TRAINING FOR ALPINE

As with rock, alpine climbing is a generic term that encompasses several subdisciplines, including ice and mixed climbing, technical alpine climbing, general mountaineering, and high-altitude mountaineering. While these are all interrelated, they are distinct enough that you can train for each.

One major difference between preparing for alpine climbing versus rock is you often don't have the luxury of practicing even simulated conditions on a regular basis. Some climbing gyms are starting to install indoor walls made from artificial ice (special sheets of foam formulated to withstand abuse). Dry tooling is also possible on a normal wall using a pair of tools—picks won't damage most holds—and boots without crampons.

Most forms of alpine climbing demand endurance and power endurance, so these should form the bulk of your training. However, as with rock climbing, power plays a greater roll at the highest levels of the sport.

PLANNING YOUR PROGRAM

Some climbers require rigid structure in their life and map out every aspect of their training—the so-called Type A personality. If you desire, there are numerous computer programs available that allow you to create charts and plot data. Several heart rate monitors and programs for PDA devices can even guide you through different workouts and allow you to download the info to your home computer. Be especially cognizant of the need to periodize your training with planned variations on a weekly, monthly, and quarterly basis.

Other climbers are Type B and are much more relaxed about training. You may find charts and schedules abhorrent but still recognize the benefits of a conditioning program. While you may not stick to a set routine, following the basic form of one is better than going about things haphazardly; consider it a plan-less plan. It is helpful to establish benchmarks in performance so you can evaluate the effectiveness of your efforts.

For either personality type, you want to start preparing for the upcoming season well ahead of time. Thus, begin getting ready for rock season in the winter. And thinking about skiing and ice climbing when there are still leaves on the trees.

BASIC PROGRAMS

The following are a selection of training routines that can serve as stepping-stones to greater levels of climbing performance. Don't try to skip ahead too fast or you could be setting yourself up for trouble. You will need to at least complete an intermediate program (the one here or its equivalent) before beginning any of the peaking programs described later in this chapter.

No single routine is appropriate for everybody. These programs are merely guidelines to help you develop your own customized routines. Based upon your self-evaluation, there will be certain weaknesses that need greater emphasis and strengths that may need less effort.

Even after you start in on a routine, it should not be cast in stone: your body isn't. If you stick with the exact same workout for too long, two things are inevitable: a plateau and boredom. In order to make gains, your muscles and nervous system constantly need to be challenged anew. Without variations in motion, intensity, and volume, you will stagnate. Given the countless exercise options—the ones presented here are just the tip of the iceberg—there is little reason to become bored unless you have limited imagination.

Don't just do an exercise because a trainer, friend, article, or book told you it would help. Always ask the question "what does this actually do for me?" If there is no sound physiological reason for the exercise, including specific muscles and energy systems involved, you may be wasting your time or risking injury.

For details on the zones that are mentioned with each of these programs, see the sidebar "Zone Play" in chapter 3.

Approach: Beginning Fitness

If you've become the proverbial couch potato, this is the program to begin your comeback (or new life). Before you can start working toward your major goals, you need to establish a base of fitness. This means strengthening major muscles, stabilizing joints, and reducing body fat. At this stage, climbing is purely for fun and is not part of your training.

Depending on how out-of-shape you are, this program could last from one to six months, maybe more. Don't rush it, particularly if you have a lot of weight to lose. During this time, you are also phasing in better nutrition and adding cross-play to your lifestyle. If you are seriously overweight, have your doctor check your heart health, then emphasize resistance training and low-impact, higher-intensity aerobic fun.

When starting out, you might only resistance train two times per week, cross-play for a half hour three times, and sneak in some stretching. That isn't much—less than six out of 120 waking hours—but it's enough to get your mind and body ready for more. As your fitness improves, and it will, you should try to add one more day of resistance and either add an extra day of cross-play or extend the duration to 45 minutes.

This program includes a full-body resistance routine with plenty of options. If you have a choice of gym exercises, perform one the first day and the other exercise the next. If only one exercise is listed (bench press, calf raise, crunch), try its variations on different days (for instance: incline, normal, and decline bench press). Use free weights most of the time as well as machines for variety.

Don't expect to see major changes: you should lose some fat, but increased muscle mass can balance it out on the scale. However, you should *feel* better and find that simple things, like walking up the stairs, are easier. Perhaps that sore back will be less bothersome or you won't be as tired after a weekend of play.

Crankin' Up: Intermediate Fitness

If you already are in reasonable shape, or are feeling comfortable with the beginning

---

APPROACH: BEGINNING FITNESS
Suggested Program

Climbing: For fun, as you can fit it in.
Stretching: 10 minutes a day, or three 20-minute sessions per week.
Aerobic conditioning: 30 to 45 minutes of cross-play, three times a week, in Zone 1 and 2.
Resistance training: Two or three 45-minute sessions per week of the following exercises:

Exercise	Volume, Intensity	Rest Period
Cycling or Running	5–10 minutes (Zone 2)	
Squat or Leg Press	2 sets, 12–15 reps	1.5 minutes
Calf Raise	1 set, 12–15 reps	
Lat Pull or Pull-up	2 sets, 12–15 reps	1 minute
Bench Press	1 set, 12–15 reps	
Bent-over or Seated Row	2 sets, 12–15 reps	1 minute
Shoulder Press or Rear Delt Row	1 set, 12–15 reps	
Internal Shoulder Rotations	1 set, 12–15 reps	
External Shoulder Rotations	1 set, 12–15 reps	
Crunch	2 sets, 12–15 reps	1 minute
Back Extension	1 set, 12–15 reps	

fitness (Approach) plan, then this program can take you to the next level of climbing performance. The goal here is to significantly strengthen the climbing muscles while continuing to improve the weak links. Because this includes an all-around gym routine tailored for climbers, it also serves as the foundation for those who intend to progress to even higher levels.

This program should take about six to eight weeks, possibly less if you are reasonably fit. Again, don't rush things, since your tendons and ligaments need time to catch up with the muscles. Hopefully by now you are eating healthier and look forward to cross-play. Climbing is still recreational, but you are doing more of it and the grades are getting harder.

Since you are looking to really improve, a greater time commitment is required. This calls for about 60 minutes of resistance training two or three days per week. You are still cross-playing, too, but the sessions are 45 to 60 minutes each and at higher intensity. It's also important to maintain flexibility with at least an hour of stretching per week. Thus you are looking at around 8 hours each week, in addition to climbing.

The resistance training described here is a full-body routine featuring both ascending and multiple sets. Three days a week is preferred for strength gains but missing a day every now and then shouldn't mess up your training, particularly if the reason was climbing or cross-play.

By the time you complete this program, you should be cranking harder climbs and notice significant changes in your body. Not only will you have visibly lost body fat, but your muscles will be more defined. Maybe you aren't quite "ripped" yet but you're getting there. Most people think you're "normal," but would say you're in good shape.

If you can plot out your life for several months, even greater progress can be made with a periodization program in the gym (see the section "Periodization" and the sidebar "Muscle Magic," in chapter 4.) Using the same set of exercises, or variations thereof, you would spend four to six weeks training low-intensity power endurance (15 to 20 reps), the same amount of time doing high-intensity power endurance (8 to 12 reps), and end the cycle with strength and power exercises (4 to 6 reps). The cycle can be repeated following a week of rest. The time spent in each stage will depend upon you and your goals. Consider hiring a coach or personal trainer to get the most out of periodization.

CRANKIN' UP: INTERMEDIATE FITNESS
Suggested Program

Climbing: For fun, as you can fit it in.

Stretching: 10 minutes a day, or three 20-minute sessions per week.

Aerobic conditioning: 45 to 60 minutes of cross-play, two or three times a week, in Zones 2 and 3.

Resistance training: Two or three 60-minute sessions per week of the following exercises:

Exercise	Volume, Intensity	Rest Period
Cycling or Running	5–10 minutes, Zone 2	
Lat Pull or Pull-up	1 set, 15–20 reps 1 set, 8–10 reps 2 sets, 4–6 reps	1 minute 2 minutes 3 minutes
Bench Press or Fly	3 sets, 8–12 reps	1 minute
Bent-over or Seated Row	3 sets, 6–10 reps	1 minute
Shoulder Press or Rear Delt Row	2 sets, 10–12 reps	1 minute
Side Raise	2 sets, 10–12 reps	1 minute
Squat or Leg Press	1 set, 12–15 reps 2 sets, 8–10 reps	1.5 minutes
Static Lunge	3 sets, 10–12 reps	1 minute
Calf Raise	1 set, 8–10 reps	
Crunch	3 sets, 8–12 reps	1 minute
Back Extension	2 sets, 8–12 reps	1 minute
Internal Shoulder Rotations	1 set, 8–12 reps	
External Shoulder Rotations	1 set, 8–12 reps	
Wrist Curl	3 sets, 8–12 reps	1 minute

Weekend Warrior: Intermediate Maintenance

Once you have raised the bar on your fitness, you have the option of holding it there or taking it even higher. After completing the intermediate fitness (Crankin' Up) program you should be fairly pleased with your climbing ability—and your appearance. But all that gym time hasn't improved your technique, and you know there's room to improve. This program will allow you to maintain those gains and prevent imbalances. Equally as important, greater emphasis on climbing-specific training at a rock gym (or home wall) develops the muscles and neural pathways necessary for serious fun on the weekends.

Because this is a maintenance program, it can last more or less indefinitely, though you need to mix it up enough to prevent stagnation. When necessary, you should be able to launch into any of the peaking programs (detailed later in this chapter) to prepare for an upcoming climbing trip. While climbing is your main release, cross-play is also a significant part of life.

The emphasis here is on time efficiency, but you can still make progress on strength.

Warning: this is a demanding full body routine—don't try it until you are ready! If the alternating agonist/antagonist sets are too hard, give yourself more time by alternating upper and lower body exercises. Switch between alternative exercises on different training days.

Ideally, this superset routine should be performed twice a week, but you can hold even with just one day if you are playing often. Cross-play can be reduced to 2 hours a week, but you'll like it so much you may do it more often. Stretching is still important at the end of workouts. So at a minimum, we're talking about 5 hours of focused training each week—plus as much climbing as you can squeeze in.

Although you aren't working for major changes, an active athletic lifestyle results in continued adaptations. After a while, your body reaches its natural set point for body fat (don't even think about going below this), but your endurance continues to increase. By now, co-workers who don't know you well think you're nuts, but are secretly jealous when you return from weekend climbing epics and still have energy.

WEEKEND WARRIOR: INTERMEDIATE MAINTENANCE
Suggested Program

Climbing: Three to four days per week (weekend excursions and a gym session or two).
Stretching: 10 minutes a day, or three 20-minute sessions per week.
Aerobic conditioning: 45 to 60 minutes of cross-play, two or three times a week, in Zone 3.
Resistance training: One or two 45-minute sessions per week of the following exercises:

Exercise	Volume, Intensity	Rest Period
Cycling or Running	5 minutes, Zone 2	
Pull-up or Lat Pull *alternating sets with* Dip or Shoulder Press	3 sets, 6–10 reps 3 sets, 8–12 reps	15 seconds
Seated or Bent-over Row *alternating sets with* Bench Press or Fly	3 sets, 6–10 reps 3 sets, 8–12 reps	15 seconds
Biceps Curl *alternating sets with* Triceps Press	2 sets, 8–12 reps 2 sets, 8–12 reps	15 seconds
Squat or Leg Press *alternating sets with* Calf Raise	3 sets, 6–10 reps 3 sets, 8–12 reps	15 seconds
Quad Extension *alternating sets with* Hamstring Curl	2 sets, 8–12 reps 2 sets, 8–12 reps	15 seconds
Crunch *alternating sets with* Back Extension	3 sets, 8–12 reps 3 sets, 8–12 reps	15 seconds
Wrist Curl or Internal Shoulder Rotation *alternating sets with* Reverse Wrist Curl or External Shoulder Rotation	2 sets, 8–12 reps 2 sets, 8–12 reps	15 seconds

Slammed: The Too-Busy-To-Work-Out Workout

Hey buddy, can you spare 45 minutes? Although you will get the best training effect from resistance-training sessions lasting about an hour, life has a way of getting in the way. Rather than blow off exercise alto-gether—the easy, but wrong, answer—you can maximize efficiency. This bare-essentials routine will get you in and out the gym door in under an hour, including changing clothes and a quick shower. If you have a few more minutes, add a set or two of rows after the inclined bench press.

SLAMMED: THE TOO-BUSY-TO-WORK-OUT WORKOUT
Suggested Program

Climbing: For fun, as you can fit it in.
Stretching: 5 minutes a day, or three 10-minute sessions per week.
Aerobic conditioning: 30 to 45 minutes of cross-play, two or three times a week, in Zone 3.
Resistance training: Two 45-minute sessions per week of the following exercises:

Exercise	Volume, Intensity	Rest Period
Cycling or Running	10 minutes, Zone 2	
Pull-up or Lat Pull	2 sets, 6–10 reps	45 seconds
Inclined Bench Press	1 set, 8–10 reps	
Squat	2 sets, 6–10 reps	45 seconds
Crunch	2 sets, 8–12 reps	15 seconds
Cycling or Running	5 minutes, Zone 2	

Hard Rock: Injury Prevention

During the height of the season, especially when the weather is good, few climbers are interested in working out in a gym of any type. While you may not be a fan of lifting weights, you're probably even less excited about getting sidelined by an injury.

This short routine can be done at home, or on a road trip, with a few dumbbells. These exercises also maybe performed with a set of therapy bands (elastic tubing with handles), which are compact to carry. The tubing comes in different flexes so you can vary the resistance.

Even during a climbing vacation, you need to take rest days occasionally. Use a fraction of this time to do a little preventive maintenance. Incorporate some cross-play and stretching into your rest days as well. Your body will thank you.

HARD ROCK: INJURY PREVENTION
Suggested Program

Climbing: 4 or 5 days per week.
Stretching: 10 minutes a day, or three 20-minute sessions per week.
Aerobic conditioning: 45 to 60 minutes of cross-play, two times a week.
Resistance training: Two 45-minute sessions per week of the following exercises:

Exercise	Volume, Intensity	Rest Period
Cycling or Running	3 minutes, Zone 2	
Squats	2 sets, 8–10 reps	2 minute
Bench Press	2 sets, 8–10 reps	1 minute
Shoulder Press	2 sets, 12–15 reps	1 minute
Internal Shoulder Rotations	2 sets, 12–15 reps	1 minute
External Shoulder Rotations	2 sets, 12–15 reps	1 minute
Reverse Wrist Curl	2 sets, 8–12 reps	1 minute
Crunch	2 sets, 8–12 reps	15 seconds

Fun Hog: Advanced Fitness

Admit it, you have a problem: being in pretty good shape isn't good enough. You know that the harder you train, the harder you can play. This means you aren't content with the routes for the masses but are looking to put up your own climbs or establish new records (faster times, longer linkups, higher fun quotient).

Since you are committed (or committable), then you are willing to put in the time and effort it takes for four to six weeks to get maximum results. At this level of fitness, individual goals will determine the specifics of your training program. But you should also know enough about your body that you can decide what areas need improvement.

This routine assumes that much of your endurance training comes from climbing and cross-play. By splitting resistance workouts into two days, your body has more time to recover. The amount of cross-play will range from a great deal for an alpinist to very little for a sport climber. With this much activity, rest days are critical and stretching should be an integral part of your workouts. Including climbing, you may well be putting in 20 or more hours each week.

With this routine, you may see little change in your body. But you should find that you have more energy in reserve on harder climbs and can pull through more difficult moves. Nonclimbing friends wonder aloud what drives you, and when you'll grow up.

FUN HOG: ADVANCED FITNESS
Suggested Program

Climbing: Possibly four or five days per week.
Stretching: 10 minutes a day or a few longer sessions of stretching or yoga.
Aerobic conditioning: 45 to 60 minutes of cross-play, three or four times a week, in Zone 3 and 4 (with some Zone 5 intervals); longer sessions (over 90 minutes) once a week.
Resistance training: Two 60-minute sessions per week:

Day 1 (Torso)

Exercise	Volume, Intensity	Rest Period
Cycling or Running	5–10 minutes, Zone 2	
Lat Pull or Pull-up	1 set, 15–20 reps 3 sets, 4–8 reps	1 minute 3 minutes
Bench Press or Fly	2 sets, 8–12 reps	1 minute

Exercise	Volume, Intensity	Rest Period
Bent-over or Seated Row	3 sets, 6–10 reps	1 minute
Shoulder Press or Rear Delt Row	3 sets, 10–12 reps	1 minute
Straight-arm Pull-down	2 sets, 8–12 reps	1 minute
Side Raise	2 sets, 10–12 reps	1 minute
Internal Shoulder Rotations	2 sets, 8–12 reps	30 seconds
External Shoulder Rotations	2 sets, 8–12 reps	30 seconds
Back Extension	3 sets, 8–12 reps	1 minute
Crunch	3 sets, 8–12 reps	1 minute

Day 2 (Arms and Legs)

Exercise	Volume, Intensity	Rest Period
Cycling or Running	5–10 minutes, Zone 2	
Squat or Leg Press	1 set, 12–15 reps 3 sets, 4–8 reps	1 minute 3 minutes
Quad Extension	3 sets, 8–12 reps	1 minute
Hamstring Curl	3 sets, 8–12 reps	1 minute
Calf Raise	3 sets, 8–10 reps	1 minute
Biceps Curl	3 sets, 6–10 reps	1 minute
Triceps Press	3 sets, 6–10 reps	1 minute
Wrist Curl	3 sets, 6–10 reps	1 minute
Reverse Wrist Curl	3 sets, 8–12 reps	15 seconds
Reverse Crunch	3 sets, 8–12 reps	1 minute
Twist Crunch or Side Raise	3 sets, 8–12 reps	1 minute

PEAKING FOR GOALS

Climbers are twisted. Instead of spending our vacation time relaxing on a warm beach drinking mai tais, we go and punish ourselves on crags and mountains. Of course, those cold drinks do taste better after a good round of suffering. But we all enjoy our climbing vacations more when our mind and body perform at optimal levels.

If you have adopted a healthy athletic lifestyle, peaking for an upcoming goal is usually just a matter of tweaking and intensifying your current regimen. Here are a half dozen programs—out of an infinite realm of possibilities—that can help maximize your performance.

Important note: The following plans all assume a solid base of fitness and therefore start at a moderately high level of intensity. Do *not* jump into these training schedules until week 1 is something you can do comfortably. Thus, if you aren't in great shape but decide to make an attempt on Denali, it's going to take at least six months of serious training instead of the four outlined here. Be careful not to hurt yourself before the big trip; back off the training if necessary.

The tables that follow give suggested training activities for each day of a program that lasts anywhere from two months (for rock climbing) to four months (for a high-mountain expedition). Here's what is meant by the abbreviations used in the tables:

ST = Strength training: 1–1.5 hours of resistance exercises in the gym.

FH = Finger hangs: 10–15 minutes of focused training.

CE = Climb endurance: 1–4 hours on long, easy routes, preferably outdoors; this could be termed "active rest."

CS = Climb strength: 1–1.5 hours of power endurance or power.

AB = Aerobic base: cross-play in Zone 2 (about 70 percent–80 percent MHR).

LT = Endurance or Lactate Threshold intervals/fartleks: Either 4–5 intervals of 8- to 15-minute bouts at moderate intensity followed by 5 minutes of cool down, or 5–6 intervals of 2- to 8-minute bouts at high intensity followed by 4–6 minutes of cool-down.

S/L = Sprint or Lactate Tolerance intervals/fartleks: Either 5–20 intervals of 10- to 30-second full-intensity bursts followed by 3–5 minutes of complete rest, or 5–10 intervals of 1- to 3-minute bouts at near maximum intensity followed by 1 minute of cool-down.

Rock Climbing: Two Months

When heading off for a week or more of trad or sport climbing, you want to arrive at your destination prepared for the type of climbing that you'll encounter. Obviously the pocketed limestone crags of southern France and Thailand have different demands than Indian Creek cracks or Joshua Tree face climbs. Tuning your body and climbing technique ahead of time can maximize your fun.

At home, it's likely that you seldom get more than two full days of climbing in a row. If this is the case, it's unrealistic to expect your body to suddenly be able to climb day after day without falling apart. This program aims to get you in a rock gym as often as possible prior to your trip. There are more days of intense training in a row than you may be used to: when it's time to rest, make it good.

This schedule should help trad climbers prepare for a serious climbing vacation. If you will mostly sport climb, your training will necessitate more power endurance and power training while backing off on—but not eliminating—endurance and aerobic training.

ROCK CLIMBING: TWO MONTHS							
	M	**Tu**	**W**	**Th**	**F**	**Sa**	**Su**
Week 1 Base	CE	0.5 hr AB, ST	CS	0.5 hr AB, ST	off	CE	0.75 hr AB, CS
Week 2 Intensity	off	0.5 hr AB, ST, FH	CS	0.75 hr AB, ST, FH	CE	CS	0.75 hr LT, CE
Week 3 Intensity	off	0.5 hr AB, ST, FH	CE	0.75 hr AB, ST, FH	CE	CS	1 hr AB, CE
Week 4 Intensity	off	0.75 hr AB, ST, FH	CS	0.75 hr LT, ST, FH	CE	CS	1 hr AB, CE
Week 5 Intensity	CE	0.75 hr AB, ST, FH	CE	0.75 hr AB, ST	CS	off	1.25 hr LT, CS
Week 6 Peak	CE	0.75 hr AB, ST	CS	0.75 hr AB	CS	CE	1.25 hr AB, CS
Week 7 Peak	off	0.75 hr AB, ST	CS	0.5 hr LT, CE	CS	CE	CS
Week 8 Taper	off	0.75 hr AB, ST	CS	0.5 hr AB, CE	off	CE	off

Big Wall Climbing: Two Months

Whether adventuring to Yosemite, Greenland, or the Baltoro, the big stone requires significant preparation and a mountain of gear. While demanding overall, climbing a big wall requires good endurance, particularly when leading in blocks (multiple pitches in a row instead of alternating each time).

Upper-body and core strength are certainly important. If you anticipate a lot of nailing or hand drilling, be sure to include shoulder presses, triceps extensions, and wrist curls. Prepare for lots of jumaring with reverse wrist curls. Your legs had better be ready too; humping haul bags to and from a climb can be serious work.

BIG WALL CLIMBING: TWO MONTHS							
	M	**Tu**	**W**	**Th**	**F**	**Sa**	**Su**
Week 1 Base	ST	0.5 hr AB, CS	ST	0.5 hr AB, CS	ST	CE	0.75 hr AB
Week 2 Intensity	ST	0.5 hr LT, CE	ST	0.75 hr AB, CS	ST	off	0.75 hr LT, CE
Week 3 Intensity	ST	0.5 hr AB, CS	ST	0.75 hr AB, CS	ST	CE	1 hr AB
Week 4 Intensity	ST	0.75 hr AB, CE	ST	0.75 hr LT, CE	ST	CS	1 hr AB
Week 5 Intensity	off	0.75 hr LT, ST	CS	0.75 hr AB, ST	CE	CS	1.25 hr AB, CE
Week 6 Peak	off	0.75 hr LT, ST	CS	0.75 hr AB, ST	CE	CS	1.25 hr AB, CE
Week 7 Peak	off	0.75 hr AB, ST	CS	0.75 hr LT, ST	CS	off	1.5 hr AB, CE
Week 8 Taper	CE	0.75 hr AB, ST	CS	0.75 hr LT	off	CE	off

Ice Climbing: Two Months

Modern ice tools and crampons have certainly made this sport easier, and high-tech clothing has made it less miserable. But the newfangled gear just means we can all push our personal limits a bit further. During a trip to playgrounds like Ouray, Valdez, and Banff, multiple days of ice climbing can fry your forearms and calves, work the rest of your body, and leave your face bloodied.

Preparation for ice season involves total body conditioning with an emphasis on endurance. Those interested in high-end, mixed climbing will train for greater power.

When possible, perform the climbing endurance and climbing strength sessions while dry-tooling and wearing your climbing boots. Resistance training should include a significant amount of shoulder presses, triceps extensions, wrist curls, and calf raises. To really get specific, attach a 1-inch-thick rope to the lat pull machine and do one-handed pulls with a few extra seconds (2 to 20) of contraction at the bottom to simulate a lock-off.

ICE CLIMBING: TWO MONTHS							
	M	**Tu**	**W**	**Th**	**F**	**Sa**	**Su**
Week 1 Base	CE	0.5 hr AB, ST	CS	0.5 hr AB, ST	off	CE	0.75 hr AB, CE
Week 2 Intensity	CS	0.5 hr AB, ST	off	0.75 hr AB, ST	CE	CS	0.75 hr LT, CE
Week 3 Intensity	off	0.5 hr AB, ST	CE	0.75 hr AB, ST	CE	CS	1 hr AB, CE
Week 4 Intensity	off	0.75 hr AB, ST	CS	0.75 hr LT, ST	CE	CS	1 hr AB, CE
Week 5 Intensity	CE	0.75 hr AB, ST	CE	0.75 hr AB, ST	CS	off	1.25 hr LT, CS
Week 6 Peak	CE	0.75 hr AB, ST	CS	0.75 hr AB	CS	CE	1.5 hr AB, CS
Week 7 Peak	off	0.75 hr AB, ST	CS	0.75 hr LT, CE	CS	CE	1 hr AB, CS
Week 8 Taper	off	0.75	CS	0.75 hr AB, CE	off	CE	off

Ski Mountaineering: Two Months

Leaving the piste behind for a week or more gets you into some fantastic ski country. Whether hut touring the Haute Route (Argentière to Saas Fee) or crossing the Columbia Icefield, you will encounter significant vertical gain and descent while wearing a moderate to heavy pack. Light, fluffy powder is the exception rather than the norm. Expect heavy crud, breakable crust, bottomless depth hoar, and frozen sastrugi.

Good aerobic conditioning is vital to your happiness—inline skating is great preparation. This is certainly quad-burning skiing, so place a heavy emphasis on squats and static lunges to strengthen the muscles and knee joints. But you still need significant upper-body and core strength for poling uphill and extricating yourself after a fall; lat pulls, dips, and crunches now will reward you later.

If you have snow, try to go skiing on your "off" days. If you have great snow, ski all weekend!

SKI MOUNTAINEERING: TWO MONTHS							
	M	**Tu**	**W**	**Th**	**F**	**Sa**	**Su**
Week 1 Base	ST	0.75 hr AB	ST	0.75 hr AB	ST	off	1 hr AB
Week 2 Intensity	ST	0.75 hr LT	ST	0.75 hr AB	ST	off	1.5 hr AB
Week 3 Intensity	ST	1 hr LT, CS	ST	1 hr AB	ST	off	1.5 hr AB
Week 4 Intensity	off	ST	1.25 hr AB	ST	1 hr LT	off	2 hr AB
Week 5 Intensity	off	ST	1 hr LT	ST	1 hr S/L	off	2 hr AB
Week 6 Peak	1 hr AB	ST	1.25 hr LT	ST	1.25 hr S/L	off	2.5 hr AB
Week 7 Peak	1 hr AB	ST	1.25 hr AB	ST	1.25 hr LT	off	2 hr AB
Week 8 Taper	off	ST	1 hr AB	off	0.75 hr LT	off	off

Alpine Climbing: Three Months

For the ultimate form of climbing—nothing else is as demanding of technique, endurance, mental power, and physical strength—your body should be tuned to its highest potential. Whether going to the Tetons, the Alaska Range, Chamonix, or Peru, you will be using everything you've got—and sometimes more.

The problem (and part of the attraction) with remote wilderness climbing areas such as the Wind Rivers or Bugaboos is you have to get there with all of your stuff—and the gear required for 15-pitch climbs isn't light.

ALPINE CLIMBING: THREE MONTHS							
	M	**Tu**	**W**	**Th**	**F**	**Sa**	**Su**
Week 1 Base	1 hr AB, CS	ST	off	ST	1 hr AB, CS	CE	2 hr AB
Week 2 Intensity	ST	1 hr LT	ST	1.25 hr AB, CS	ST	off	3.5 hr AB
Week 3 Intensity	ST	1.25 hr LT, CS	ST	1.25 hr AB, CS	ST	CE	4.5 hr AB
Week 4 Intensity	off	ST	1.25 hr AB, CS	ST	1.25 hr LT	CE	3.5 hr AB
Week 5 Intensity	.75 hr AB, CS	ST	1 hr LT, CS	ST	1 hr AB	CE	3 hr AB
Week 6 Intensity	.75 hr AB, CS	ST	1.25 hr LT, CS	ST	1.25 hr LT	off	3.5 hr AB
Week 7 Intensity	.75 hr S/L	ST	1.25 hr AB, CS	ST	1.25 hr LT	CE	4.0 hr AB
Week 8 Peak	off	1 hr S/L, CS	ST	1.25 hr LT, CS	ST	CE	4.0 hr AB
Week 9 Peak	1 hr S/L	ST	1.25 hr AB, CS	ST	1.25 hr LT, CS	off	4.5 hr AB
Week 10 Peak	1 hr AB, CS	1 hr S/L	1 hr AB, ST	1 hr LT, CS	1 hr AB	off	4 hr AB
Week 11 Peak	ST	1 hr S/L	ST	1.25 hr LT, CS	1 hr AB	CE	3.5 hr AB
Week 12 Taper	1 hr AB	ST	1.25 hr AB, CS	ST	1.25 hr LT	off	1.5 hr AB

Porters aren't an option, and horse and llama packers don't come cheap. Which leaves you and your partners with big, heavy packs.

In addition to a fair amount of climbing and resistance training, this plan calls for a lot of aerobic conditioning. The long days should be a low-impact activity—power hiking, road biking, ski touring, snowshoeing—and include hills if you have them.

It takes a demanding training program to prepare for a demanding sport. In the alpine world, you need to be ready for anything and must perform at a high standard, sometimes for days on end. As Mark Twight puts it, your goal is "to make yourself as indestructible as possible."

High Mountain Expedition: Four Months

The lack of oxygen turns the big peaks—Denali, Aconcagua, the eight-thousanders—into a struggle against time. Most climbers have a very limited window of opportunity when logistics, weather, and health all come together for a summit bid. Although the climbing usually isn't very technical, it is always physically demanding and often very exposed.

Obviously, aerobic and muscular endurance are essential for high-altitude climbing. But you also want big, strong muscles when you head in, partly because physical strength is useful up there and partly because your muscles may wither.

For this type of climbing, you must be prepared to work hard day after day when the weather is good. Since summit snow slopes seem to last forever, it takes mental stamina to tough them out. Those long, sweaty hours of training will reward you at the top—even more so when you make it down in one piece.

HIGH MOUNTAIN EXPEDITION: FOUR MONTHS							
	M	**Tu**	**W**	**Th**	**F**	**Sa**	**Su**
Week 1 Base	1 hr AB	ST	1 hr AB	ST	off	CE	2 hr AB
Week 2 Base	ST	1 hr LT	ST	1.25 hr AB	ST	CE	2 hr AB
Week 3 Base	ST	1.25 hr LT	ST	1 hr AB, CE	ST	CE	2.5 hr AB
Week 4 Base	off	ST	1.25 hr AB	ST	1.25 hr LT	CE	2.5 hr AB
Week 5 Intensity	off	ST	1 hr LT, CE	ST	1 hr AB	off	3 hr AB
Week 6 Intensity	CE	ST	1 hr LT, CE	ST	1.25 hr LT	off	3 hr AB
Week 7 Intensity	1hr AB	ST	.75 hr S/L, CE	ST	1.25 hr LT	CE	3.5 hr AB
Week 8 Intensity	off	1.25 hr AB, CS	ST	1.25 hr LT, CE	ST	off	3.5 hr AB
Week 9 Intensity	1 hr AB	ST	1 hr S/L, CE	ST	1.25 hr LT	off	4 hr AB
Week 10 Intensity	CE	1 hr S/L	1 hr AB, ST	1 hr LT	1 hr AB, ST	off	4.5 hr AB
Week 11 Intensity	1 hr AB, ST	1 hr S/L	ST	1.25 hr LT	1 hr AB, ST	off	4 hr AB
Week 12 Intensity	ST	1 hr S/L	ST	1.25 hr LT	ST	off	4 hr AB
Week 13 Peak	ST	1 hr S/L	ST	1.25 hr AB	1.25 hr LT, ST	off	3.5 hr AB
Week 14 Peak	1 hr S/L	ST	1.25 hr AB	ST	1.25 hr LT	CE	3 hr AB
Week 15 Taper	1 hr S/L	ST	1.25 hr AB, CE	ST	1.25 hr LT	off	2 hr AB
Week 16 Taper	1 hr AB	ST	off	ST	1.25 hr LT	off	1.5 hr AB

217

Appendix A: Dining Out

When you dine out, especially if you're traveling, it's harder to control your diet. If you normally enjoy a healthful diet, there are no forbidden foods for the climber in training—just fewer indulgences. And keep exercising while you travel.

TRADITIONAL

Better: grilled, baked, or broiled fish; barbecued or grilled chicken sans skin; turkey; lean steak (filet mignon or sirloin); roast beef or tri tip; lean hamburger; gardenburger; soups sans cream; whole grain bread sans butter; salad bars (careful with the dressing and toppings); baked or mashed potato; baked sweet potato; roasted garlic; rice; steamed veggies; sherbet; angel food cake with fruit.

Worse: fried anything; most toppings on baked potatoes; pot pies; fatty steaks (New York strip, porterhouse, T-bone); grilled cheese or Philadelphia sandwich; Caesar salad; creamy salad dressings; buffalo wings; potato skins; ice cream; crème brûlée; cheesecake, mousse.

FAST FOOD

Better: submarine with lean meat; thick-crust veggie pizza (request half the cheese); soft taco; broiled or grilled chicken (remove skin); chicken burrito; roast beef sandwich; chili and crackers; single broiled or grilled burger; baked potato sans topping; pancakes, bagel, breakfast burrito; low-fat milk shake.

Worse: supersize meals; french fries or onion rings; extra hamburger patties; bacon cheeseburger; fried chicken; fish sand-wiches; special sauce and mayo; sodas; milk shake; granola; kids' cereals; break-fast biscuit; hash browns; muffins; Danish pastries; donuts.

CHINESE

Better: stir fries; chow meins; chop sueys; moo goo gai pan; Mongolian beef; black bean and garlic sauce; hot and sour or wonton soup; spring rolls; steamed rice (order extra); steamed dumplings; fortune cookie (just one for good luck).

Worse: fried rice; crispy or batter-coated dishes; egg rolls; fried wonton; lo mein; pork ribs; duck; sweet and sour dishes; kung pao dishes; cashew, lemon, or sesame chicken (okay if not fried); orange beef; General Tso's chicken; lobster sauce; MSG.

MEDITERRANEAN

Better: gyros; cucumber salad; baba ganoush; tabouli; humus; olive bread.

Worse: feta cheese; spanikopita; falafel; baklava.

INDIAN

Better: tandori chicken; shish kebabs; curries sans coconut milk; biriyani; tikka and vindaloo dishes; chapatti, naam, and roti breads; steamed rice; mulligatawny and dhal soups; low-fat lassi (yogurt drink).

Worse: pakori, samosas; paratha; poori; palak and saag paneer; dishes with makkhani (butter) or malai (cream).

ITALIAN

Better: pasta with red, primavera, or clam sauce; thick-crust veggie pizza; chicken cacciatore; minestrone; bread sans butter.

Worse: calamari; antipasto; garlic bread; bread dips; alfredo or pesto sauce; cannelloni, lasagna, ravioli, and tortellini; parmagiana dishes; pepperoni or sausage pizza; parmesan topping.

JAPANESE

Better: sushi and sashimi (from a reliable source); edamame; sunomono (cucumber salad); tofu dishes; soba noodles; ramen; sukiyaki; yakitori; green tea.

Worse: tonkatsu (fried pork); tempura; agemono; smoked fish.

MEXICAN

Better: grilled fish and chicken; rice and bean burritos; tostadas; soft tacos; fajitas; tamales and enchiladas sans cheese; salsa and baked chips; gazpacho and bean soups; ceviche; black or red beans; refried beans sans lard; Spanish rice.

Worse: fried chips; nachos; guacamole; sour cream; normal refried beans (with lard); mole; chimichangas; chili relleno; hard tacos; quesadilla; flautas; fried ice cream.

THAI

Better: tom yum soups; pad thai; Thai salads (many have meat or seafood); steamed rice; curries sans coconut milk; gratium (garlic pepper) sauce.

Worse: tom kha gai (coconut chicken soup); satay with peanut sauce; mee krob; gang, massamon, and panang curry (lots of coconut milk); Thai iced tea.

Appendix B: Glycemic Index

The glycemic index is a rating system developed for people with diabetes to approximate how fast sugars enter the bloodstream: 0 to 60 is low and slow, 60 to 85 is moderate, 85 to 100 is high and fast. If you are not sugar-sensitive, the main value of this chart is for planning meals and snacks before, during, and after exercise. See Chapter 1, page 31 for more information.

Beans

Soy beans 18
Kidney beans 27
Lentils 29
Black beans 30
Split peas, yellow 32
Lima beans.. 32
Garbanzo beans (chickpeas) 33
Navy beans 38
Pinto beans 39
Black-eyed peas 41

Breads and Cakes

Sponge cake 46
Banana bread 47
Oat bran bread 48

Mixed grain bread 48
Pumpernickel 50
Pound cake.. 54
Pita bread, white 57
Muffin, bran 60
Hamburger bun 61
Rye bread 64
Angel food cake 67
Croissant 67
Wheat bread, whole grain 69
Crumpet 69
Wheat bread, white 70
Bagel, white 72
Kaiser roll.. 73
Donut 76
Waffles... 76

French baguette 95

Cereals

Rice Bran 19
All-Bran 42
Special K 54
Oat Bran 55
Honey Smacks 55
Muesli 56
Bran Chex 58
Just Right 59
Oatmeal 61
Life 66
Nutri-Grain 66
Grape-Nuts 67
Shredded Wheat 69
Cream of Wheat 70
Golden Grahams 71
Puffed Wheat 74
Cheerios 74
Corn Bran 75
Total 76
Coco Pops 77
Corn Flakes 77
Rice Krispies 82
Corn Chex 83
Crispix 87
Rice Chex 89

Dairy

Yogurt, low fat, artificially sweetened 14
Milk, full fat 27
Milk, skim 32
Yogurt, low fat, fruit sweetened 33
Milk, chocolate 34
Ice cream, low fat 50
Ice cream 61

Drinks

Soy milk 30
Apple juice 41
Orange juice 57
Soft drink 68
Gatorade 91

Fruits

Cherries 22
Grapefruit 25
Apricots, dried 31
Apple 36
Pear 36
Plum 39
Peach 42
Orange 44
Pineapple juice 46
Grapes 52
Kiwi fruit 53
Banana, ripe 54
Fruit cocktail 55
Apricot 57
Raisins 64
Cantaloupe 65
Pineapple 66
Watermelon 72

Grains

Rye 34
Bulgur 48
Sweet corn 55
Rice, brown 55
Rice, white 58
Couscous 65
Taco shells 68
Cornmeal 68
Rice, instant 91

Pasta

Spaghetti, protein enriched	27
Fettuccine	32
Spaghetti, whole wheat	37
Ravioli, durum, meat filled	39
Macaroni	45
Linguine	46
Instant noodles	47
Tortellini, cheese	50
Spaghetti, durum	55
Macaroni and cheese	64
Rice pasta	92

Snacks

Peanuts	14
Peanut M&Ms	32
Nutella spread	32
PowerBar	35
Snickers	40
Twix	43
Jams and marmalades	49
Chocolate	49
Potato chips	54
Oatmeal cookies	55
Popcorn	55
Clif Bar	58
Mars bar	64
Shortbread	64
Stoned Wheat Thins	67
Skittles	69
Life Savers	70
Corn chips	73
Graham crackers	74
Vanilla wafers	77
Jelly beans	80

Pretzels	81
Rice cakes	82
Dates	103
Tofu frozen dessert	115

Soups

Tomato soup	38
Lentil soup	44
Split pea soup	60
Black bean soup	64
Green pea soup	66

Vegetables

Green peas	48
Yam	51
Sweet potato	54
Sweet corn	55
Potato, white	60
Beets	64
Carrots	71
Potato, mashed	73
French fries	75
Pumpkin	75
Potato, instant	83
Potato, baked	85

Sugars

Fructose	23
Lactose	46
High fructose corn syrup	62
Sucrose (table sugar)	65
Honey	73
Glucose	100
Maltodextrin	105

Appendix C: Glossary

abduction. The movement of a limb away from your body, such as raising your arm or leg straight off to the side.

adduction. The movement of a limb toward your body, such as lowering your arm or leg back to the side.

aerobic capacity. See *VO₂max*.

aerobic exercise. Anything that elevates the heart rate to over 50 percent of the maximum heart rate without exceeding the anaerobic threshold.

aerobic metabolism. Chemical pathways in muscle cells that consume oxygen to produce energy.

agonist. The muscle (or group) that moves a limb, such as the biceps that contract to flex the elbow. See *antagonist*.

anabolic. The building of larger molecules and body tissues. Medium-intensity resistance training tends to be anabolic, so muscles get bigger.

anaerobic metabolism. Chemical pathways in muscle cells that do not consume oxygen to produce energy and lactic acid.

anaerobic threshold. The point during exercise where demand for energy cannot be met by aerobic metabolism alone. See *lactate threshold*.

antagonist. The muscle (or group) that opposes the prime mover, such as the triceps that slows the flex of the elbow. See *agonist*.

antioxidant. Enzymes that remove free radicals from within cells. Supplementing your diet with antioxidants may be beneficial to health, but the evidence is not as strong as many people believe. See *free radicals*.

ATP (adenosine triphosphate). A phosphate molecule that is the ultimate source of energy to make muscles move. When a phosphate is released, energy is produced that contracts the filaments in a muscle fiber. The resulting molecule,

ADP, must be restored by aerobic or anaerobic processes before it may be re-used for energy.

bioavailability. The ability of a food to be utilized by the body. When you consume a food or supplement, the body digests a portion and the rest is excreted. Higher bioavailablity means greater absorption and utilization. However, different tests can change the ranking of products, so the term is often abused by marketers.

calorie. For biological systems, energy is measured by the amount of heat a reaction produces. A nutritional calorie is the amount of heat energy it takes to raise 1 kilogram of water by 1°C at 15°C.

capillarity. The ratio of the smallest blood vessels (capillaries) to muscle fiber. The capillaries are vital for providing oxygen and removing wastes to and from muscle fibers. With endurance training, the capillarity increases.

carbohydrate. A major source of energy for animals, these are organic compounds made of carbon, hydrogen, and oxygen in a 1:2:1 ratio. Sugars and starches are carbohydrates that are the body's most readily accessible form of energy; each gram of carbohydrate provides 4 calories.

catabolic. The breakdown of big things into little things, such as proteins into amino acids, often with a release of energy. High amounts of endurance training tend to be catabolic to muscles—making them wither.

closed chain. A movement where the last segment in a kinetic chain is fixed; for example, the squat is a closed chain exercise because the feet are immobile. Generally considered more functional exercises that promote joint stability. See *open chain* and *kinetic chain.*

compound movement. A movement that involves bending two or more joints, such as a pull-up (elbows and shoulder).

Compound exercises are considered very functional because muscles work in coordination. See *simple movement.*

concentric. A movement that shortens the muscle(s), such as flexing the biceps. Also called the positive phase. See *eccentric.*

distal. The part of a limb that is farthest from the heart. See *proximal.*

DOMS (delayed onset muscle soreness). Pain that sets in two or three days after a workout. Although eccentric movement tends to increase DOMS, the mechanism is still under investigation. It is generally harmless (unless pain persists) and is not a requirement for strength gains nor is it a gauge of effectiveness. See *eccentric.*

eccentric. A movement that lengthens the muscle(s). Also called the negative phase. See *concentric.*

ergogenic. Used in reference to a supplement that is said to increase performance. Some work, most don't.

extension. Usually the movement of bones farther apart, such as straightening a bent elbow or knee. However, raising your arm straight behind you is also considered shoulder extension. See *flexion.*

fartlek. A Swedish word for speed-play. It basically means to throw occasional bursts of hard effort into your aerobic workouts and have fun.

fat. The most dense form of energy and the slowest to digest. Unsaturated vegetable fats (fewer hydrogen bonds) are generally regarded as the healthiest, while saturated animal fats are less healthy. Eating too much fat does not make you fat; eating too many calories does; each gram contains 9 calories.

flexion. Generally means bringing bones together, such as upper and lower arms or legs. However, raising your arm straight in front of you is also considered shoulder flexion. See *extension.*

free radical. A molecule containing oxygen and an unpaired electron that makes it highly reactive. Free radicals can cause oxidative damage to cells but proper training and nutrition mollify the effects. Reactive oxygen species (ROS, the technical term) are not inherently evil; they are only bad for you in excess quantities.

frontpointing. Climbing steep snow or ice by kicking the crampons straight in and standing on the front three or four points. Even with rigid mountaineering boots, this can be very tiring on the calves.

glycogen. This is the form of carbohydrate that your body stores in your muscles and liver for fast energy. This power source can quickly be converted to glucose, but the supply is limited to around 100 minutes.

hypertrophy. To grow larger; commonly describes an increase in muscle size.

hypoxia. Reduced oxygen content of the air, generally from increased altitude.

isokinetic. A contraction that occurs at a constant velocity while the resistance varies. Hyper-expensive hydraulic isokinetic machines are often found in physical therapy offices but are rare in gyms.

isometric. A static contraction of the muscle (neither shortens nor lengthens), such as a lock-off when climbing. Strength gains tend to be very localized and specific to the angle of force.

isotonic. The term means "same tension," but it's often misapplied as a reference to free weights. Although the weight of a dumbbell is constant, the resistance a muscle feels varies considerably within the range of movement. (A more accurate description of free-weight training is "dynamic constant external resistance," though the phrase doesn't exactly roll off the tongue.)

kinetic chain. A linkage that consists of all the joints involved in a movement, such as the shoulder, elbow, and wrist when pulling up on a hold. In the real world, our joints seldom work in isolation but often work together. A weak point in the chain makes the entire movement less effective. See *closed chain* and *open chain.*

lactate threshold. The point during exercise where lactate accumulates faster than it is metabolized; closely associated with the anaerobic threshold. Higher lactate thresholds are good indicators of superior aerobic performance. See *anaerobic threshold.*

lactic acid. One of the by-products of anaerobic energy production that is soon converted into a salt called lactate. When these metabolites accumulate faster than they can be removed, the muscle starts shutting down. See *anaerobic metabolism.*

lateral. Close to the body's middle

medial. Farther from the body's middle

negative phase. See *eccentric.*

onsight. When you climb a route with no rehearsal or prior knowledge.

open chain. A movement where the last segment in a kinetic chain is free to move; for example, the quad extension is an open chain exercise because the feet are mobile. Generally considered less functional exercises that isolate muscles. See *closed chain* and *kinetic chain.*

positive phase. See *concentric.*

pronation. Inward rotation of a limb about its horizontal axis. The elbow pronates when your thumb rotates inward, and the ankle pronates when it rolls toward the arch. See *supination.*

protein. The source of amino acids, which are the building blocks of the body. Each gram of protein provides 4 calories, but this is an inefficient source of energy.

proximal. The part of a limb that is closest to the heart. See *distal.*

redpoint. When you lead a route without falling, after practicing the moves.

simple movement. A movement that only flexes a single joint, such as a biceps curl. Simple exercises isolate muscles that need to be targeted. See *compound movement.*

sport climb. A rock or ice route with all of the protection placed ahead of time, typically as bolts; removes this layer of difficulty, so the climber can focus on harder moves.

supination. Outward rotation of a limb about its horizontal axis. The elbow supinates when your thumb rotates outward, and the ankle supinates when it rolls away from the arch. See *pronation.*

traditional (trad) climb. A rock or ice route where the climber places most of the protection (nuts, cams, pitons) as he or she ascends; more challenging than sport climbing.

vitamins. Molecules that make things happen in the body, serving as catalysts. You don't burn vitamins, nor are they a source of energy, but you need an adequate intake.

VO$_2$max. The maximum amount of oxygen that the body can consume during heavy exercise. Usually measured in milliliters per kilogram of body weight per minute (ml/kg/min), it can be a good estimation of fitness but a poor predictor of athletic performance. Also called aerobic capacity.

Appendix D: Resources

General

MEDLINEplus (*www.medlineplus.gov*). A free resource operated by the National Library of Medicine and the National Institutes of Health. Contains a wealth of information on health, diseases, and drugs.

The Physician and Sportsmedicine Online (*www.physsportsmed.com*). Medical review articles (technical, but not overly so), in addition to many excellent articles for the layperson in the Personal Health section.

PubMed (*www4.ncbi.nlm.nih.gov/pubmed*). The largest online database of scientific research articles. Operated by the National Library of Medicine. Before trusting ad claims, verify references here, because they are often taken out of context or misinterpreted.

SportScience (*www.sportsci.org*). A superb, peer-reviewed collection of information on all aspects of the science of sport.

Wilmore, Jack, and David Costill. *Physiology of Sport and Exercise*, 2nd edition. Champaign, Illinois: Human Kinetics, 1999. A superb college text that provides an overview of human performance.

Chapter 1: Performance and Nutrition Fundamentals

Antonio, Jose, and Jeffrey Stout. *Sports Supplements*. Philadelphia: Lippincott Williams & Wilkins, 2001. A well-referenced text that gets into the nitty-gritty of what supplements do and don't do.

Clark, Nancy. *Sports Nutrition Guidebook*, 2nd edition. Champaign, Illinois: Human Kinetics, 1997. Clear explanations for the layperson, with lots of good recipes in the back.

Dorfman, Lisa. *The Vegetarian Sports Nutrition Guide*. New York, NY: John Wiley & Sons, 1999. Though a bit evangelical, this is a good source of information and recipes for non-meat-eating athletes.

Food and Nutrition Board, Institute of Medicine. *Dietary Reference Intakes*. Washington, DC: National Academy Press. If you really need to know all the details behind the new recommendations for vitamins and minerals, here they are. The online version is free (*www.nap.edu*), or you can buy the six printed volumes.

Gatorade Sport Science Institute (*www.gssiweb.com*). No snake oil here—just heaps of good information on endurance training and sports nutrition with only a hint of bias.

Girard Eberle, Suzanne. *Endurance Sports Nutrition*. Champaign, Illinois: Human Kinetics, 2000. Written for serious athletes, this is a very good source of nutrition information with excellent advice for vegetarians.

Healthwell.com. Despite a strong leaning to the New Age (operated by a producer of natural-products magazines and trade shows), this site offers a lot of information (with references) on supplements, herbs, drug interactions, and nutrition (*www.healthwell.com*).

Manore, Melinda, and Janice Thompson. *Sport Nutrition for Health and Performance*. Champaign, Illinois: Human Kinetics, 2000. A college textbook for those who want a strong science background to decipher the mumbo jumbo.

Quackwatch.com. Perhaps a bit zealous in the battle against evil, but full references are provided, so you can decide for yourself (*www.quackwatch.com*).

Supplementwatch.com. An independent website that isn't selling anything and doesn't accept advertising. Well-researched and referenced articles (*www.supplementwatch.com*).

Chapter 2: Mind and Body: Mental and Flexibility Training

Alter, Michael. *Sport Stretch*, 2nd edition. Champaign, Illinois: Human Kinetics, 1998. A more technical approach, with many advanced stretches for dancers and martial artists.

Anderson, Bob. *Stretching*, 20th anniversary edition. Bolinas, California: Shelter Publications, 2000. The latest edition of this classic book now has more than fifty routines, including one for rock climbing, that only take 2 to 8 minutes each.

Williamson, Jed, editor. *Accidents in North American Mountaineering*. Golden: American Alpine Club Press, annual. Learn from other people's mistakes.

Chapter 3: Aerobic Conditioning

Armstrong, Lawrence E., and Larry Armstrong. *Performing in Extreme Environments*. Champaign, Illinois: Human Kinetics, 1999. A compilation of research on how the body reacts in less than ideal conditions.

Janssen, Peter. *Lactate Threshold Training*. Champaign, Illinois: Human Kinetics, 2001. Though horribly edited, there is a lot of good information on maximizing aerobic performance.

Sleamaker, Rob, and Ray Browning. *SERIOUS Training for Endurance Athletes*, 2nd edition. Champaign, Illinois: Human Kinetics, 1996. A book for the dedicated triathlete willing to plan life months in advance, though most aerobic animals can benefit.

Ward, Michael, J. S. Milledge, and J. B. West. *High Altitude Medicine and Physiology* 3rd edition. London: Oxford University Press, 2000. This definitive medical text is not for the lay reader, but it has exceptional content for those seriously interested in performance at altitude and the history of research.

Chapter 4: Strength Conditioning

Aaberg, Everett. *Muscle Mechanics*. Champaign, Illinois: Human Kinetics, 1998. One of the better introductions to resistance training, this provides good explanation of the pros and cons of exercises that are safe and effective.

Baechle, Thomas, and Roger Earle. *Essentials of Strength Training and Conditioning*, 2nd edition. Champaign, Illinois: Human Kinetics, 2000. The National Strength and Conditioning Association's textbook for personal trainers. It is an excellent reference for those interested in the science of training.

Brooks, Douglas. *Effective Strength Training*. Champaign, Illinois: Human Kinetics, 2001. Intended for personal trainers but useful for athletes, this provides a good analysis of resistance exercises.

Fleck, Steven, and William Kraemer. *Designing Resistance Training Programs*, 2nd edition. Champaign, Illinois: Human Kinetics, 1997. Though somewhat old, this remains a good textbook for those interested in the research behind the theories.

Chapter 5: Recovery: Rest and Rehab

Horrigan, Joseph, and Jerry Robinson. *7-minute Rotator Cuff Solution*. Los Angeles: Health For Life, 1991. Provides a good explanation of shoulder problems and exercises to help them.

Musnick, David, and Mark Pierce. *Conditioning for Outdoor Fitness*. Seattle, Washington: The Mountaineers Books, 1999. Good source for functional exercises used in rehabilitation.

Chapter 6: Synergy: Coalescing and Planning

Goddard, Dale, and Udo Neumann. *Performance Rock Climbing*. Mechanicsburg, Pennsylvania: Stackpole Books, 1993. Though some of the information is dated, this remains a good starting point for sport and high-level trad climbers.

Horst, Eric. *Training for Climbing*. Helena, Montana: Falcon Books, 2002. An update of his popular book for sport climbers.

Sagar, Heather Reynolds. *Climbing Your Best: Training to Maximize Your Performance*. Mechanicsburg, Pennsylvania: Stackpole Books, 2001. Another good book for sport and trad climbers.

Twight, Mark. *Extreme Alpinism*. Seattle, Washington: The Mountaineers Books, 1999. An excellent how-to-push-the-envelope manual. Those with no desire to imitate Dr. Doom can still pick up some good tidbits.

Index

About the Author

Clyde Soles is a freelance writer, photographer, and consultant with a passion for adventure.

For seven years, he was an editor at *Rock & Ice* magazine, during which time he wrote most of the gear reviews and several feature articles. This tenure culminated with *Rock & Ice Gear: Equipment for the Vertical World* (The Mountaineers Books, 2000), which is a comprehensive guide to climbing gear. He is also the founder of *Trail Runner* magazine and has contributed many articles to that publication.

After three decades of climbing, Soles enjoys all aspects of the sport—from bouldering to Himalayan summits. He is equally devoted to trail running, road biking, mountain biking, telemark skiing, track skiing, and scuba diving.

Soles has a B.A. in nature photojournalism from the University of Colorado in Boulder and attended graduate school (ABD) at the Brooks Institute of Photography in Santa Barbara, California.

THE MOUNTAINEERS, founded in 1906, is a nonprofit outdoor activity and conservation club, whose mission is "to explore, study, preserve, and enjoy the natural beauty of the outdoors. . . . " Based in Seattle, Washington, the club is now the third-largest such organization in the United States, with 15,000 members and five branches throughout Washington State.

The Mountaineers sponsors both classes and year-round outdoor activities in the Pacific Northwest, which include hiking, mountain climbing, ski-touring, snowshoeing, bicycling, camping, kayaking and canoeing, nature study, sailing, and adventure travel. The club's conservation division supports environmental causes through educational activities, sponsoring legislation, and presenting informational programs. All club activities are led by skilled, experienced volunteers, who are dedicated to promoting safe and responsible enjoyment and preservation of the outdoors.

If you would like to participate in these organized outdoor activities or the club's programs, consider a membership in The Mountaineers. For information and an application, write or call The Mountaineers, Club Headquarters, 300 Third Avenue West, Seattle, WA 98119; 206-284-6310.

The Mountaineers Books, an active, nonprofit publishing program of the club, produces guidebooks, instructional texts, historical works, natural history guides, and works on environmental conservation. All books produced by The Mountaineers Books fulfill the club's mission.

Send or call for our catalog of more than 500 outdoor titles:

The Mountaineers Books
1001 SW Klickitat Way, Suite 201
Seattle, WA 98134
800-553-4453
mbooks@mountaineersbooks.org
www.mountaineersbooks.org

The Mountaineers Books is proud to be a corporate sponsor of Leave No Trace, whose mission is to promote and inspire responsible outdoor recreation through education, research, and partnerships. The Leave No Trace program is focused specifically on human-powered (nonmotorized) recreation.

Leave No Trace strives to educate visitors about the nature of their recreational impacts, as well as offer techniques to prevent and minimize such impacts. Leave No Trace is best understood as an educational and ethical program, not as a set of rules and regulations.

For more information, visit *www.LNT.org,* or call 800-332-4100.

Other titles you might enjoy from The Mountaineers Books

Available at fine bookstores and outdoor stores, by phone at 800-553-4453, or on the Web at *www.mountaineersbooks.org*

Mountaineering: The Freedom of the Hills, 7th Edition by The Mountaineers, edited by Steven M. Cox and Kris Fulsaas. $37.95 hardbound, 0-89886-426-7. $26.95 paperbound, 0-89886-427-5.

Extreme Alpinism: Climbing Light, High, and Fast by Mark Twight and James Martin. $27.95 paperbound. 0-89886-654-5.

Ice World: Techniques and Experiences of Modern Ice Climbing by Jeff Lowe. $29.95 paperbound. 0-89886-446-1.

Rock & Ice Gear: Equipment for the Vertical World edited by Clyde Soles and Dougald MacDonald. $24.95 paperback. 0-89886-695-2.

Medicine for Mountaineering: And Other Wilderness Activities, 5th Edition edited by James A. Wilkerson, M.D. $19.95 paperbound. 0-89886-799-1.

Fifty Favorite Climbs: The Ultimate North American Tick List by Mark Kroese. $32.95 paperbound. 0-89886-728-2.

Staying Alive in Avalanche Terrain by Bruce Tremper. $17.95 paperbound. 0-89886-834-3.

Glacier Travel & Crevasse Rescue, 2nd Edition by Andy Selters. $18.95 paperbound. 0-89886-658-8.

Conditioning for Outdoor Fitness: A Comprehensive Training Guide by David Musnick, M.D. and Mark Pierce, A.T.C. $21.95 paperbound. 0-89886-450-X.

GPS Made Easy: Using Global Positioning Systems in the Outdoors, 4th *Edition* by Lawrence Letham. $15.95 paperbound. 0-89886-802-5.

Mount Rainier: A Climbing Guide by Mike Gauthier. $17.95 paperbound. 0-89886-655-3.

Alaska: A Climbing Guide by Michael Wood and Colby Coombs. $24.95 paperbound. 0-89886-724-X.